D1359854

THE SOCIAL PROGRESS
OF NATIONS

Richard J. Estes

PRAEGER

PRAEGER SPECIAL STUDIES • PRAEGER SCIENTIFIC

New York • Philadelphia • Eastbourne, UK
Toronto • Hong Kong • Tokyo • Sydney

303.4
E 79

Library of Congress Cataloging in Publication Data

Estes, Richard J.
    The social progress of nations.

    Bibliography: p. 211
      1. Social history—1970–   2. Progress.   3. Social
indicators. I. Title.
HN17.5.E79   1984   303.4′4   84–9802
ISBN 0–03–059582–7 (alk. paper)

Part of Chapter 6 of the present work appeared in a slightly different version as "World Social Progress, 1969–1979," in *Social Development Issues*, 1984, 8(1). © 1984 by the University of Iowa.

Published in 1984 by Praeger Publishers
CBS Educational and Professional Publishers
a Division of CBS, Inc.
521 Fifth Avenue, New York, New York 10175, U.S.A.

© 1984 by Praeger Publishers

456789 052 987654321
Printed in the United States of America
on acid-free paper

For my children and all the children of the world
whose future depends on
the raw courage and willingness of their parents
to risk the creation of a
more equitable international social order.

Acknowledgments

Since beginning the project described in this volume, many persons, institutions, and research organizations have contributed to its completion. Central among all of them, however, is Kate Katzki who, as then Secretary-General of the International Council on Social Welfare, stimulated me to pursue the development of a more objective approach to measuring changes in world *social* progress over time. Kate's belief in the importance of the project provided invaluable inspiration during the often difficult early phases of beginning work on such a complex comparative welfare research effort.

My colleague, John S. Morgan, then Kenneth L. M. Pray Professor of Social Policy at the University of Pennsylvania School of Social Work, worked with me in developing the theoretical model that guided the research through to its completion. John's many years of experience in comparative social policy analysis simplified considerably the many difficult analytical problems that were encountered during the project's first two phases.

Administrative support at the University of Pennsylvania for the multi-year effort was provided by Louise P. Shoemaker, Dean of the School of Social Work. Louise made possible the time needed to pursue the project and, as opportunities became available, for me to accept appointments as visiting professor to the University of Teheran, Iran (fall 1978), the University of Trondheim, Norway (spring 1979), and the University of Hawaii at Manoa (fall 1982 and spring 1983). Her generous help in resolving the sometimes difficult administrative issues involved with these critical field research, teaching, and consultative experiences is deeply appreciated.

Financial support for the field testing of the project's research instruments was provided, in part, by the U.S. Department of State in the form of a Fulbright-Hays Senior Lecturer Award. Without this financial assistance it is doubtful that the project could have progressed as quickly beyond its first several phases.

More than a dozen undergraduate and graduate students from a variety of social science disciplines contributed to the work as research assistants between 1975 and 1981. The most significant contributions to the project's completion were made by John Reed, John McQueen, Dorothy Linder, Cynthia Golden, and Melanie DeMatto. Others who contributed to the research effort included Vatsala Vivek, Shujaat H. Zaidi, and Hisae Tachi. I am deeply thankful to each of these persons, both for their willingness to use the investigation to enhance their own comparative research skills and for their patience in completing what, at times, was experienced to be an impossible task.

Robert Spena of Systems and Computer Technology, Inc. (SCT) provided valuable assistance with the data analysis portion of the study. Graham Clifford (social policy), Ivar Bjørgen (sociology), Frøde Meland (education), Ola Kindseth (computers), Michael Jones (social geography), and Maurine Kuebekk (librarian)—all of the University of Trondheim in Norway—provided specialized consultation to me within their areas of comparative social science specialization. Sir Geoffry Vickers of the United Kingdom was kind enough to comment on early versions of the research instruments as was Katherine Kendall, then Secretary General of the International Association of Schools of Social Work.

The volume's several drafts were typed by Joan Habres (University of Pennsylvania), Linda Loui (University of Hawaii), and Donna Colabella (Los Angeles). I am grateful to each of these persons for their skill in transforming what at times were barely legible notes into readable text.

A very special acknowledgement belongs to my friend and colleague of several years, Daniel S. Sanders, Dean of the University of Hawaii at Manoa School of Social Welfare. In his multiple capacities as dean, president of the Inter-University Consortium for International Social Development and as a personal friend, Dan has been a continuing source of intellectual support and enthusiasm for me and for the project. I am especially grateful to him for making it possible for me to spend the 1982/83 academic year in Hawaii as a visiting professor. This visit provided the ideal location and much-needed time to complete work on the project. Mahalo nui loa, Dan.

My good friends Arthur Schwartz of the University of Maryland School of Social Work and Community Planning, Virgil Renzulli of the University of Pennsylvania, and James Midgley of the London School of Economics were kind enough to review earlier drafts of the manuscript. I thank each of them for their critical comments and many helpful suggestions. Bonnie Clause, of Honolulu, Hawaii, brought considerable editorial skill in helping me to revise and complete the last draft of the manuscript. I am deeply indebted to her for helping to make the volume far more readable than it otherwise would have been. Lynda Sharp, my editor at Praeger, is thanked for her patience in awaiting completion of the volume's final manuscript. Lynda commented generously on all aspects of the manuscript with the result that, because of her, several important discussions in the volume have been elaborated upon more fully.

Finally, this volume could not have been completed in as timely a manner without the special encouragement and assistance provided by Arleen Kahn. I am especially grateful to Arleen for her generous hospitality while the initial draft was being written.

Richard J. Estes
January 1984

Contents

List of Charts, Figure, and Tables

1

Introduction

World development is not merely an economic process. . . . The new generations of the world need not only economic solutions, they need ideas to inspire them, hopes to encourage them, and first steps to implement them. They need a belief in man, in human dignity, in basic human rights; a belief in the values of justice, freedom, peace, mutual respect in love and generosity, in reason rather than force.

Willy Brandt

in *North-South: A Program for Survival*

When the research reported in this volume was beginning, the world was moving steadily toward increased social chaos. In 1974, terrible wars were being fought in Southeast Asia, Latin America, and Africa, and the prospects of a more serious war in the Middle East loomed ever large. The capitals of many of the world's nations were centers of unrelenting civil strife, political protest demonstrations, and not infrequently, assassinations and large-scale political deaths and murders. The exodus of hundreds of thousands, ultimately millions, of political refugees from the war-torn nations of Africa and Asia had already begun. National expenditures for defense, for the military, and in support of regional and international wars were escalating at an alarming rate. Respect for basic human rights and freedoms was on the decline almost everywhere on the planet.

In most parts of the world, women continued to eke out subsistence levels of existence for themselves and their children. Comparatively few participated in the political prerogatives that had been granted to men for decades, or even centuries before. Most women lacked independence of movement due to restrictions of marriage, obligations toward the extended family, or lack of recognition as autonomous persons with legal identities of their own.

1

And the children were suffering too. Left abandoned or orphaned by the hundreds of thousands, millions were eventually to die each year from the ravages of war, famine, natural disasters, and manmade social problems of an enormous magnitude. Millions more were to become permanently handicapped as well, the victims of brutality and impersonal terrorism. Others were to die the slower death of damaged brains forever encased in bodies deprived of essential nutrients, or as the victims of wanton environmental pollution and poisoning.

It was in 1974, too, that the majority of the world's international development assistance organizations declared the first "Developmental Decade" to be something "less than a success." Exclusively economic approaches to solving the world's massive social problems were recognized as inadequate to the task. So, too, were the largely fragmented, often highly politicized, bilateral aid programs organized by the world's rich countries to selected developing nations. Money, human talent, material resources all had proven inadequate in reversing the global social declines that followed the end of colonialism and the birth or rebirth of half the world's nations during the late 1950s and early 1960s.

Leaders of the world's nations were confronted, too, with a dim prognosis concerning the future of the planet, given what were perceived as real limits to growth stemming from dramatic increases in the global population, environmental pollution, the increasing scarcity and eventual loss of nonrenewable natural resources, and so on. "Global catastrophe" was a phrase commonly used to describe the predicament of mankind at that juncture of history.

The research reported in this volume was undertaken with considerable apprehension, and out of a deeply felt concern for the human condition as it existed in various parts of the world. As a human being I felt a deep compassion for people who, simply because of the facts of history and their place of birth, were condemned to live out their lives in comparative deprivation and suffering. As a researcher I wanted to better understand the nature and causes of these massive international problems. As a social worker active in the international community I wanted to contribute toward an implementation of more effective and long-lasting solutions to mankind's most difficult social problems. For me, carefully conducted research on the changing nature, extent, and adequacy of social provision on the global level offered the most satisfying approach for acting upon my various concerns.

ASSESSING WORLD SOCIAL PROGRESS

The project reported in this volume began in 1974 with a request from Kate Katzki, then Secretary-General of the International Council on Social Welfare (ICSW).[1] Like so many persons responsible for directing social development assistance efforts internationally, Kate Katzki was increasingly concerned about the apparent drift of many developing nations into deeper poverty and even more profound social chaos. The widening gap in development between the richest and poorest nations was of special concern to her, as was the escalation in political tensions between Eastern and Western nations with its inevitable negative impact on the fragile economic and political systems of the majority of non-aligned countries. She was concerned, too, about the over-emphasis that nearly all leading multinational development assistance organizations were placing on various aspects of economic development, often with little or no concern for the even more profound social problems that existed alongside economic needs. In some cases, national and international efforts directed toward rapid economic development within particular nations or world regions created, or at least contributed significantly to, social problems at a level previously unknown in many developing nations. For example, the rapid exodus of peasants from rural, essentially agricultural, communities to urban centers, "new towns," "squatter villages," and so forth; unemployment; the need for elaborate social security and social welfare measures required to deliver services previously performed by the extended family; pollution; destruction of the natural environment for essentially industrial purposes, and so on.

The ICSW Secretary-General identified the need to develop objective approaches to the assessment of changes in world social welfare development over time. In particular she was interested in seeing emerge an analytical and planning tool that could be used by the ICSW and ministries of social welfare throughout the world to assist them in responding more effectively to the changing needs of the world's growing population. Use of the tool in assessing the changing social needs among the hundreds of millions of persons living in countries that are officially designated by the United Nations as "least developing countries" (LDCs) was to be a special priority. Her interests in the model were twofold: (1) it should assign higher priority to the *social* aspects of development rather than to indicators of economic development; and (2) the model should reflect the fundamental humanitarian values that are shared by social development specialists throughout the world (see Piettre 1968; Howard 1969; United Nations 1978b; International Council on Social Welfare 1978).

---

[1]Founded in 1928, the ICSW is made up of persons and groups that are committed to the promotion of international cooperation in the field of social welfare. The ICSW encourages and conducts studies and research into matters affecting international social welfare. It has been granted special consultative status to the United Nations. The Council is located in Vienna, Austria, and has a membership consisting of 80 national committees and 28 international organizations (Kruzas 1982, 388).

Unfortunately, neither the ICSW nor other international social development assistance organizations had funds available to support work on the model's development. Work was begun nevertheless but proceeded at a slower pace than had been anticipated.[2] Essentially, between 1975 and 1982 the effort progressed in six stages:

Stage I (1974–76)—Review of Literature and Consultations: Extensive reviews of the then available theoretical and empirical international social development literature were conducted. Consultations also took place between the investigator and other specialists in international social development working in various parts of the world.

Stage II (1976)—Formulation of the Index of National Social Vulnerability (NSV): The study's initial conceptual framework—referred to as the "Index of National Social Vulnerability" (NSV)—was formulated and disseminated internationally for review and comment (Estes and Morgan 1976).

Stage III (1978–79)—Preliminary Data Collection and First Field Testing: Data collection from available international statistical data-gathering sources was begun. Field-testing of the NSV in some 20 countries located in Western and Northern Europe, the Middle East, and the Near East was made possible through Fulbright-Hays Senior Lecturer awards to the investigator.

Stage IV (1979)—Creation of the Index of National Social Progress (ISP): In response to the data collection and preliminary field testing of Stage III, the NSV was expanded along several dimensions and was reconceptualized as the "Index of National Social Progress" (ISP).

Stage V (1980)—Global Analysis and Field Testing of the Revised ISP: The ISP was applied to 107 politically autonomous nations with 1969 populations equal to or greater than one million persons. The preliminary findings obtained from these global statistical analyses were reported at three conferences of international social development scholars and practitioners meeting in Hong Kong (1980).

A second field testing of the analytical model also took place as part of Stage V; this time, however, the model was tested in 15 nations located within the Asian, Pacific, and Western European regions.

Stage VI (1980–82)—Final Data Analysis: Refined analyses of both the statistical data and field visit observations gathered during the study's earlier stages were completed. These final results were presented to international social development researchers, academicians, and practitioners

---

[2]My early collaborator in this effort was John S. Morgan, a Canadian, who was then Kenneth L. M. Pray Professor of Social Policy at the University of Pennsylvania School of Social Work. Professor Morgan retired in 1976.

attending the biennial meetings of the Inter-University Consortium for International Social Development held in Brighton, England (Estes 1983). Work on the study's final report was begun at the University of Hawaii at Manoa in Honolulu, Hawaii, during fall and spring 1983.

Throughout the study's various stages, a single research purpose was central: to develop a paradigm of world social development—subsequently referred to as the Index of Social Progress (ISP)—that: (a) would reflect changes in the capacity of individual nations to provide more adequately for the basic social and material needs of their populations; and (b) would be a relatively more objective approach to assessing these changes in the context of gains and losses in global social provision *over time*. Analyses of the data collected as part of the research, including data obtained through field visits to some 40 of the 107 countries included in this study, were to be used as a basis for developing a "social agenda for mankind." This agenda was to serve as a stimulus for practical action among the world's political leaders, international social development specialists and citizens-at-large in formulating integrated solutions to the world's most pressing social problems.

ORGANIZATION OF THE VOLUME

This volume describes a new approach to assessing the world social situation over time. It builds consciously on the research efforts of earlier investigators and, hopefully, extends their work in meaningful ways. A deliberate effort has been made to incorporate as fully as possible many of the often hard-earned learnings of these investigators into my own work.

Readers should not confuse the research reported in this volume with research on "quality of life." For the reasons outlined above, this latter research is of a highly subjective nature and, ultimately, deals with questions of personal happiness and satisfaction with life. Except in very limited ways, large-scale comparative research on quality of life throughout the entire world is not possible. Research on "adequacy of social provision," however, tends to be somewhat more objective in nature and, therefore, reasonable comparisons can be made between the capacity of various nations to provide more or less adequately for the basic material and social needs of their people. Such research also allows for assessments to be made concerning changes over time in the capacity of nations to increase or decrease their ability to provide better for the basic needs of their people.

The present study reports "social progress" data—that is, the extent of national and global changes in adequacy of social provision as measured by the Index of Social Progress (ISP)—for 107 of the world's politically autonomous nations; all are member states of the United Nations. In 1980, the population of these nations totaled approximately 2.7 billion persons, 63 percent of the world's total population. Future studies of world social progress will include an even larger proportion of the world's population. Data are reported at two time intervals, 1969–70 and 1979–80. Plans currently exist for the research to be updated at five-year intervals so that progress in achieving various international social development objectives can be gauged on a timely basis.

The volume is divided into eight chapters and three appendixes. Readers who are interested only in the study's major findings will want to turn first to Chapter 6, which provides these findings in summary format and, then to Chapters 4 and 5, which discuss the findings in greater detail. The implications and global actions that follow from the study's findings are discussed in Chapter 7. Chapter 8 provides an update on the major social, political, and economic events that have taken place throughout the world since 1980, the last year for which statistical analyses were made, and early 1984.

Readers who are interested in the methodological basis of the present study should read Chapters 2 and 3 and Appendixes A and B. These sections of the volume contain detailed information concerning the theoretical base, research design, and methodological considerations governing the selection of specific indicators of social change, as well as the statistical procedures used throughout the study. A comprehensive bibliography on international and comparative social welfare research appears at the end of the volume.

Researchers who have undertaken international comparative investigations of their own are already familiar with the enormous conceptual and methodological problems inherent in a study of the magnitude reported in this volume; for them the need for the various methodological conveniences used to complete the study will require little elaboration. Other readers should understand that this is one of the few studies that have attempted to incorporate such a broad range of complex social phenomena for so many nations into one research design. As such, the present study should be viewed as a beginning effort to describe more accurately changes in world social progress over time. Future reports on this subject will reflect the sensible advice given to the author by international social development scholars and experts, and by others who share a deep interest in improving the world social situation. These future studies should be more methodologically sophisticated, and I hope they will offer even more explicit guidance for reducing the world's myriad social problems.

2

Assessing Global Social Progress

Since the mid-1940s a number of significant efforts have been undertaken by social scientists toward developing research tools that could effectively assess changes in the capacity of nations to provide for the basic needs of their people. Referred to as research on "level of living," "social well-being," "quality of life," "physical quality of life," and "human welfare," among others, each of these various efforts has attempted to measure a range of human social phenomena broader than economic factors alone. All approaches have sought to combine various social welfare and welfare-related social indicators (for instance, health care, education, food and nutrition) into composite indices that could be used for purposes of both cross-national comparative studies and, within individual nations, for application to the changing social needs of discrete population groups that make up a nation (for example, men versus women, children versus older people, minorities, urban versus rural dwellers, and so on). An extensive body of literature exists that describes the conceptual and methodological issues involved in constructing social indicators for purposes of international comparative welfare research (Bauer 1966; Sheldon and Moore 1968; OECD 1976a, 1976b).

The majority of cross-national comparative efforts in social welfare, however, have been impaired by enormous conceptual problems (Seers 1972; Drenowski 1972, 1974; Morris 1979), by problems of missing, incomplete, or otherwise unavailable data (Merritt and Rokkan 1966; Przeworski and Teune 1970) and by the worldwide shortage of researchers and statisticians trained to undertake welfare-relevant research (Vogel and Lund 1972; Bubeck 1972; Estes 1983). Problems of national and international political tensions have contributed to the difficulties of cross-national data collection (Warwick and Osherson 1973; Adelman and Morris 1971), as have the not entirely unreasonable concerns of governments regarding the potential misuses to which politically sensitive welfare data might be put (Henriot 1972; Graycar 1979). Consequently, international comparative studies using the world as the unit of analysis tend to be sparse (Ward 1971; McGranahan 1972; Harbison 1970) and, when available, often to be either more statistical (for example, ILO 1981; USDHHS 1980) or theoretical in nature than empirical (for example, Pusic 1972; George and Wilding 1976).

Despite these obstacles to cross-national research, a substantial body of comparative welfare inquiry does exist. The great bulk of this literature analyzes patterns in the administration of welfare services in countries that share similar (Morgan 1966; Rodgers 1968, 1979; Jenkins 1969; Kahn and Kamerman 1976) or, in some cases, contrasting social, political, or economic ideologies (Pryor 1968; Rimlinger 1971; Wilensky 1975). However, almost all of these inquiries are either national (for instance, Hansen 1971; Connor 1972; Radask 1976; Smith 1973; Naipaul 1977) or regional in design (Myrdal 1968; Badgley 1971).

Unfortunately, there are relatively few studies in the comparative literature that examine patterns of welfare administration on a global basis (for instance, Lally 1970; USDHHS 1980; ILO 1981). Studies are available, though, that report international findings on recurrent welfare issues related to, among others, population trends (United Nations 1979e; Shanas 1968), refugees (United Nations 1973c; Berry and Soligo 1979), unemployment (Reubens 1970; ILO 1977; Squire 1979), housing (Wendt 1963; United Nations 1975b), the changing status of women and children (Nash 1977; U.S. Commissioner for Civil Rights 1978), political oppression (Jalee 1968; Goulet 1971; Gutierrez 1973), human rights violations (United Nations 1979f, 1982), and hunger (for example, Cox 1970; Scrimshaw and Gordon 1968). A few internationally influential studies make use of past and current economic and social growth trends to forecast the emerging welfare dilemmas of the future (Meadows 1972; Pestel and Mesarovic 1974; Tinbergen 1976; Leontief et al. 1977; Ehrlich and Ehrlich 1977).

Because of the problems incurred in carrying out large-scale comparative studies, the development of new analytical tools for use in assessing the extent of national and international success in meeting the basic human needs of the world's growing population constitutes an urgent priority before the international social welfare community. These research tools are needed to provide welfare ministers, planners, service directors, researchers, and others with ongoing, reliable information for use in formulating more realistic social development objectives. They also are needed to establish more rational priorities among the competing alternatives for international development assistance. They are needed, too, to provide greater accountability among development assistance organizations for the substantial expenditures being made by them to promote social and economic development objectives internationally.[1]

APPROACHES TO ASSESSING NATIONAL AND INTERNATIONAL DEVELOPMENT

At least four closely related initiatives have been attempted by international development assistance organizations to construct the research and planning tools needed by specialists in national and international social development. Various degrees of success have been realized from these efforts.

Gross National Product (GNP)

The most successful approach used to assess changes in patterns of national and global development has been Gross National Product (GNP). As an analytical tool, GNP measures the monetary value of all the goods and services produced by nations at various points in time. Developed during the 1930s and 1940s in response to widespread global economic recession, unemployment and underproductivity (Morris 1979), GNP has served well the needs of economists and political leaders for an effective tool that reliably measures changes in national and international economic trends.

As a measure of "human welfare" or social development, however, GNP has never been very satisfactory.[2] The reasons for these are twofold: (a) GNP measures only those economic activities to which a discrete monetary value (a "price tag") can be attached; and (b) GNP was never designed to take into account subjective valuations that people place on critical noneconomic experiences that are essential to human "fulfillment," that is, personal happiness, satisfaction with life. As a specialized social science tool

---

[1]Chapter 8 contains a listing of development assistance expenditures of nation-state members of the Organization for Economic Cooperation and Development (OECD) and the Organization of Petroleum Exporting Nations (OPEC) for selected years beginning 1960.

[2]The majority of centrally-planned economy nations use the concept of "Gross Domestic Product" (GDP) to measure changes within their economies. Unlike GNP, GDP "measures the total final output of goods and services produced by an economy—that is, within a country's territory by residents and nonresidents, regardless of its allocation to domestic and foreign claims. It is calculated without making deductions for depreciation" (World Bank 1980, 158–59). Though perhaps useful as a measure of economic changes within the borders of these nations, GDP has not been shown to be any more sensitive to changes in *social* development than has GNP and, therefore, is not widely used by development specialists as an indicator of the capacity of nations to provide for the basic social and material needs of their populations.

proven to be useful in economic analyses, forecasting and planning, GNP simply cannot incorporate all of the diverse social phenomena required to assess changes in "human welfare" over time. Indeed, efforts to equate GNP with human welfare, or even to use GNP as an indicator of the differential levels of human welfare that characterize nations at various points in their development, have been sharply criticized (Drenowski 1974; Juster 1977; Morris 1979).

United Nations

With the exception of the pioneering work of economists Joseph Davis (1945) and M. K. Bennett (1951), the most significant work on developing more inclusive approaches to assessing changes in the global *social* situation was initiated under the auspices of the United Nations. Acting in conformity with Article 55 of its Charter, the United Nations established an Expert Group that was charged:

> . . . to prepare a report on the most satisfactory methods of defining and measuring standards of living and changes therein in the various countries, having regard to the possibility of international comparison. . . . (United Nations 1954).

After meeting for two years, the Expert Group was unable to produce a definitive response to such an ambitious charge but did, nonetheless, identify the need to distinguish between the concepts of "standard," "norm," and "level of living." Its report emphasized the need for quantitative measures of human welfare in the areas of *health, nutrition, housing, employment,* and *education* (United Nations 1954). The group believed that the development of quantitative "indicators" of human welfare was essential to the establishment of objective standards which then could be applied to analysis and comparison of the "level of living" that characterized member states of the United Nations over time.

The 1954 report stimulated considerable discussion both within the Economic and Social Council (ECOSOC) of the United Nations as well as within the General Assembly itself. An interagency commission was formed to promote cooperation between the various specialized agencies of the United Nations—the International Labor Organization (ILO), the World Health Organization (WHO), and so on—and a second Expert Group was formed to implement the recommendations outlined by the 1954 committee. In 1961 the second Expert Group produced its report entitled, "An Interim Guide to the International Definition and Measurement of Levels of Living" (United Nations 1961). This report advanced considerably the work of the first Expert Group and expanded from five to twelve the number of components to be included in the level of living concept: *health, food and nutrition, education* (including literacy and skills training), *conditions of work, employment situation, aggregate consumption and savings, transportation, housing, clothing, recreation and entertainment, social security* and *human freedoms*.

In addition to formulating a more inclusive list of components that defined level of living, the committee also identified discrete indicators that could be used to operationalize each of the components. These more or less objective, almost always quantifiable, measures of human welfare were to be used in making comparisons in the level of living that characterized member states over time (for example, expectation of life at birth, infant mortality rate, and crude annual death rate were to serve as valid indicators of level of living in relation to health). The various conceptual and data collection principles formulated by the committee were adopted with relatively few changes and, subsequently, were outlined in handbook format for use by the United Nations and its specialized agencies in collecting national *social* reporting information from member countries (see United Nations 1964).

Recognizing the peace-keeping importance of promoting social development more systematically throughout the world, the United Nations established the Research Institute on Social Development (UNRISD) in Geneva, Switzerland in 1961. The purpose of the UNRISD then, as now, was to engage in systematic research on the nature and dynamics of social development nationally and in the context of world economic development. Not accidentally, the initial work of the Institute focused on highly technical, but very influential, studies that identified more effective approaches to assessing level of living in a variety of crosscultural contexts (see Baster and Scott 1967, 1969; Drenowski 1970, 1974). A very important study undertaken by a UNRISD team headed by Donald McGranahan examined "the correlates of socio-economic development" (McGranahan 1972). The McGranahan team emphasized the need for basic economic transformations within nations as a precondition for higher levels of *social* development, as did many other studies of this type.

Equally ambitious approaches at both conceptualizing and measuring the nature and dynamics of level of living throughout the world have been undertaken by other units of the United Nations. The Research Division of the United Nations Educational, Scientific and Cultural Organization (UNESCO) in Paris, for example, has made invaluable contributions to this effort (for instance, UNESCO 1976; Gostkowksi c. 1973). So, too, has the United Nations European Social Development Programme (UNESDP 1972, 1974, 1976). Even though the research efforts of each of these United Nations agencies carries its own theoretical stamp, as well as its particular approach to concept operationalization and data collection, each shares with all other United Nations agencies the same fundamental commitment to the development of reliable approaches to the assessment of human welfare that incorporate a broad range of social and economic phenomena. Most are committed to a "basic needs" approach to level of living, however, one that emphasizes the degree to which the most fundamental needs of people are satisfied irrespective of their country of residence or the specific type of political or economic system under which they live.

Organization for Economic Cooperation and Development (OECD)

A very different approach to assessing adequacy of national and international social provision has been undertaken by the Paris-based Organization for Economic Cooperation and Development (OECD).

Made up of 24 of the world's richest nations, the OECD serves as one of several multinational organizations through which these countries direct their financial contributions and technical assistance to less-developed nations. As such, OECD nations are seeking to formulate a somewhat different approach to measuring and influencing patterns of international development from that undertaken by the United Nations (see OECD 1977a, 1977b, 1977c). This approach involves four discrete phases:

Phase I—establish consensus on a list of social concerns for which social indicators are to be developed.

Phase II—develop a set of social indicators ". . . designed to reveal with validity the level of 'well-being' for each social concern . . . and to monitor changes in those levels over time" (OECD 1976, 20).

Phase III—measure the social indicators developed in Phases I and II.

Phase IV—link "well-being" conditions to practical policy measures and options.

Of the four projected phases, only Phase I has been completed. Essentially, the OECD Working Party on Social Indicators was able to achieve consensus on eight categories of social concerns that are grouped into 24 "fundamental social concerns" and 56 "sub-concerns" (see OECD 1973; Christian 1974). The eight categories of OECD social concerns differ in only minor respects from the twelve components of level of living identified by the UN Expert Groups: *health, individual development through learning, employment and quality of working life, time and leisure, command over goods and services, physical environment, personal safety and the administration of justice,* and *social opportunity and participation.* The degree to which these concerns have been operationalized into "fundamental social concerns" and "sub-concerns," however, differs significantly with respect to the specificity that has been achieved by the United Nations and by its specialized agencies (see OECD, 1977b, 1977c).

The full significance of the OECD effort has yet to be determined, inasmuch as its work is still not complete (OECD 1982). The organization's 1976 interim progress report, however, suggests that the effort is not producing the results intended (OECD 1977a). Much as the United Nations did, the OECD staff assessed the conceptual and methodological problems required to produce a composite index of social well-being as too difficult to solve. The continuing need for such an instrument, however, is emphasized repeatedly throughout the interim report and in other reports published by the OECD (OECD 1976; Beckerman 1978).

Physical Quality of Life Index (PQLI)

The social indexing work of Morris D. Morris and his colleagues at the Washington-based Overseas Development Council (ODC) has received considerable international attention in recent years (Sewell et al. 1977). Interest in the council's work stems in large measure from the simplicity of the Morris model for global social assessment, especially in comparison with the more comprehensive models sought after by the United Nations, UNESCO, the OECD, and other international development assistance organizations.

Essentially, in an effort to minimize the awesome conceptual and methodological problems that blocked the work of other investigators, the Morris team constructed a three-item Physical Quality of Life Index (PQLI). The PQLI examines variations over time in national rates of *infant mortality*, years of *average life expectation* at birth and *rates of adult literacy*. These indicators of social development were selected on the basis of: (a) their relative theoretical independence from measures of economic development; and (b) their results-orientation, that is, all three indicators focus attention on the social accomplishments of nations over time rather than on the nature, extent, or amount of resources required to bring about these achievements (time, money, human effort, and so on).

Morris applied the PQLI to 74 nations at varying points in time between 1947 and 1973 (Morris 1979). His results were quite intriguing and provided even further evidence concerning the inappropriateness of GNP as the primary indicator of changes in level of national social development. He also showed that a simplified approach to assessing world social progress over time can yield results that are both analytically interesting and politically useful in redirecting global development assistance resources to those nations with the most urgent social needs.

The simplicity of the PQLI model, however, also is its major weakness. Of the three indicators used to construct the index, two (rates of infant mortality and years of average life expectation) are essentially measures of the quality of national health care services and the third (rates of adult literacy) assesses the adequacy of basic educational services. The PQLI makes no reference to other equally important spheres of social development activity, for example, improvements in the changing status of women and children, protection of internationally guaranteed human rights, participation in political decision making, quality of housing and the living environment, and so forth. No valid index that attempts to measure changes in levels of national—and global—social development over time can exclude indicators of these critical social development activities.

In constructing the PQLI, of course, Morris did not attempt to produce a measure of "total welfare," but did, indeed, create an index that "promises to serve as a creative complement to the GNP" (Morris 1979, 93). It does, as Morris writes, "show how successful a country is in providing specific social qualities to its population and how it performs over time" (Morris 1979, 96). Even with its serious limitations with respect to the range of social development activities reflected in the index, the PQLI does contribute usefully to international development analysis and planning. The PQLI, however, is not the more comprehensive index of national social development that international development assistance organizations have sought to formulate since the mid-1950s.

Subjective Approaches to Human Well-Being

In sharp contrast to the objective, highly statistical "basic needs" approaches to changes in human welfare taken by the world's major development assistance organizations, a number of investigators have sought to assess more subjective aspects of human well-being. Working in the early and mid-1970s, these researchers drew heavily from the psychological "needs-hierarchy" theories of Abraham Maslow (Maslow 1968). Their interest was in identifying the cross-cultural correlates of "felt satisfaction with life," "happiness," and "sense of personal security" (for instance, Kennedy et al. 1978; Andrews and Inglehart 1979). The investigators were concerned not so much with the extent to which the basic material needs of respondents were satisfied, but rather with the value they placed on their perceived satisfaction with life within whatever social context they found themselves.

Nearly all of the studies on the subjective aspects of human well-being, however, have been conducted on people living in a limited number of Western-oriented, democratic societies. Relatively few investigators have attempted to broaden their research focus to incorporate the majority of the world's population that live in developing nations and for whom the satisfaction of basic social and material needs cannot be taken for granted. The reason for this is obvious—the relative nontransferability of basic psychological concepts from one culture to another. Interpretations of concepts such as "happiness" or "satisfaction with life," for example, differ significantly among people living within the same society and differ even more dramatically among people living in entirely different societies. The nontransferability (that is, nonequivalence) of concepts from one culture to another has been a major stumbling block for all comparative investigators, irrespective of their philosophical inclination or methodological approach.

Relatively few large-scale comparative efforts on the subjective aspects of human well-being are currently in progress.[3]

---

[3]A useful review of this research appears as *Correlates of Happiness* by Ruut Veenhoven and his colleagues at the Erasmus University of Rotterdam (1977).

3

The Index of Social Progress (ISP)

INTRODUCTION

Since 1974 the author has sought to construct and validate an operational-ized model of world *social welfare* development (Estes and Morgan 1976). The model—referred to as the Index of Social Progress (ISP)—was de-signed to include a variety of social, economic, and political factors that could serve as valid indicators of the differential levels of human depriva-tion and suffering experienced by people living anywhere in the world. More particularly, the ISP was to serve as a reliable tool for assessing shifts in the capacity of nations to provide for the basic needs of their populations. These assessments were to be made independent of the type of political or economic system characteristic of a country.

Another purpose of the ISP was to facilitate the analysis of welfare-relevant data at regular intervals, thereby providing social development planners with a tool that could be used to direct the world's increasingly scarce resources for development assistance to those social sectors within developing nations experiencing the most urgent human needs (health care, education, human rights, and the like).

The general research design and analytical premises that were to guide the development of the ISP were summarized and published for dissemi-nation to an audience of international social welfare scholars during the summer of 1976 (Estes and Morgan 1976). These design premises included the following:

1. The ISP should include measures of a broad range of social, po-litical, and cultural phenomena that reliably assess changes over time in the capacity of nations to provide for the basic social and material needs of their population.

17

2. The ISP should portray economic development as only one of many social factors that contribute to or inhibit international, national, and subnational social welfare development.

3. The ISP should serve as an operationalized definition of "social development" for purposes of specialized research study and world human welfare analysis.

4. The ISP should assess the "state of welfare" at discrete points in time and not concentrate on the "flow of welfare" programs and services over the long- or short-term (Drenowski 1974).

5. The ISP should recognize the unique nature of each society's social, political, and cultural traditions as they interface with current human needs and the resources that are available to a nation to respond to these needs.

6. For ministries of social welfare (and for world welfare planners in general) the ISP should provide critical planning data needed to redirect scarce resources for national and international development assistance to those social sectors within nations—indeed within world regions and groups of nations—experiencing the most urgent social needs. At a minimum, the ISP should:

a. Suggest discrete indicators of social progress for which reliable data could be collected and analyzed at regular time intervals;

b. Assist in assigning differential intervention priorities to the multiplicity of international, national, and subnational social needs that characterize the world's population at various points in time;

c. Aid in the choice of specialized programs of national and international social action and social intervention that can be targeted at specific social problems or needs;

d. Serve as a baseline data source for use in helping to assess the relative effectiveness and efficiency of various strategies of national and international social intervention aimed at solving recurrent human welfare problems.

7. As a general model of world social welfare development, the ISP should be sufficiently flexible, especially in its early stages of development, so that the index can be adapted for use at various geopolitical levels of analysis (for example, to world regions, groups of nations, or within nations, to particular subnational entities including states, cities, communes, or to subgroups within a national population, and so on). This requires that selected indicators of social progress can be substituted for others (expanding or contracting the number of indicators included in some subindexes) and that individual nations can assign differential weights to index indicators so as to better reflect the salience of particular social phenomena within their own national or regional contexts.

8. The ISP should contain both quantitative and qualitative indica-

tors of change in the adequacy of national social provision over time, albeit non-quantitative measures of social progress eventually will need to be converted to numerical values for purposes of statistical analysis.

9. The ISP should be capable of measuring national social progress in both *real* (actual changes) and *relativistic* terms (changes that occur within one nation or group of nations relative to social changes that occur within other nations during the same time period).

10. The ISP should be both *descriptive* and *prescriptive*, that is, specific action implications should follow from analysis of ISP changes in adequacy of social provision over time.

11. As an analytical tool, the ISP should be parsimonious, operationally stable, statistically reliable, and possess at least face validity.

NATIONAL SOCIAL VULNERABILITY

The study's initial theoretical work was organized around the major analytical concept of national social vulnerability. As advanced in the original model of world social welfare development, social vulnerability refers to the extent to which people reside in adverse social, political, and/or economic situations that expose them to injurious or otherwise socially debilitating experiences. Level of social vulnerability is directly related to degree of exposure to such experiences which, when protection is inadequate, can render exposed individuals less competent in dealing with the routine tasks of daily living (Maloney 1973). When applied to a nation (Schlegel 1977, 81–100), social vulnerability is conceptualized as existing to the extent that available national resources—including both material (food, shelter, wealth) and non-material (social welfare programs and services) resources—are inadequate relative to the unmet human and social needs that exist within a nation's population (for example, malnutrition, illiteracy, poverty, contaminated environment, and so on). The gap that results from significant disparities between social needs and resources is conceptualized to be a direct indicator of the actual and potential social risks to which national populations are exposed. Within the context of this study, national social vulnerability (NSV) is assessed to be higher for those countries in which social needs significantly exceed the social resources that are available to respond to those needs; conversely, national social vulnerability is conceptualized as being lower for those countries in which resources and needs converge so that the seriousness of the social risks to which national populations are exposed is minimal.

In the original model of world welfare development (Estes and Morgan 1976) the level of national social vulnerability (NSV) was conceptualized as assessable in terms of six dimensions. They are: (1) the prevailing *social philosophy and purpose* of a nation as reflected in its constitution, official documents, and major public policy statements; (2) the level of *national human needs* as reflected through standardized statistical reporting procedures; (3) the level of *national social resources* available to meet the social needs of the nation's population; (4) the degree of *political stability* characteristic of a nation at particular moments in time; (5) forces within a society that either support or disrupt the structure of *the family* as the basic social unit; and (6) the presence of countervailing *cultural forces* that contribute to intergroup conflicts and disrupt historic traditions, values, customs, and beliefs.

The interactive nature of these universally powerful societal forces is illustrated in the theoretical scheme presented in Figure 3–1. As shown in the figure, each factor occupies one dimension of the six-sided cube. For

FIGURE 3–1   Three-Dimensional Model of National Social Vulnerability

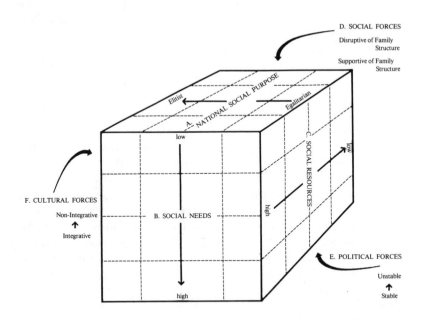

analytical purposes, arrows are used to indicate the direction of highest social vulnerability (that is, lowest level of national social provision). Social vulnerability, for example, is conceptualized as being highest among those nations that are: (1) elitist in social organization (in which emphasis is placed on mass subservience to the needs of a limited number of persons who occupy positions of preeminence or power); (2) high in unmet human needs; (3) low in available social resources; (4) politically unstable; and in which both (5) family structures and (6) traditional cultural forces are in a state of disintegration. Conversely, nations possessing the opposite characteristics are conceptualized as being characterized by lower levels of national social vulnerability. One should not conclude from these inferences, however, that nations characterized by comparatively low levels of social vulnerability are socially invulnerable. To assert such a conclusion would represent a serious fault in both logic and practical judgment. In any event, even a cursory examination reveals many nations that already are highly developed economically to be subjected to very high levels of vulnerability in selected sectors of their national life (that is, a relatively high incidence of poverty, increasing crime rates, political discontent, urban blight, family disorganization, social malaise, and so on). One can reasonably expect, however, that nations that are assessed to be relatively low in social vulnerability will experience more rapid success in achieving their social goals than will those nations whose social needs are escalating while their resources either remain constant or actually diminish (for reasons related to uncontrolled population growth, war, famine, political instability, and the like).

CONSTRUCTING THE INDEX OF SOCIAL PROGRESS (ISP)

In many respects operationalization of the national social vulnerability concept was a more difficult task to accomplish than its conceptualization. Problems of language, of differences in cross-cultural definitions of critical social development concepts ("social need," "social resource," "poverty," "crime," and so on), and of serious limitations in the choice of comparative social indicators, as well as the availability of acceptable international time-series data were the most difficult to solve. Methodological issues related to statistical weighting, index and subindex construction, and techniques of comparative analysis initially were found to be somewhat elusive but were resolved more readily.[1] Indeed, several of the fundamental value and

---

[1]A variety of specialized cross-cultural and comparative research methodology reference books are available to assist investigators with conceptual and methodological problems encountered in comparative analysis. As examples, see Merritt and Rokkan 1966; Przeworski and Teune 1970; Warwick and Osherson 1973.

conceptual dilemmas concerning the goals, objectives, method, and assessment of national development that impeded the work of earlier investigations continued to evidence themselves throughout the early phases of the present study (see, for example, United Nations 1954; Harbison 1970; Drenowski 1974; McGranahan 1972; UNESCO 1976; OECD 1976). The majority of these issues were resolved satisfactorily, however, and as a result, national social vulnerability was operationalized as the Index of Social Progress (ISP).

In its present form, the Index of Social Progress (ISP) consists of 44 welfare-relevant social indicators distributed among eleven subindexes:

1. Education (4 items)
2. Health (3 items)
3. Status of Women (5 items)
4. Defense Effort (1 item)
5. Economics (4 items)
6. Demography (5 items)
7. Geography (3 items)
8. Political Stability (5 items)
9. Political Participation (6 items)
10. Cultural Diversity (3 items)
11. Welfare Effort (5 items)

Each subindex measures a different dimension of changes over time in the capacity of nations to provide for the basic social and material needs of their populations. Each subindex measures, too, a specific area of organized social welfare activity that is recognized internationally as constituting a critical dimension of social development (Pusic 1972; Paiva 1977; Sanders 1982; Cummings 1983). The various indicators that form the ISP are grouped by subindex in Chart 3–1.

Briefly, transformation of national social vulnerability (NSV) from an analytical concept into the operationalized ISP required that the original model of world social welfare development be expanded from six to eleven dimensions (see Chart 3–2). The original dimension of *national social purpose*, for example, was concerned with the degree of political egalitarianism present within different nations (Dahl 1971). This concern was operationalized through the six-item Political Participation subindex, which assesses changes over time in the extent to which citizens of a nation are permitted to participate actively in the political decision making of that nation (through regularly scheduled and held popular elections, the formation of political parties, election to national assemblies, and the like). The subindex also assesses the extent to which military authorities influence either directly

CHART 3–1   Index of Social Progress (ISP) Indicators by Subindex (N = 44 Indicators, 11 Subindexes)

---

1. EDUCATION SUBINDEX

   School Enrollment Ratio, First Level (+)[a]
   Pupil Teacher Ratio, First Level (−)
   Percent Adult Illiteracy (−)
   Percent GNP in Education (+)

2. HEALTH STATUS SUBINDEX

   Rate Infant Mortality Per 1000 Liveborn (−)
   Population in Thousands Per Physician (−)
   Male Life Expectation at 1 Year (+)

3. WOMEN STATUS SUBINDEX

   Percent Age Eligible Girls Attending First Level Schools (+)
   Percent Children in Primary Schools Girls (+)
   Percent Adult Female Illiteracy (−)
   Years Since Women Suffrage (+)
   Years Since Women Suffrage Equal to Men (+)

4. DEFENSE EFFORT SUBINDEX

   Percent GNP in Defense Spending (−)

5. ECONOMIC SUBINDEX

   Economic Growth Rate (+)
   Per Capita Estimated Income ($) (+)
   Average Annual Rate of Inflation (−)
   Per Capita Food Production Index (1970 = 100) (+)

6. DEMOGRAPHY SUBINDEX

   Total Population (Thousands) (−)
   Crude Birth Rate Per 1000 Population (−)
   Crude Death Rate Per 1000 Population (−)
   Rate of Population Increase (−)
   Percent of Population Under 15 Years (−)

7. GEOGRAPHY SUBINDEX[b]

   Percent Arable Land Mass (+)
   Number Major Natural Disaster Impacts (−)
   Lives Lost in Major Natural Disasters Per Million Population (−)

8. POLITICAL STABILITY SUBINDEX

   Number of Political Protest Demonstrations (−)
   Number of Political Riots (−)
   Number of Political Strikes (−)
   Number of Armed Attacks (−)
   Number of Deaths From Domestic Violence Per One Million Population (−)

CHART 3–1   Continued

---

9. POLITICAL PARTICIPATION SUBINDEX

Years Since Independence (+)
Years Since Most Recent Constitution (+)
Presence of Functioning Parliamentary System (+)
Presence of Functioning Political Party System (+)
Degree of Influence of Military (−)
Number of Popular Elections Held (+)

10. CULTURAL DIVERSITY SUBINDEX

Largest Percent Sharing Same Mother Tongue (+)
Largest Percent Sharing Same Basic Religious Beliefs (+)
Ethnic-Linguistic Fractionalization Index (−)

11. WELFARE EFFORT SUBINDEX

Years Since First Law—Old Age, Invalidity, Death (+)
Years Since First Law—Sickness & Maternity (+)
Years Since First Law—Work Injury (+)
Years Since First Law—Unemployment (+)
Years Since First Law—Family Allowances (+)

---

[a]Signs indicate directionality of indicators.
[b]Excluded in computing scores for the Index of Net Social Progress (INSP).

or indirectly the major political affairs of a nation (Blondel 1973; Fidel 1975).[2]

The dimension of *national human need* was operationalized in four subindexes: Health, Education, Economics, and Demography. The sixteen indicators that make up these subindexes assess national progress over time in satisfying discrete social welfare needs (for health and educational services, population control, and so on). The subindexes of Welfare Effort and Defense were required to operationalize the original dimension of *national*

---

[2]For four of the six items contained in the *Political Participation* subindex data are reported for the five-year period 1972 and 1977 *only*, i.e., "functioning partiamentary system," "functioning political party system," "influence of military," and "number of popular elections held." The source of the 1972 data is Blondel (1973). Jodice and Taylor (1981) collected the political events data for 1977. Unfortunately, reliable sources of political data prior to 1972 and after 1977 were not identified by this author. Therefore, the reader is cautioned to keep in mind that the majority of the items used to form this subindex cover only a five-year, rather than ten-year, period of political activity within nations. For the reader's reference, subindex raw score values for nations grouped by economic development classification are reported in Table C–1 of Appendix C. As more timely data become available, these subindex indicators will be updated so as to more accurately reflect levels of national political participation within nations for the two modal years of this study, that is, 1969–70 and 1979–80.

CHART 3–2   Operationalization of the Six Dimensions of the National Social Vulnerability Concept (NSV) into the 11 Subindexes of the Index of Social Progress (ISP)

1. NATIONAL SOCIAL PURPOSE

Political Participation Subindex

2. NATIONAL HUMAN NEEDS

Health Subindex
Education Subindex
Demography Subindex
Economics Subindex

3. NATIONAL SOCIAL RESOURCES

Welfare Effort Subindex
Defense Effort Subindex

4. POLITICAL STABILITY

Political Stability Subindex

5. FAMILY STABILITY

Status of Women Subindex

6. CULTURAL DIVERSITY

Cultural Diversity Subindex
Geography Subindex[a]

[a]The Geography Subindex was not included in the original model of national social vulnerability. The subindex was added to the ISP following its initial field-testing in Europe and the Middle East during summer 1979.

social resources. In the ISP, for example, favorable assessments are made for increases in the level of organized social welfare effort. Increases in level of national defense expenditures, however, are treated negatively on the ISP.

The Women Status subindex operationalizes the original model's concern with the social status of women vis-à-vis that of men. The five items contained in the subindex assign priority to advanced educational and legal entitlements for women and girls, and less priority to the homemaking, care-giving and nurturing roles that women traditionally have performed for and on behalf of families. Because of its socially progressive nature (that is, with a focus on literacy, primary school involvement, and political suffrage), the subindex does not measure the impact of those changes affecting women on traditional family life. Similarly, the index does not measure the impact on the family of such broadly based social forces as migration, urbanization, industrialization, social mobility, and so on. Additional subindexes would be needed to detail the social consequences of these phenomena on families nationally and internationally. The need for women to enjoy more secure forms of social provision in their own right, however, is without question. As such, the subindex created here highlights global trends in providing for the basic legal and educational needs of women along the several dimensions indicated.

A reasonable level of *political stability* is required for nations to progress in a more or less orderly fashion toward the achievement of national social goals (Organski 1967; Dahl 1971; Blondel 1973). This dimension of national social vulnerability is operationalized on the ISP as the Political Stability subindex. Consisting of five indicators, the subindex measures the frequency with which selected politically disruptive events occur over time (politically induced strikes, riots, protest demonstrations, and so on). Nations are conceptualized as being more socially vulnerable as the frequency of these destabilizing events increases.[3]

Within the ISP, however, no assumption is made to the effect that political stability per se should be the exclusive or even the preeminent objective of a national government. Rather, stability is only one of several critical dimensions that should be used to assess the quality of the political life within a given nation; political participation is a second dimension. In the ISP, variations in levels of political participation *and* political stability over time are examined in relation to one another. That is, nations characterized by high levels of political stability but low levels of political participation—such as those that exist in autocratically governed countries (Benin, Mali, Niger, Kampuchea, and so on)—receive less favorable scores on the *composite* ISP than do those nations in which both political stability and political participation are high (Switzerland, New Zealand, Austria, Belgium, and so on). Similarly, countries low in political stability but high in political participation—such as many democratically governed nations (India, the United Kingdom, and so on)—receive more favorable ISP scores than do nations in which both political stability and political participation are low (Argentina, Peru, Uganda, among others). In this way, *composite* ISP scores correct for distortions that may occur when only one or another dimension of polit-

---

[3]The reader should note that the data used in the *Political Stability* subindex are for the eight-year period 1969 and 1977 *only*—not 1969–70 and 1979–80. The reason for this is that the last year for which these data were gathered was 1977 (Jodice and Taylor 1981). Consequently, critical politically stabilizing or destabilizing events that occurred within many nations during the three-year period 1978–80 are not reflected in 1980 subindex scores. This is especially important to keep in mind as one attempts to interpret subindex scores for individual nations in terms of political events that occurred within these countries after December 31, 1977. Also, the reader is referred to Appendix C, which contains raw score values for all of the indicators used to form the *Political Stability* subindex. These values appear by economic development grouping and for individual nations both for 1969 and 1977.

ical events is examined in isolation from other relevant characteristics that make up the political life of a nation. In this way, too, *composite* ISP scores assure that a better balance will exist among all of the relevant dimensions that must be considered together in order to arrive at a reasonable assessment of changes over time in the capacity of nations to provide for the orderly and regular participation of their citizens in shaping the political decisions by which the nation as a whole will be governed.

The final dimension of world social development conceptualized on the original NSV model is related to those universal *cultural forces* that operate within societies and that either promote or inhibit national social integration. Emphasis was given to the particularly powerful contribution of religion, language, and ethnicity in melding an otherwise heterogeneous population of individuals and subgroups into a nation of people possessing a common identity, language, and widely shared social values, beliefs, and national goals. Changes over time in these socially integrative forces are assessed on the three-item Cultural Diversity subindex of the ISP (Deutsch 1953; Rice 1962; Taylor and Hudson 1972).

Though widely recognized as critical factors in national and international development planning (Hewitt and Burton 1971; Ehrlich and Ehrlich 1972; Ominde 1975; Berkol 1976; Burton 1978), naturally occurring geological and environmental forces were excluded from the original model of world social welfare development. This was deemed appropriate given the low level of human intervention that is possible in controlling the nature, frequency, or impact of these phenomena. Because of their significance to development planners (United Nations 1976), however, in constructing the ISP the investigator decided to include a limited number of welfare-relevant environmental factors in the index as a separate Geographic subindex. This three-item subindex assesses the amount of arable land mass available to nations for use in food production and measures the frequency with which nations are subjected to recurrent natural disasters (tornadoes, earthquakes, floods, tidal waves, and the like).

Recognizing that individual readers may wish to assign varying degrees of importance to geographic factors as valid indicators of national social progress, two sets of composite index scores are reported in the present analysis: (1) those that include the Geographic subindex as part of the composite index score (the Index of Social Progress—ISP—with its 44 indicators distributed among 11 subindexes); and (2) those that do not, (the Index of Net Social Progress—INSP—consisting of 41 indicators distributed among 10 subindexes). The majority of the summary statistical tables printed in this volume report composite scores for both indexes (the ISP and the INSP). In the narrative portion of the report, however, the more inclusive ISP scores are reported unless otherwise indicated.

Directionality of Indicators

Each indicator used to form the ISP is associated with a particular directional sign that specifies: (a) the normative nature of the indicator; and (b) its contribution toward national social development as increases and decreases in the numerical value of the indicator change over time. These indicator directional values are shown as a series of plus (+) and minus (−) signs that appear next to each indicator in Chart 3-2. On the Education subindex, for example, *higher* School Enrollment Ratio(s) (+) are judged to be more desirable from a social development perspective than are lower ratios; conversely, *lower* Pupil-Teacher Ratios (−) and *lower* rates of Adult Illiteracy (−) are more socially desirable than are higher numerical values on these indicators. Similarly, *lower* Rate(s) of Infant Mortality (−) but *higher* levels of Male Life Expectation at One Year (+) are more socially desirable than are opposite values on these indicators. Hence, levels of national ·social vulnerability (NSV), too, can be thought of as *decreasing* as *reductions* occur in Pupil-Teacher Ratios, Rates of Adult Illiteracy, and so on, but as *increasing* as the score on these indicators of social progress move upward over time.

A variety of conceptual (Schlegel 1977; Drenowski 1974; Paiva 1977) and empirical (Harbison 1970; McGranahan 1972) comparative welfare research studies were consulted prior to establishing the normative value directions incorporated into the ISP. Because of the unique international debates that lead to its construction, however, the Universal Declaration of Human Rights (United Nations 1978b) was selected as the primary documentary source for identifying both the types of humanistically oriented indicators to be included on the ISP and the value standards against which the desirability of selected national social, political, and economic changes over time on these indicators would be assessed.

For readers who are unfamiliar with the Universal Declaration of Human Rights, the document consists of some 30 articles that proclaim the universal right of all persons to life, liberty, and security of person; to freedom from arbitrary arrest; to freedom of movement and residence, of speech, press, assembly and worship; and to the other legal rights commonly protected by democratic constitutions. The Declaration also proclaims the rights of people to social security, education, and opportunities to earn a living (Coyle 1960).

Adopted by the General Assembly of the United Nations on December 10, 1948, without a dissenting vote, the substance of the Declaration was divided into two Covenants in 1966. A nation ratifying the first Covenant—the "International Covenant on Economic, Social and Cultural Rights" (31 articles)—binds itself to make and enforce laws protecting its own people against unjust and cruel treatment. A nation ratifying the second Covenant—the "International Covenant on Civil and Political Rights" (53 articles)—acknowledges its responsibility to do all that it can to promote better living conditions. In connection with this general duty toward its citizens, a signatory nation also recognizes certain legal rights connected with economic and social security, including the right to join trade unions as a necessary economic right to promote the public welfare (Coyle 1960).

Though no formal power has been granted to the United Nations to force a signatory nation to uphold specific provisions of the Declaration, the document does, nonetheless, serve as a powerful international moral force for encouraging governments to work toward optimal realization of the principles contained within it. As of December, 1978, 58 (38 percent) of the United Nations' 152 member-states were signatories of Covenant I of the Declaration and 55 (36 percent) were signatories of Covenant II (United Nations 1982, 258).

Other United Nations human rights agreements, covenants, and conventions were consulted (see United Nations 1978b) in assigning specific value directions to ISP indicators. These included human rights agreements pertaining to women (1952), children (1959), war victims (1950), and refugees (1951). United Nations statements on freedom of the press (1948), slavery (1956), genocide (1948), discrimination (1957), racism (1963), and the arms race (see United Nations 1978a, 1981b), among others, also significantly influenced the choice of particular directional signs (including the assignment of a negative directional sign to the one-item Defense Effort subindex—Percent GNP in Defense Spending). For this model at least, all expenditures for defense—including those for military personnel as well as armaments—are conceptualized as constituting a drain on scarce national resources, which otherwise could be available to provide more adequately for the basic human needs of a nation's population (Wilensky 1975; United Nations 1978a; United Nations 1981b).

Altogether, then, the standards against which changes in levels of national social progress are assessed on the ISP depend heavily on those widely shared humanistic values and principles that repeatedly have been enunciated, ratified, and promulgated through various declarations, agreements, and covenants of the member states of the United Nations.

STUDY TIME FRAME

A central concern of this inquiry from the outset has been to measure more objectively changes that take place *over time* in the capacity of nations to provide for the basic social and material needs of their populations. The reasons underlying this concern are three-fold: (1) to better assess the short- and long-term significance of social development gains (and setbacks) that

occur within nations; (2) to better understand the complex interplay of social, political, and economic forces that contribute so critically to differential
patterns of national and international social development; and (3) to provide more objective evidence concerning the short-term successes (and fail-
ures) of international assistance efforts in reducing the sizeable gap in social
development that long has existed between the world's richest and most impoverished nations. Imbedded in each of these concerns is the goal of better
understanding the importance of *time* as a critical dimension in the social
development process.

The present inquiry examines adequacy of social progress at two points
in time over a ten-year period, 1969–70 and 1979–80. These intervals were
selected for study for reasons of timeliness and the general availability of
acceptable social indicator data. Also, the 20-year period, 1960–80, was
marked by an extraordinarily high level of cooperation internationally to
reduce the levels of human suffering and deprivation that characterize
much of life in the world's developing and least developing countries (see
Commission of International Development 1969; Djukanovic and Mach
1975; ILO 1977; Brandt 1980; United Nations 1981a). The author's expectation was that, through application of a properly validated and tested ISP,
many of the most significant social development shifts that occurred within
these nations over the last 20-year period could be discerned. The 10-year
period, 1970–80, was selected, too, so as to capture comparative baseline
data needed to better assess future progress in achieving national and international social development objectives—for example, by the years 1985,
1990, and so on.

DATA AND DATA COLLECTION

Between 1977 and 1981, a data reservoir of some 91 international and comparative social, political, and economic indicators were collected. The majority of these data were obtained from the published statistical archives of
major international organizations (the United Nations, World Bank, Organization for Economic Cooperation and Development, International Social
Security Association, International Labour Organization, and so on). Other
data were obtained from the published works of independent comparative
research scholars (Taylor and Hudson 1972; Blondel 1973; Gastil 1978; Regulska 1980; Reed 1981). In the case of current political events data, special
permission was granted to the author to use unpublished original data gathered by two investigators as part of their more comprehensive international
comparative political events inventory (Jodice and Taylor 1981).

Four criteria were applied to the reservoir of indicators prior to their
selection into the final data set.

Timeliness: Indicators reflect the designated social phenomena for the two time intervals selected for study, 1969–70 and 1979–80. The majority of indicators that form the ISP satisfy this criteria. Several, however, do not (for instance, political events and selected health indicators). These slightly older data were included in the present analysis for these reasons: (a) the importance of three indicators as measures of significant social development activity; (b) the absence of acceptable alternative indicators; and (c) the provisional nature of the present analysis. Table 4–1 identifies the base years of all indicators that form the ISP. As the ISP is revised and ideally gains recognition as a tool useful in facilitating national social development planning, the author anticipates that timely measures for all indicators contained on the ISP will be taken and reported internationally at regular intervals.

Accuracy: Indicators included in the final data set are judged to give a reasonable portrayal of the designated social condition in each country. In reality, of course, most internationally reported social indicators result, not from timely sample surveys of the population, but rather from estimates made by planning and research personnel in various national ministries of social welfare, health, education, and so on. In any event, these estimates are the best sources of data available to the investigator and, therefore, are judged to be adequate for purposes of the present analysis. Readers should be aware, however, that the accuracy of estimates provided to international data collection and reporting organizations does vary depending on the differential capacity of nations to provide accurate information. Occasionally, problems of political oppression or social ideology may influence the accuracy of data reported to international organizations as well.

Representativeness: To the fullest extent possible, indicators selected for inclusion on the ISP reflect the total population of a given nation. Indicators that reflected characteristics of any one or another subset of the population (for "whites only" in the case of South Africa) were dropped from the final data set. For detailed information concerning representational qualifications of various ISP indicators, readers are referred to the original source documents from which these data have been obtained. Space limitations prohibit the reprinting here of the protracted footnotes and other qualifying statements that normally accompany publication of international comparative statistical data.

Equivalence: Problems of comparability in concept definition, operationalization and methods of data collection constitute a major problem in comparative analysis (see Przeworski and Teune 1970, 113–34). Given the analytical care with which indicators were selected for inclusion on the ISP, the investigator judges that individual indicators possess a reasonable level of conceptual and methodological equivalency.

Problems of missing, incomplete, or otherwise unreliable data also received considerable attention prior to an indicator's inclusion on the ISP. Indicators for which data could not be obtained for the majority of countries included on the analysis were dropped entirely (comparative statistics on crime and criminal behavior, human rights violations, quality of the physical environment, selected mental health statistics, and the like). Indicators for which needed data were missing for only a few or several countries were retained when reasonable estimates of these data could be obtained through computation of subregional averages using the geographic groupings identified in Chart 3–3 (rates of illiteracy, infant mortality, population growth, and so on). Indicators for which reasonable estimates of missing data could not be obtained, however, also were excluded from the ISP data pool.

Given this study's emphasis on the *social* aspects of development, every effort was made to avoid inclusion in the ISP of a large number of indicators that favor one or another form of economic development. Numbers of automobiles, televisions, radios, type of indoor plumbing, grams of animal protein consumed, square meters of living space per person, for example, all are closely associated with industrial forms of economic development; so, too, are indicators related to rates of employment and unemployment, distribution of the labor force by particular sectors of the economy, and so on (McGranahan 1972). In constructing the ISP, priority was given to those indicators that (1) reflect one or another dimension of *social* development (political, cultural, and related social behavior); (2) indicate the extent to which *basic* material or social needs are being met (for food, shelter, health and education services); or (3) represent significant areas of organized social welfare activity internationally (welfare programs and services).

Insofar as economic indicators were to be included in the ISP, those chosen were to be few in number, and then selected from among those that reflect only the most fundamental aspects of national economic activity (per capita gross national product, production rates, income levels, savings-consumption ratios, rates of inflation, and so forth). Preference was to be given to economic indicators that adequately measure critical economic aspects of social development irrespective of the dominant economic philosophy of a given nation or group of nations ("open market," "centrally planned," or "mixed" economic systems).[4]

Finally, factor analytic techniques were used to reduce the total number of indicators to be included in the ISP. These procedures also were used to organize the remaining indicators into the ISP's relevant subindexes. For

---

[4]For a discussion of the social welfare implications of the major differences that exist in these alternative systems of national economic activity, see Pryor 1968, Rimlinger 1971, Wilensky 1975.

CHART 3–3   Nations Grouped by Continents and Geographic Subregions
(N = 107)

AFRICA

Western Africa (N = 13)
Benin[a]
Ghana
Guinea[a]
Ivory Coast
Liberia
Mali[a]
Mauritania
Niger[a]
Nigeria
Senegal
Sierra Leone
Togo
Upper Volta[a]

Eastern Africa (N = 11)
Burundi[a]
Ethiopia[a]
Kenya
Madagascar
Malawi[a]
Rwanda[a]
Somalia[a]
Uganda[a]
United Republic of Tanzania[a]
Zambia
Zimbabwe

Northern Africa (N = 6)
Algeria
Egypt
Libyan Arab Republic
Morocco
Sudan[a]
Tunisia

Middle Africa (N = 4)
Central African Empire[a]
Chad[a]
United Republic of Cameroon
Zaire

Southern Africa (N = 1)
South Africa

NORTHERN AMERICA

Canada
United States (including Hawaii)

LATIN AMERICA

Tropical South America (N = 6)
Bolivia
Brazil
Colombia
Ecuador
Peru
Venezuela

Middle America (Mainland) (N = 7)
Costa Rica
El Salvador
Guatemala
Honduras
Mexico
Nicaragua
Panama

Temperate South America (N = 4)
Argentina
Chile
Paraguay
Uruguay

Caribbean (N = 5)
Cuba
Dominican Republic
Haiti[a]
Jamaica
Trinidad and Tobago

UNION OF SOVIET SOCIALIST REPUBLICS

OCEANIA

Australia
New Zealand

ASIA

East Asia (N = 2)
Japan
Republic of Korea

Middle South Asia (N = 5)
India
Iran
Nepal[a]
Pakistan
Sri Lanka

CHART 3–3   Continued

Eastern South Asia (N = 8)
    Burma
    Democratic Kampuchea
    Indonesia
    Malaysia
    Philippines
    Singapore
    Socialist Republic of Vietnam
    Thailand

Western South Asia (N = 7)
    Iraq
    Israel
    Jordan
    Lebanon
    Syrian Arab Republic
    Turkey
    Yemen, PDR[a]

EUROPE

Western Europe (N = 6)
    Austria
    Belgium
    France
    Germany, Federal Republic of
    Netherlands
    Switzerland

Southern Europe (N = 6)
    Albania
    Greece
    Italy
    Portugal
    Spain
    Yugoslavia

Eastern Europe (N = 5)
    Bulgaria
    Czechoslovakia
    Hungary
    Poland
    Romania

Northern Europe (N = 6)
    Denmark
    Finland
    Ireland
    Norway
    Sweden
    United Kingdom

---

[a]Indicates nations officially designated by the United Nations as "Least Developing Countries."

reasons of greater analytical efficiency, the total number of indicators included in the ISP was reduced to 44, its present size.

    Altogether, then, a rather rigorous set of conceptual and methodological criteria was applied to indicators that form the ISP. Appendixes A and B contain detailed technical information concerning the statistical construction of the ISP: indicator operational definitions, primary statistical data sources, estimation of missing data, formulae used to compute standardized and nonstandardized subindex and overall ISP scores, and interindex correlation coefficients.

STATISTICAL WEIGHTING

During the early phases of the ISP's operationalization, a serious effort was made to assign differential statistical weights to each indicator used to form the index. Factor analysis and the judgements of international specialists in social development both were utilized for this purpose.

It soon became clear, however, that although statistical weighting generally does serve a variety of theoretical and statistical purposes in index construction, the assignment of statistical weights to ISP indicators was not achieving the original analytical purposes of the ISP, that is, greater importance was being placed on the statistical precision of the index rather than on the substantive importance of its composite indicators. Consider, for example, the differential value that persons residing in very prosperous countries place on the "food versus freedom" issue relative to persons living in very impoverished nations. With a full and satisfied stomach one can easily espouse the protection of personal freedom to be the central obligation of the state toward its citizens. Such is not commonly the case in nations where hundreds of thousands, indeed millions, of persons die each year because of widespread famine, disease, and war. Clearly, the importance that persons residing in these two groups of nations would place on freedom versus food would differ substantially.

Consequently, early in the data analytical process the investigator decided not to assign differential statistical weights to the component indicators of the ISP. In addition to recognizing the selective importance of each ISP indicator to different clusters of nations, the decision was also justified by the uneven data quality of some indicators that make up the ISP (for many nations, reported data are little more than general estimates of the social conditions prevailing within the country at one or another point in time). The preliminary nature of this first application of the ISP to such a large number of the world's nations also contributed to this decision.

Thus, all 44 items that make up the ISP are treated as statistical equivalents; that is, they are assigned an equal statistical weight. Indicator values are averaged within subindex(es), however, because of the variations in the number of indicators that make up each of the ISP's 11 subindexes, as well as to reduce statistical distortions produced by extreme scores in several indicators (rates of inflation, incidence of natural disasters, and so on). Subindex averaging also minimizes the statistical impact of estimation errors in nations' reporting of their social indicator data to international data collection organizations. The statistical procedures used to generate these subindex averages are described in Step 4 of Appendix B. The appendix also describes the computational procedures used to combine the subindex averages into composite ISP scores.

NATION-STATE SELECTION

During the early phase of the project every effort was made to maximize the number of countries that could be included in the analysis. Problems of missing, incomplete, unreliable, or otherwise non-comparable data, however, required that guidelines be developed and applied systematically in the selection of individual countries for inclusion in the study. To assure a reasonable degree of uniformity with respect to social indicator operational definitions as well as data collection procedures, then, four selection guidelines were used in considering countries for inclusion in the analysis.

1.   Only *politically independent nations* would be included. Trust territories (such as the Pacific Islands of Micronesia), city-states (East and West Berlin), and politically dependent territories (for example, Hong Kong, Puerto Rico) were dropped from the list.

2.   Only *member states of the United Nations* in 1969—the baseline year of the study—would be included. In that year, 127 countries were member states of the United Nations (Dolmatch, 1981, 324).

3.   Only *nations with populations equal to or larger than one million persons* in 1969 would be included.

4.   Only *countries with data missing* for no more than four of the ISP's 44 indicators would be selected. Further, nations with missing data would be selected only if reasonable estimates of these data could be obtained on the basis of subregional averages or through other acceptable statistical procedures.

Application of the first three selection criteria—political independence, member state of the United Nations, and population size—resulted in a list of 121 countries. Severe problems of data quality and data availability, however, necessitated that 14 countries—including the People's Republic of China—be dropped from the analysis (see note at bottom of Chart 3–4 for a complete listing of excluded nations). Overall, 107 politically independent nations satisfied the study's four selection criteria.

Regional and Development Level Groupings

An analytical problem encountered early in the study was the need to develop a system for classifying the 107 nations selected for inclusion in the study into smaller, more statistically manageable groupings. Consideration was given to classifying nations by *per capita* income level (from very rich to very poor), by type of dominant political system (democratic to autocratic), by type of dominant economic system (open versus closed market), and by geographic location (by regions, continents, and so on). Consideration also was given to classifying nations in terms of their history of political independence (young versus old), religious and ethnic mix, and so on. None of these approaches alone, however, fully discriminated between the world's most socially advantaged and least socially advantaged nations.

Instead, the decision was made to group nations along three dimensions: (1) by type of dominant economic system; (2) by level of current economic development; and (3) by geographic location. The classification scheme adopted and used by the United Nations (1977b) proved to be the most useful typology for meeting the various analytical needs of this investigation, especially in distinguishing the world's most impoverished nations—the so-called Fourth World—from the larger group of "developing" nations that comprises these countries and others. Essentially, the typology classifies nations into more or less similar economic groupings, using the following criteria:

- Per capita gross domestic product (GDP)
- Percent population living in rural areas
- Percent adult illiteracy
- Dominant type of economic system
- Percent GDP in manufacturing
- Degree of centralized versus decentralized social and economic planning
- Import/export patterns.

Using these criteria, the Economic and Social Council of the United Nations classifies each of its 154 member states (1982) into one of four categories:

1. *Developed Market Economy Nation (DME):* Consisting primarily of Western-oriented democracies, characterized by open-market economic systems. The majority of these nations are located in Western Europe and North America, but this grouping also includes Japan, Israel, Australia, and New Zealand.

2. *Eastern Trading Area (ETA):* Consisting primarily of the Soviet Union and its Eastern European allies with the exception of Yugoslavia, which is classified as a DME nation. The ETA is basically a closed economic system, characterized by a strong, centrally planned and controlled economic system.

3. *Developing Country (DC):* Consisting mostly of middle-income countries with gross national products (GNP) averaging $350 in 1970. The majority of these nations are located in Africa, Latin America, the Caribbean, and Asia. Seventy percent of the populations of developing nations live in rural areas.

4. *Least Developing Country (LDC):* Characterized as the poorest of the poor or as the Fourth World, the majority of LDCs are located in Africa and Asia. The economies of these mostly young nations tend to be of a mixed nature (to include elements of both open and centrally planned systems)

CHART 3–4   Country List by Continent and Economic Development Grouping (N = 107)

Continent	DMEs (N = 24)	Eastern Trading Area (N = 7)	DCs, excluding LDCs (N = 58)	LDCs (N = 18)
AFRICA	South Africa		Algeria, Egypt, Ghana, Ivory Coast, Kenya, Liberia, Libya, Madagascar, Mauritania, Morocco, Nigeria, Senegal, Sierra Leone, Togo, Tunisia, United Republic of Cameroon, Zambia, Zaire, Zimbabwe	Benin, Burundi, Chad, Central African Empire, Ethiopia, Guinea, Malawi, Mali, Niger, Rwanda, Somalia, Sudan, Uganda, United Republic of Tanzania, Upper Volta
EUROPE	Austria, Belgium, Denmark, Finland, France, West Germany, Greece, Ireland, Italy, Netherlands, Norway, Portugal, Spain, Sweden, Switzerland, United Kingdom, Yugoslavia	Albania, Bulgaria, Czechoslovakia, Hungary, Poland, Romania, Union of Soviet Socialist Republics		
NORTH AMERICA	Canada, United States			

LATIN AMERICA	Argentina	Honduras	Haiti
	Bolivia	Mexico	
	Brazil	Nicaragua	
	Chile	Panama	
	Colombia	Paraguay	
	Costa Rica	Peru	
	Ecuador	Uruguay	
	El Salvador	Venezuela	
	Guatemala		
CARIBBEAN	Cuba		
	Dominican Republic		
	Jamaica		
	Trinidad + Tobago		
OCEANIA	Australia		
	New Zealand		
ASIA	Israel		
	Japan		
	Burma	Pakistan	Democratic Yemen
	Democratic Kampuchea	Philippines	Nepal
	India	Singapore	
	Indonesia	Sri Lanka	
	Iran	Syrian Arab Republic	
	Iraq	Thailand	
	Jordan	Turkey	
	South Korea	Republic of Vietnam	
	Lebanon		
	Malaysia		

Note: Countries with populations greater than 1 million in 1969 excluded from this analysis for reasons of incomplete data include: Afghanistan, Angola, Bangladesh, China, Democratic People's Republic of Korea, Democratic Republic of Vietnam, Ifni, Laos, Mozambique, Mongolia, Papua New Guinea, Saudi Arabia, Taiwan, and Yemen. The city states of East and West Berlin were excluded from the analysis as were the politically dependent territories of Hong Kong and Puerto Rico.

with per capita gross domestic product (GDP) averaging less than $100 in 1970 prices. Literacy in LDCs averages less than 20 percent of the adult population aged 15 years or older. Countries designated by the United Nations as LDCs are targeted for priority international development assistance (World Bank 1980; U.N. 1979d). At the present time, 24 (16 percent) of the United Nations' member states are classified as LDCs.

Chart 3-4 groups the 107 nations included in the present study by type and level of economic development and by geographic location. As seen in that chart, the present study includes 24 Developed Market Economy nations (DME), 7 Eastern Trading Area nations (ETA), 58 Developing nations (DCs), and 18 Least Developing Countries (LDCs). The six LDCs for which adequate social indicator data could not be obtained and which, therefore, were ineligible for inclusion in the analysis are: Lesotho, Afghanistan, Bhutan, Laos, Arab Yemen, and Bangladesh.

As shown in Table 3–1, these 107 nations included 70 percent of the world's total population in 1969–70 and 63 percent of the world's total in 1979–80. Given the preliminary nature of the present investigation, then, the inclusion of such a large proportion of the world's total population is judged to be more than adequate to justify inferences concerning the changing capacity over time of all the world's nations in providing more adequately for the material and social needs of their populations.

FIELD TESTING OF THE ISP

Field testing of the ISP took place in two stages. The first field testing occurred in late 1978 and early 1979 as part of a series of consultative visits to some 20 nations located in Northern and Western Europe, the Middle East, and areas of the Near East.[5] These visits involved meetings with social welfare planners and researchers and with staff members of various national ministries of social welfare. They also included on-site visits to various social welfare service agencies, including centers of local social development activity. During all of these visits the research and planning purposes of the ISP were described. As appropriate, preliminary findings from the application of the ISP to individual countries were shared and discussed.

Following several slight revisions in the choice of indicators and, in some cases, the number included in four of the model's subindexes (which

[5]These visits were made possible through Fulbright-Hays Senior Lecturer awards to the author for fall 1978 (Iran) and spring 1979 (Norway). The International Communications Agency (ICA) of the U.S. Department of State, the Ministry of Education of the Government of Iran, and the University of Trondheim, Norway, are thanked for their financial assistance to the author during these time periods.

TABLE 3–1   Population Size by Type of Economic Development and Year
(N = 107 world total)

	1969–70 (millions)	Percent of total		1979–80 (millions)	Percent of total	
All nations	3612	100.0		4258	100.0	
Developed Market Economies (N = 24)	704	28.0		724	26.8	
Eastern Trading Area (N = 7)	329	13.1		328	12.1	
Developing Countries (N = 58)	1379	54.8 ⎫		1534	57.0 ⎫	
Least Developing Countries (N = 18)	104	4.1 ⎬ 58.9		115	4.3 ⎬ 61.3	
Study total (N = 107)	2516	100.0		2701	100.0	
As percentage of all nations		69.7			63.4	

then totaled ten), the ISP then was applied to analysis of welfare develop-
ments over time in all 107 nations selected for inclusion in the study. The
results of this more refined analysis were presented subsequently to two international congresses of experts in social welfare that met in Hong Kong
during summer 1980.[6]

The ISP's second field testing occurred during summer 1980, again
through a series of consultative visits to national ministries of social welfare
and voluntary social welfare organizations located in various parts of the
world. During this three-month period, though, meetings were held in various parts of East, Middle South, and Eastern South Asia, including India,

---

[6]The Inter-University Consortium for International Social Development and the International Congress of Schools of Social Work.

Pakistan, Malaysia, Thailand, and Japan. Again, the purpose and organization of the revised ISP was described to welfare specialists in these countries. Nation-specific and subregional findings also were shared with these international social development specialists who, in turn, made suggestions to the author concerning ways in which the analytical power of the ISP could be enhanced. Again, several of the ISP subindexes were revised slightly through the substitution of what were judged to be more reliable indicators of social progress. The Defense subindex was added to the ISP as a consequence of these visits.

Between fall 1980 and summer 1982, analytical work on the revised ISP—including validity and reliability studies (Appendix A)—was completed.[7] The preliminary findings resulting from these analyses were reported to a gathering of specialists in an international social development meeting in Brighton, England, during summer 1982 (Estes 1984). The present report is based on ISP analyses completed for presentation at that time.

ISP VALIDITY AND RELIABILITY

The ISP is characterized by both *face* and *content* validity. That is, the ISP measures exactly what it was intended to measure (a broad range of welfare-relevant social phenomena) and provides an adequate sample of these phenomena (44 indicators distributed among 11 subindexes). The ISP also is characterized by a reasonable degree of *concurrent* validity as well, that is, it does succeed in distinguishing subtle shifts in the adequacy of social provision characterizing nations at different points in time.

Formal tests of the ISP to assess degree of statistical reliability (with respect to index stability, equivalence and homogeneity) were not undertaken. Factor analysis was performed to eliminate redundant indicators from the index, however, as were inter-index correlational analyses for both 1969–70 and 1979–80. The results of these latter analyses appear as Table B–18 in Appendix B. Consultations with international specialists in comparative social welfare, however, suggest a high level of reliability for the ISP. Subsequent index scores for the four major clusters of nations used in the analysis offer additional evidence in support of the measure's reliability.

[7]Thanks are due the Center for the Study of Social Work Practice of the University of Pennsylvania School of Social Work for its support of the data analysis portion of this study.

4

Global Trends in Social Provision

As a development planning tool the ISP is only as good as the quality of the data on which it is based and the nature of the analyses that it makes possible.

This chapter reports the study's major findings obtained from application of the ISP to 107 nations over the ten-year period 1969–70 to 1979–80. It illustrates the versatile uses of the ISP in analyzing welfare shifts that have occurred at various levels of inquiry, including adequacy of social provision for the world as a whole and for various economic development groupings and geopolitical regions. Discussed here is the impact of national welfare changes on the level of living characteristic of the world's population studied at various levels of aggregation. ISP findings for individual nations are reported in the next chapter.

SOCIAL PROVISION WORLDWIDE

The study's major findings are summarized in Tables 4–1 through 4–10. Table 4–1, for example, reports the mean raw scores for the 44 indicators that make up the ISP. These scores are grouped in the table by the study's two modal years—1969–70 and 1979–80—and by the four economic development groupings used to classify the 107 nations for which the analysis was undertaken. Global composite scores also are reported in these tables.

Table 4–2 reports the percentage change observed on indicator raw scores between 1970 and 1980.[1] Changes reported in parentheses ( ) indicate a general trend toward *less adequate* levels of social provision over the

---

[1]Percentages were computed as follows: $(('79/80) - ('69/70)/('69/70))$; thus, School Enrollment Ratio for all countries $(N = 107) = ((85.8 - 83.1)/83.1) = +3.2$ percent.

TABLE 4–1 Mean Raw Scores on Index of Social Progress (ISP) by Subindex and Development Classification

Subindex Indicators	Modal Data Years(s)	All Countries (N = 107) X̄	(S.D.)	Developed Market Economies (N = 24)	Eastern Trading Area (N = 7)	Developing Countries (N = 58)	Least Developing Countries (N = 18)
1. Education Subindex							
School enrollment ratio, First level (+)ᵃ	1969–70	83.1	(31.3)	104.1	102.3	87.1	34.4
	1980	85.8	(27.5)	97.6	100.0	91.3	46.9
Pupil-teacher ratio, First level (−)	1969	34.9	(11.3)	25.4	21.4	38.0	42.9
	1980	32.8	(12.7)	21.7	16.9	35.4	45.6
Percent adult illiteracy (−)	1969	42.8	(33.6)	7.3	8.7	48.3	85.9
	1980	42.1	(34.2)	6.2	7.7	47.3	86.5
Percent GNP in education (+)	1969–70	4.1	(1.6)	5.0	5.1	3.7	3.6
	1980	4.5	(1.9)	5.6	5.1	4.2	3.6
2. Health Status Subindex							
Rate infant mortality per 1000 live born (−)	1969	73.8	(55.3)	27.7	41.6	78.7	131.9
	1980	69.3	(58.8)	18.5	33.2	77.7	124.3
Population in thousands per physician (−)	1969	11.2	(17.8)	0.8	0.7	7.5	41.2
	1978	9.4	(15.7)	0.7	0.4	6.0	35.5

Life expectation at 1 year, males (+)	1969	55.8	(11.8)	68.8	68.0	54.0	39.6
	1979	55.1	(12.0)	68.8	66.5	52.8	39.9
3. Women Status Subindex							
Percent age eligible girls attending first level schools (+)	1970	74.8	(35.1)	102.4	101.3	75.8	24.3
	1979	82.7	(29.3)	102.3	97.6	85.9	40.2
Percent children in primary schools girls (+)	1970	43.1	(7.9)	49.2	48.3	43.2	32.9
	1977	44.6	(6.4)	49.4	48.7	44.7	36.4
Percent adult female illiteracy (−)	1970	47.1	(37.5)	5.3	5.8	55.6	91.5
	1980	40.4	(34.8)	3.8	4.9	45.9	85.3
Years since women suffrage (+)	1969	27.5	(18.7)	46.0	40.9	22.2	14.7
	1979	37.0	(19.6)	56.0	50.9	31.4	24.1
Years since women suffrage equal to men (+)	1969	22.6	(16.1)	37.8	33.1	17.8	13.6
	1979	31.9	(17.1)	47.7	43.1	27.0	22.4
4. Defense Effort Subindex							
Percent GNP in defense spending (−)	1969	3.6	(3.9)	4.3	4.2	3.5	2.7
	1979	3.9	(3.7)	3.7	4.7	4.3	2.9

45

TABLE 4-1   Continued

Subindex Indicators	Modal Data Years(s)	All Countries (N = 107) $\overline{X}$ (S.D.)		Developed Market Economies (N = 24)	Eastern Trading Area (N = 7)	Developing Countries (N = 58)	Least Developing Countries (N = 18)
5. Economic Subindex							
Economic growth rate (+)	1967–68 1979	4.6 4.5	(4.1) (2.4)	4.7 3.8	8.3 5.3	4.3 5.1	3.8 3.3
Per capita income (est. U.S. dollars) (+)	1969 1979	771.5 2235.6	(909.6) (2767.0)	1961.1 6259.0	2100.0 3355.1	334.5 1076.1	76.8 171.7
Average annual rate of inflation (−)	1960–70 1970–79	6.8 15.4	(18.7) (25.9)	4.9 11.9	0.0 0.0	9.2 20.3	4.0 10.5
Per capita food production index (1970 = 100) (+)	1976–78	101.8	(12.8)	108.4	114.6	100.4	92.8
6. Demography Subindex							
Total annual population (Thousands) (−)	1970 1979	23519.0(62025.8) 25248.0(62394.8)		29342.0 30180.5	47000.1 46857.7	23781.5 26446.4	5777.1 6406.1

46

Crude birth rate per 1000 population (−)	1969	36.4	(13.3)	18.5	19.9	42.2	47.9
	1980	34.1	(13.9)	15.5	19.3	39.6	47.0
Crude death rate per 1000 population (−)	1969	14.5	(6.3)	10.2	9.4	14.2	23.0
	1974–78	12.6	(12.6)	9.5	10.1	11.4	21.8
Rate population increase (−)	1963–69	2.2	(0.9)	1.1	0.9	2.7	2.4
	1978	2.2	(1.1)	0.8	1.0	2.7	2.7
Percent of population under 15 years (−)	1970	39.8	(0.1)	26.7	26.1	43.7	43.8
	1979	38.9	(0.4)	27.3	26.0	43.7	43.6
7. Geography Subindex							
Percent arable land mass (+)	1971	39.6	(21.8)	50.5	54.1	33.6	39.1
Number disaster impacts (−)	1947–79	8.8	(32.3)	21.7	2.4	6.4	1.7
Lives lost in disasters per million population (−)	1947–79	249.1	(511.6)	70.3	12.4	369.6	191.4
8. Political Stability Subindex							
Political protest demonstrations (−)	1969	5.0	(17.1)	10.8	19.1	2.3	0.2
	1977	3.7	(9.1)	10.3	5.9	1.7	0.6

TABLE 4-1 Continued

Subindex Indicators	Modal Data Years(s)	All Countries (N = 107) X̄ (S.D.)		Developed Market Economies (N = 24)	Eastern Trading Area (N = 7)	Developing Countries (N = 58)	Least Developing Countries (N = 18)
Political riots (−)	1969	1.9	(5.3)	3.8	0.7	1.8	0.1
	1977	1.7	(5.3)	4.6	0.1	1.1	0.1
Political strikes (−)	1969	1.0	(3.0)	1.9	0.0	1.0	0.0
	1977	0.6	(1.8)	1.4	0.1	0.5	0.2
Armed attacks (−)	1969	17.5	(127.7)	8.0	0.1	28.6	1.0
	1977	8.6	(33.0)	22.8	0.3	5.3	3.7
Deaths from domestic violence (−)	1969	274.1	(1949.3)	0.0	0.1	497.0	28.3
	1977	12.0	(56.6)	0.3	0.0	10.3	37.9
9. Political Participation Subindex							
Years since independence (+)	1969	78	(73)	140.0	79.0	65.0	36.0
	1979	88	(73)	150.0	89.0	75.0	46.0
Years since most recent constitution (+)	1969	28	(42)	67.0	20.0	19.0	7.0
	1979	29	(41)	68.0	17.0	20.0	12.0
Functioning parliamentary system (+)	1972	2.4	(1.2)	2.9	3.0	2.3	1.5
	1977	2.0	(1.2)	2.9	2.3	1.9	1.1

48

Functioning political party system (+)	1972	.6	1.2	1.0	1.8	(.8)	1.2
	1977	.7	1.0	1.0	2.0	(.7)	1.2
Influence of military (−)	1972	1.0	.7	.1	.1	(.9)	.6
	1977	1.6	1.0	1.0	.1	(.8)	.9
Number of popular elections held (+)	1969	.2	.5	.6	1.3	(1.7)	.6
	1977	.3	.4	.3	1.1	(1.0)	.5
10. Cultural Diversity Subindex							
Largest percent sharing same mother tongue (+)	1952–66	52.8	71.3	82.6	85.6	(25.9)	72.1
Largest percent sharing same basic religious beliefs (+)	1980	67.5	83.8	74.9	90.0	(18.1)	81.6
Ethnic-linguistic fractionalization index (−)	1964	.56	.46	.26	.28	(.30)	.42
11. Welfare Effort Subindex							
Years since first law—old age, invalidity, death (+)	1969	1.2	2.0	5.1	5.5	(2.1)	2.9

TABLE 4–1 Continued

Subindex Indicators	Modal Data Years(s)	All Countries (N = 107) $\overline{X}$ (S.D.)		Developed Market Economies (N = 24)	Eastern Trading Area (N = 7)	Developing Countries (N = 58)	Least Developing Countries (N = 18)
Years since first law—sickness and maternity (+)	1969	3.0	(2.3)	5.3	6.1	2.1	1.3
Years since first law—work injury (+)	1969	4.7	(2.0)	7.0	6.4	4.2	2.9
Years since first law—unemployment (+)	1969	1.3	(2.1)	4.6	1.3	0.4	0.1
Years since first law—family allowances (+)	1969	1.5	(1.5)	2.9	3.0	0.9	0.8

^aSigns indicate directionality of indicators, that is, a positive sign (+) indicates that *more* of factor "X" is more desirable than less of factor "X"; similarly, a negative sign (−) indicates that *less* of factor "X" is more desirable.

period of the decade, that is, toward increased levels of national social vulnerability (NSV). Otherwise, changes reported—regardless of the mathematical sign associated with the change—indicate progress within these nations in providing *more adequately* for the basic social needs of their populations along the dimensions shown. Changes greater than ± 10 percent are judged to be *substantial* given the extraordinary national commitment (or lack of it, in the case of diminished social progress) that was required to effect social change of any type at this level of accomplishment.

Between 1970 and 1980, for example, the ISP shows that the most substantial gains worldwide occurred on the indicators that make up the subindexes of Education, Women Status, Defense Effort, and Political Stability. Movement on the 15 indicators that make up these subindexes all occurred in the desired direction. For example, a larger percentage of age-eligible children were enrolled in primary school, adult illiteracy declined, the percentage of GNP devoted to basic and advanced education rose, the percentage of GNP allocated to defense expenditures declined, the incidence of destabilizing political events dropped, and so on. These shifts forward in global social provision indicate substantial and real gains on the part of the world's nations in providing more adequately for the basic needs of their populations.

Similarly, substantial gains in social progress occurred on the Health Status subindex, albeit the average world life expectation for males at one year of age dropped slightly (down an average of 1.3 percent from 55.8 years in 1969 to 55.1 years in 1979). The Demography subindex also reflects real progress on the part of the world's nations in reducing mortality rates of both infants (-6 percent) and in general (-13 percent). World progress in reducing global death rates, however, resulted in the average population size of nations increasing by some 7.4 percent—an increase in some 650 million persons overall—during the decade, a factor that is assessed negatively on the ISP.

The most profound global setbacks in levels of previously attained social progress occurred on the Economic and Political Participation subindexes. Five of the ten indicators that make up these subindexes moved toward increased levels of national and global social vulnerability. The negative findings on the Economic subindex, for example, reflect the severe economic problems experienced by the majority of the world's nations during much of the second half of the 1970s (high rates of inflation coupled with reduced rates of economic expansion).

Even more alarming, however, are the reductions in levels of participatory governance observed to have occurred for many of the world's nations on the Political Participation subindex. Sharp declines are found on three of the subindex's six indicators: presence of a functioning parliamentary system (-17 percent); number of popular elections held (-17 per-

TABLE 4–2   Percent Change in Mean Raw Scores for Selected Indicators of Social Progress Between Modal Years 1969–70 and 1979–80 by Subindex and Development Classification Groupings (N = 107)

Subindex Indicators	Modal Data Years(s)	All (N = 107)	Developed Market Economies (N = 24)	Eastern Trading Area (N = 7)	Developing Countries (N = 58)	Least Developing Countries (N = 18)
1. Education Subindex						
School enrollment ratio, First level (+)	1969–70 1980	+3.2	(−6.2)[a]	(−2.2)	+4.8	+36.3
Pupil-teacher ratio, First level (−)	1969 1980	−6.0	−14.6	−21.0	−6.8	(+6.3)
Percent adult illiteracy (−)	1980	−1.6	−15.1	−11.5	−2.1	(+0.7)
Percent GNP in education (+)	1969–70 1980	+9.8	+12.0	NC[b]	+13.5	NC
2. Health Status Subindex						
Rate infant mortality per 1000 live born (−)	1969 1980	−6.1	−33.2	−20.2	−1.3	−5.8
Population in thousands per physician (−)	1969 1978	−16.1	−12.5	−42.9	−20.0	−13.8

Life expectation at 1 year, males (+)	1969 1978	(−1.3)	NC	(−2.2)	(−2.2)	+0.8
3. Women Status Subindex						
Percent age eligible girls attending first level schools (+)	1970 1979	+10.6	NC	(−3.7)	+13.3	+65.4
Percent children in primary schools girls (+)	1970 1977	+3.5	+0.4	+0.8	+3.4	+10.6
Percent adult female illiteracy (−)	1970 1980	−14.2	−28.3	−15.5	−17.4	−6.8
Years since women suffrage (+)	1969 1979	+34.5	+21.7	+24.4	+41.4	+63.9
Years since women suffrage equal to men (+)	1969 1979	+41.2	+26.2	+30.2	+51.7	+64.7
4. Defense Effort Subindex						
Percent GNP in defense spending (−)	1969 1979	(+8.3)	−14.0	(+11.9)	(+22.9)	(+7.4)

TABLE 4–2 Continued

Subindex Indicators	Modal Data Years(s)	All (N = 107)	Developed Market Economies (N = 24)	Eastern Trading Area (N = 7)	Developing Countries (N = 58)	Least Developing Countries (N = 18)
5. Economic Subindex						
Economic growth rate (+)	1967–68 1979	(−2.2)	(−19.1)	(−36.1)	+18.6	+13.2
Per capita income (est. U.S. Dollars) (+)	1969 1979	+189.8	+219.2	+59.8	+221.7	+123.6
Average annual rate of inflation (−)	1960–70 1970–79	(+126.5)	(+142.9)	NC	(+120.7)	(+162.5)
Per capita food production index (1970 = 100) (+)	1976–78	+1.8	+8.4	+14.6	+0.4	(−7.2)
6. Demography Subindex						
Total annual population (Thousands) (−)	1970 1979	(+7.4)	(+2.8)	(+0.3)	(+11.2)	(+10.9)

Crude birth rate per 1000 population (−)	1969 1980	−6.3	−16.2	−3.0	−6.2	−1.9
Crude death rate per 1000 population (−)	1969 1974–78	−13.1	−6.9	(+7.4)	−19.7	−5.2
Rate population increase (−)	1963–69 1978	NC	−27.2	(+11.1)	NC	(+12.5)
Percent of population under 15 years (−)	1970 1979	−2.3	(+2.2)	−0.4	NC	−0.5
7. Geography Subindex^c						
Percent arable land mass (+)	1971	NC				
Number disaster impact (−)	1974–79	NC				
Lives lost in disasters per million population (−)	1974–79	NC				
8. Political Stability Subindex						
Political protest demonstrations (−)	1969 1977	−26.0	−4.6	−69.1	−26.1	(+200.0)

TABLE 4-2   Continued

Subindex Indicators	Modal Data Years(s)	All (N = 107)	Developed Market Economies (N = 24)	Eastern Trading Area (N = 7)	Developing Countries (N = 58)	Least Developing Countries (N = 18)
Political riots (−)	1969 1977	− 10.5	(+21.1)	−85.7	−38.9	NC
Political strikes (−)	1969 1977	−40.0	−26.3	(+10.0)	−50.0	(+20.0)
Armed attacks (−)	1969 1977	−50.9	(+185.0)	(+200.0)	−81.5	(+270.0)
Deaths from domestic violence (−)	1969 1977	−95.6	(+30.0)	−10.0	−97.9	(+33.9)
9. Political Participation Subindex						
Years since independence (+)	1969 1979	+ 12.8	+7.1	+12.7	+ 15.4	+27.8
Years since most recent constitution (+)	1969 1979	+3.6	+1.5	(− 15.0)	+ 5.3	+71.4
Functioning parliamentary system (+)	1972 1977	(− 16.7)	NC	(−23.3)	(− 17.4)	(−26.7)

Functioning political party system (+)	1972 1977	NC	+11.1	NC	(−16.7)	+16.7
Influence of military (−)	1972 1977	(+50.0)	NC	(+900.0)	(+42.9)	(+60.0)
Number of popular elections held (+)	1969 1977	(−16.7)	(−15.4)	(−50.0)	(−20.0)	+50.0
10. Cultural Diversity Subindex^c						
Largest percent sharing same mother tongue (+)	1952–66	NC				
Largest percent sharing same basic religious beliefs (+)	1980	NC				
Ethnic-linguistic fractionalization index (−)	1964	NC				
11. Welfare Effort Subindex^c						
Years since first law—old age, invalidity, death (+)	1969	NC				

TABLE 4-2   Continued

Subindex Indicators	Modal Data Years(s)	All (N = 107)	Developed Market Economies (N = 24)	Eastern Trading Area (N = 7)	Developing Countries (N = 58)	Least Developing Countries (N = 18)
Years since first law—sickness and maternity (+)	1969	NC				
Years since first law—work injury (+)	1969	NC				
Years since first law—unemployment (+)	1969	NC				
Years since first law—family allowances (+)	1969	NC				

[a]Brackets indicate unfavorable changes in modal year 1979 relative to 1969 social progress level(s).
[b]NC = no measurable change(s) between modal years 1969–70 and 1979–80.
[c]Data reported in these subindexes were treated as statistical constants for both modal time periods.

58

cent); and influence of the military in the civilian affairs of a nation (+50 percent). As shown in Table 4–3, the number of nations controlled either directly or indirectly by military authorities nearly doubled over the decade, from 33 to 65. This trend was most dramatic for nations in all economic development classifications with the exception of those Developed Market Economy countries (DMEs) of Western Europe, North America, Oceania, and Asia (see Chart 3–4 for a country-specific listing).

The Geography, Cultural Diversity and Welfare Effort subindexes were treated as statistical constants for each nation for both time periods of the study. This decision was judged to be an appropriate one given the slow pace at which the indicators used to form these subindexes change over time (that is, weather patterns tend to remain more or less constant; ethnic, linguistic, and religious patterns are very slow to change; and, in general, significant patterns of formal social welfare provision tend to remain relatively stable once implemented). As a result, no gains or losses in social progress are reported for the indicators contained on these subindexes. As reported in Table 4–1, however, enormous variations do exist throughout the world with respect to these critical dimensions of social development. Not coincidentally, the most unfavorable changes in levels of social progress attained over the decade occurred within those nations characterized by higher than average levels of cultural diversity ($r = .57$), recurrent exposures to serious natural disasters ($r = .84$), and in which level of organized social welfare programs and services continued to be minimal ($r = .84$). These findings are discussed in greater detail in the next section of this chapter where standardized versions of the study's two composite indexes (the ISP and INSP) are reported.

Table 4–4 reports the same data as Table 4–1, but, this time, as *standardized* versions of the raw scores (as Z-scores).[2] Transformation of raw data values into these standardized Z-scores was a necessary first step in the creation of the study's several composite indexes and subindexes (see Appendix B, Step 2, for a description of the computational procedures and formulae used to compute these standardized scores).

---

[2]Transformation of raw data into standardized Z-scores generates a new variable with a *group* mean of 0 and a *group* standard deviation of 1, the same mathematical properties assigned to the bell-shaped curve of the normal distribution. As such, Z-scores reflect the relative location—measured in units of standard deviations—of a particular observation, or set of observations, along such a distribution (usually ranging between ±3 of 0). Percent changes in standardized scores, inasmuch as the group mean has been set at a constant value of 0, whatever its raw score value, always reflect changes *relative* to those that occur in other parts of the world (Table 4–6). Changes in raw score values reflect *actual* increases or decreases in the social phenomena captured by the indicator or index. These actual and relative changes in ISP and subindex values are important elements in the present analysis. (For a fuller discussion of the purposes and uses of Z-scores in index construction, see Blalock 1979.)

TABLE 4-3   Role of Military in Civilian Affairs by Development Classification and Modal Year (N = 107)

Economic Developing Grouping	Modal Year					
	1970[a]			1977[b]		
	Quasi-Military	Direct Military	Total Military	Quasi-Military	Direct Military	Total Military
Developed market economies (N = 24)	—	1 (4%)	1 (4%)	2 (8%)	—	2 (8%)
Eastern trading area (N = 7)	1 (14%)	0	1 (14%)	7(100%)	—	7(100%)
Developing countries (N = 58)	4 (7%)	18 (31%)	22 (38%)	19 (33%)	20 (34%)	39 (67%)
Least developing countries (N = 18)	—	9 (50%)	9 (50%)	5 (28%)	12 (67%)	17 (94%)
All countries (n = 107)	5 (5%)	28 (26%)	33 (31%)	33 (31%)	32 (30%)	65 (61%)

[a]Blondel (1972)
[b]Castil (1978)

TABLE 4-4 Mean Transformed Raw Scores by Social Progress Subindexes and Development Classification Groupings (N = 107)[a]

Subindex Indicators[b]	Modal Data Year(s)	All (N = 107) X̄ (S.D.)	Developed Market Economies (N = 24)	Eastern Trading Area (N = 7)	Developing Countries (N = 58)	Least Developing Countries (N = 18)
1. Education Subindex						
School enrollment ratio, First level (+)[c]	1969–70	0.0 (1.0)	.674	.615	.130	−1.556
	1980	0.0 (1.0)	.429	.515	.199	−1.414
Pupil-teacher ratio, First level (−)	1969	0.0 (1.0)	−0.847	−1.197	.274	.711
	1980	0.0 (1.0)	−0.874	−1.255	.201	1.004
Percent adult illiteracy (−)	1980	0.0 (1.0)	−1.059	−1.017	.163	1.283
			−1.051	−1.006	.153	1.300
Percent GNP in education (+)	1969–70	0.0 (1.0)	.566	.616	−0.218	−0.290
	1980	0.0 (1.0)	.559	.294	−0.125	−0.456
2. Health Status Subindex						
Rate infant mortality per 1000 live born (−)	1969	0.0 (1.0)	−0.833	−0.583	.089	1.052
	1980	0.0 (1.0)	−0.865	−0.615	.142	.934
Population in thousands per physician (−)	1969	0.0 (1.0)	−0.589	−0.592	−0.209	1.688
	1978	0.0 (1.0)	−0.558	−0.577	−0.217	1.668

TABLE 4–4   Continued

Subindex Indicators[b]	Modal Data Year(s)	All (N = 107) X̄ (S.D.)	Developed Market Economies (N = 24)	Eastern Trading Area (N = 7)	Developing Countries (N = 58)	Least Developing Countries (N = 18)
Life expectation at 1 year, males (+)	1969 1978	0.0 (1.0) 0.0 (1.0)	1.104 1.138	1.041 .947	−0.155 −0.192	−1.378 −1.269
3. Women Status Subindex						
Percent age eligible girls attending first level schools (+)	1970 1979	0.0 (1.0) 0.0 (1.0)	.787 .669	.756 .509	.030 .112	−1.440 −1.451
Percent children in primary schools girls (+)	1970 1977	0.0 (1.0) 0.0 (1.0)	.768 .742	.649 .643	.004 .013	−1.290 −1.281
Percent adult female illiteracy (−)	1970 1980	0.0 (1.0) 0.0 (1.0)	−1.116 −1.053	−1.103 −1.020	.227 .158	1.183 1.292
Years since women suffrage (+)	1969 1979	0.0 (1.0) 0.0 (1.0)	.991 .969	.713 .709	−0.284 −0.283	−0.683 −0.656
Years since women suffrage equal to men (+)	1969 1979	0.0 (1.0) 0.0 (1.0)	.951 .924	.659 .656	−0.299 −0.289	−0.561 −0.556

4. Defense Effort Subindex						
Percent GNP in defense spending (−)	1969	0.0 (1.0)	.180	.143	−0.020	−0.230
	1979	0.0 (1.0)	−0.076	.194	.092	−0.271
5. Economic Subindex						
Economic growth rate (+)	1967–68	0.0 (1.0)	.037	.903	−0.064	−0.195
	1979	0.0 (1.0)	−0.310	.325	.249	−0.517
Per capita income—(est. U.S. Dollars) (+)	1969	0.0 (1.0)	1.308	1.461	−0.480	−0.764
	1979	0.0 (1.0)	1.454	.405	−0.419	−0.746
Average annual of inflation (−)	1960–70	0.0 (1.0)	−0.100	−0.363	.132	−0.150
	1970–79	0.0 (1.0)	−0.137	−0.594	.188	−0.191
Per capita food production index (1970 = 100) (+)	1976–78	0.0 (1.0)	.516	.997	−0.114	−0.707
6. Demography Subindex						
Total annual population (Thousands) (−)	1970	0.0 (1.0)	.094	.379	.004	−0.286
	1979	0.0 (1.0)	.079	.346	.019	−0.302
Crude birth rate per 1000 population (−)	1969	0.0 (1.0)	−1.343	−1.244	.438	.863
	1980	0.0 (1.0)	−1.335	−1.063	.395	.919

TABLE 4-4   Continued

Subindex Indicators[b]	Modal Data Year(s)	All (N = 107) X̄ (S.D.)	Developed Market Economies (N = 24)	Eastern Trading Area (N = 7)	Developing Countries (N = 58)	Least Developing Countries (N = 18)
Crude death rate per 1000 population (−)	1969 1974–78	0.0 (1.0) 0.0 (1.0)	−0.684 −0.487	−0.806 −0.398	−0.045 −0.193	1.371 1.427
Rate population increase (−)	1963–69 1978	0.0 (1.0) 0.0 (1.0)	−1.141 −1.257	−1.338 −1.062	.557 .494	.247 .497
Percent of population under 15 years (−)	1970 1979	0.0 (1.0) 0.0 (1.0)	−1.355 −1.293	−1.421 −1.438	.557 .544	.564 .532
7. Geography Subindex						
Percent arable land mass (+)	1971	0.0 (1.0)	.499	.665	−0.279	−0.026
Number disaster impacts (−)	1947–79	0.0 (1.0)	.400	−0.197	−0.074	−0.220
Lives lost in disasters per million population (−)	1947–79	0.0 (1.0)	−0.350	−0.463	.236	−0.113

8. Political Stability Subindex

Political protest demonstrations (−)	1969	0.0 (1.0)	.342	.831	−0.156	−0.277
	1977	0.0 (1.0)	.718	.233	−0.219	−0.341
Political riots (−)	1969	0.0 (1.0)	.358	−0.227	−0.015	−0.341
	1977	0.0 (1.0)	.564	−0.290	−0.107	−0.296
Political strikes (−)	1969	0.0 (1.0)	.320	−0.317	.004	−0.317
	1977	0.0 (1.0)	.417	−0.272	−0.060	−0.259
Armed attacks (−)	1969	0.0 (1.0)	−0.074	−0.136	.087	−0.129
	1977	0.0 (1.0)	.431	−0.253	−0.101	−0.150
Deaths from domestic violence (−)	1969	0.0 (1.0)	−0.141	−0.141	.114	−0.126
	1977	0.0 (1.0)	−0.207	−0.212	−0.031	.458

9. Political Participation Subindex

Years since independence (+)	1969	0.0 (1.0)	.851	.018	−0.174	−0.583
	1979	0.0 (1.0)	.851	.018	−0.174	−0.583
Years since most recent constitution (+)	1969	0.0 (1.0)	.929	−0.186	−0.209	−0.492
	1979	0.0 (1.0)	.944	−0.290	−0.223	−0.428
Functioning parliamentary system (+)	1972	0.0 (1.0)	.428	.531	−0.023	−0.704
	1977	0.0 (1.0)	.740	.236	−0.096	−0.768
Functioning political party system (+)	1972	0.0 (1.0)	.746	−0.262	−0.020	−0.827
	1977	0.0 (1.0)	1.078	−0.230	−0.206	−0.684

TABLE 4-4 Continued

Subindex Indicators[b]	Modal Data Year(s)	All (N = 107) X̄ (S.D.)	Developed Market Economies (N = 24)	Eastern Trading Area (N = 7)	Developing Countries (N = 58)	Least Developing Countries (N = 18)
Influence of military (−)	1972 1977	0.0 (1.0) 0.0 (1.0)	−0.553 −0.992	−0.485 .113	.136 .133	.488 .849
Number of popular elections held (+)	1969 1977	0.0 (1.0) 0.0 (1.0)	.358 .551	−0.037 −0.209	−0.059 −0.136	−0.273 −0.216
10. Cultural Diversity Subindex						
Largest percent sharing same mother tongue (+)	1952–66	0.0 (1.0)	.521	.403	−0.033	−0.744
Largest percent sharing same basic religious beliefs (+)	1980	0.0 (1.0)	.447	−0.386	.108	−0.792
Ethnic-linguistic fractionalization index (−)	1964	0.0 (1.0)	−0.470	−0.512	.103	.496

11. Welfare Effort Subindex

Years since first law—old age, invalidity, death (+)	1969	0.0 (1.0)	1.239	1.089	−0.396	−0.800
Years since first law—sickness and maternity (+)	1969	0.0 (1.0)	1.047	1.406	−0.378	−0.727
Years since first law—work injury (+)	1969	0.0 (1.0)	1.124	.857	−0.281	−0.928
Years since first law—unemployment (+)	1969	0.0 (1.0)	1.525	−0.019	−0.444	−0.595
Years since first law—family allowances (+)	1969	0.0 (1.0)	.991	1.048	−0.390	−0.472

[a]Raw data were transformed into Z-scores using the following formula:

$$\frac{x_i - \overline{x}}{SD}$$

where: x_i is the original value of the ith case
$\overline{x}$ is the mean of the variable
SD is the standard deviation

[b]Sources for data used in this table are referenced in the notes section of Appendix A.

[c]Signs indicate direction of national social vulnerability.

Average standardized scores for the ISP and INSP and for their component subindexes are summarized in Table 4–5. These scores are reported both by economic development grouping and by modal year. The average scores for all 107 nations—set statistically at 100 for the two composite indexes and at 9.1 for the eleven subindexes—also appear in the table.[3] ISP scores range from a low of − 12 for Ethiopia in 1980 to a high of + 201 for Denmark that same year; INSP scores range from − 19 (Ethiopia, 1980) to + 201 (Sweden, 1970). The ranges for subindex scores are less variable than those for the composite indexes, with a high of 67 for the Defense Effort subindex in 1970 and a low of 31 for the Education subindex in 1970 and the Women Status and Demography subindexes in 1980. The average range for all subindexes is 38. Table B-17 of Appendix B reports measures of central tendency and dispersion for all index and subindex values. The Appendix also contains intercorrelational coefficient values for all indexes and subindexes in 1969 (Table B-18).

The major global findings that result from analysis of the data contained on Table 4–5 are discussed in the next two sections of this chapter. These sections examine global changes in adequacy of social provision with respect to shifts that occurred within the study's four economic development groupings and within the world's major geopolitical regions and subregions.

DEVELOPMENT GROUPINGS AND
ADEQUACY OF SOCIAL PROVISION

The data reported in Tables 4–2, 4–5, 4–6, and 4–7 detail the differences that exist in the level of social provision characteristic of the study's four economic development groupings. Analysis of the data summarized in Table 4–5, for example, locates the most favorable ISP scores for both modal periods with the group of Developed Market Economy nations (hereafter referred to as DME or DMEs). ISP scores also are very favorable for the seven nations that make up the Eastern Trading Area (ETA or ETAs). Though average ISP scores are generally higher in DME nations (mean = 161.4) than in the ETAs (mean = 148.4), the ISP scores of four of the seven ETA nations are higher than the average score for the group of 24 DMEs— Czechoslovakia (163), Hungary (169), Poland (168), Rumania (163). ISP scores for the Soviet Union (113) reduce sharply ISP averages for the ETA group which is otherwise characterized by a level of social provision com-

---

[3]See Appendix B, Steps 4–6, for an explanation of the statistical procedures used to compute these standardized index scores.

parable in most respects to that found in DME nations. In any event, the 31 nations that make up the DME and ETA groupings are the most socially advanced nations on earth and can properly be referred to as the world's "rich" nations.

Average ISP scores are substantially lower for both the group of 58 developing nations (DCs) and the group of 18 Least Developing Countries (LDCs). Indeed, average 1980 ISP scores for developing nations (mean = 89.0) are only about half (57 percent) of those observed for DME and ETA nations (combined mean = 154.9) and average ISP scores for the LDCs (mean = 40.8) are only about one-fourth (26 percent) of those attained by DME and ETA nations. Indeed, average ISP scores for the LDCs dropped by more than eight percent during the decade!

The data reported in Table 4–5 show that over the decade the gap in development that long has existed between the world's richest and poorest nations (Ward 1971) continued to widen, rather than narrow, for many nations. Average ISP scores in 1970 for the LDCs (mean = 44.4), for example, were 28 percent of those attained by ETA nations (mean = 155.9) and 27 percent of those observed for DME countries (mean = 160.4) in 1970. By 1980, average ISP scores for the LDCs were 27 percent of those achieved by ETA nations, but only 25 percent of DME average values.

Shifts in adequacy of social provision found among the group of 58 developing nations present a more varied picture than that observed for the LDCs, however. Between 1970 and 1980, for example, average ISP scores for developing nations increased by 4.3 percent (up from 85.3 to 89.0). Indeed, higher ISP scores were found for three out of every five (60 percent) developing nations compared with only one in three (33 percent) found for the LDCs (Table 4–6). Also, when considered as a percentage of average ISP scores attained by DME nations, average ISP scores for developing nations increased from 53 percent of DME scores in 1970 to 55 percent in 1980; as a percentage of ETA average scores, average developing nation scores increased from 55 percent in 1970 to 60 percent in 1980.

Social gains within developing nations are substantial and do reflect real, if fragile, progress on the part of many countries in providing more adequately for the basic social and material needs of their populations. For some developing nations at least, the gap in adequacy of social provision that historically has characterized rich and poor countries is beginning to close, albeit if at a less rapid rate than that hoped for by many development specialists. For two out of every five developing nations (40 percent), however, social progress is not occurring and, indeed, less favorable ISP scores were found for these nations in 1980 than in 1970. The difficult social situation found within these countries is not unlike that observed in the LDCs more generally.

TABLE 4-5 Mean Standardized Scores on the Index of Social Progress (ISP) and the Index of Net Social Progress (INSP) by Subindex, Economic Development Groupings and Year (N = 107)

	Index of Social Progress	Education Subindex	Health Subindex	Women Subindex	Defense Subindex	Economic Subindex	Demographic Subindex	Geographic Subindex	Political Stability Subindex	Political Participation Subindex	Cultural Diversity Subindex	Welfare Effort Subindex	Index of Net Social Progress
Developed Market Economies (N = 24)													
1968–70	160.4	16.1	17.5	18.3	7.3	13.9	17.9	10.7	7.5	15.5	13.8	21.0	158.8
1978–80	161.4	16.3	17.6	17.8	9.8	13.6	17.7		5.3	17.6			159.8
Eastern Trading Area (N = 7)													
1968–70	155.9	17.9	16.4	16.9	7.7	18.1	18.0	13.7	9.1	9.9	11.0	18.0	151.9
1978–80	148.4	17.0	16.3	16.1	7.0	15.0	16.4		10.6	8.1			144.3
Developing Countries (N = 58)													
1968–70	85.3	7.8	9.0	7.5	9.2	6.7	6.1	7.6	9.1	8.1	9.0	5.3	86.9
1978–80	89.0	8.4	8.7	7.9	8.2	8.0	6.6		10.1	7.4			88.6

70

Least Developing Countries (N = 18)													
1968–70	44.4	−0.4	−4.6	−1.2	11.4	6.3	3.6	10.2	11.7	3.5	2.4	2.1	43.4
1978–80	40.8	−1.4	−3.9	−1.3	11.8	4.6	3.0		10.2	3.3			39.6
All countries (N = 107)													
1968–70	100.0	9.1	9.1	9.1	9.1	9.1	9.1	9.1	9.1	9.1	9.1	9.1	100.0
1978–80	100.0	9.1	9.1	9.1	9.1	9.1	9.1	9.1	9.1	9.1	9.1	9.1	100.0

TABLE 4–6   Advances and Declines on the Index of Social Progress (ISP) by Economic Development Classification, 1970–80 (N = 107)

	Advances N (%)	Declines N (%)	No Change 1980–70 N (%)	Totals N (%)
Developed market economics	15 (63)	9 (38)	0	24 (100)
Eastern trading area	1 (14)	4 (57)	2 (29)	7 (100)
Developing countries	35 (60)	22 (38)	1 (2)	58 (100)
Least developing countries	6 (33)	11 (61)	1 (6)	18 (100)
All countries	57 (53)	46 (43)	4 (4)	107 (100)

The Social Development "Gap"

Analysis of the indicator data reported in Table 4–2 provides an explanation of the complex national and international forces that have contributed to the social gains and losses found among the world's four economic development groupings. Of the 33 movable ISP indicators,[4] for example, LDC nations suffered losses over earlier social gains on 13; losses for DME nations were observed on only nine of the indicators. For LDCs, these losses, as seen in the percentage subindex changes summarized in Table 4–7, were most significant on the subindexes of Education (−250 percent), Health Status (−15 percent), Women Status (−8 percent), Economic (−27 percent), Demographic (−17 percent), Political Stability (−13 percent), and Political Participation (−6 percent).[5] All LDC losses were substantial (inflation amounted to 163 percent over the decade; GNP expenditures on defense increased by 7 percent; average population size rose by more than 10

---

[4]As used here, the term "movable" refers to those 33 indicators that form the eight subindexes for which data are reported separately for each of the study's two baseline years. The reader will recall that because of the relative slowness with which indicators change on the Cultural Diversity, Welfare Effort and Geographic subindexes these subindexes were treated as "non-movable," that is, as statistical constants, for both years of the study.

[5]As with percentage change on individual indicators (Table 4–2), net percentage changes on these composite indexes equal to or greater than 10 percent are judged to reflect significant efforts (or lack thereof in the case of diminished social progress) on the part of governments to provide more adequately for the basic social needs of their populations over the decade.

percent; the incidence of political protest demonstrations, strikes, armed attacks, and deaths from domestic violence increased by 200, 20, 270, and 34 percent respectively; and critical political participation indicators dropped precipitously as well).

Subindex losses for developing nations, though serious, were not as substantial as those found in the LDCs. They occurred mainly on the Health Status (-3 percent), Defense Effort (-11 percent), and Political Participation (-9 percent) subindexes. Moderate average gains, however, were found for developing nations on the Education ($+8$ percent), Women Status ($+5$ percent), Economic ($+19$ percent), Demographic ($+8$ percent), and Political Stability ($+11$ percent) subindexes (Table 4–7).

Between 1970 and 1980 significant losses were observed on seven of the eight movable subindexes for ETA nations: Education (-5 percent), Health Status (-1 percent), Women Status (-5 percent), Defense Effort (-9 percent), Economic (-17 percent), Demographic (-9 percent), and Political Participation (-18 percent). A social gain of 17 percent was found among ETA nations in the Political Stability subindex, however.

Social losses over the decade within DME nations, in contrast to those found for both the LDCs and ETA nations, were very small and were concentrated in only four of the eight movable subindexes: Women Status (-3 percent), Economic (-2 percent), Demographic (-1 percent), and Political Stability (-29 percent).

Subindex averages reported in Table 4–5 also reveal the very great differences that exist within developmental groupings on the Geography, Cultural Diversity, and Welfare Effort subindexes. Without exception, the least favorable scores on each of these subindexes is associated with the study's 76 developing and least developing nations. LDCs, for example, are characterized by the greatest mix of cultural diversity (mean = 2.4) and the least well-established system of organized welfare programs and services (mean = 2.1); the group of developing nations (n = 58), on the other hand, registered the lowest scores on the Geography subindex (mean = 7.6). Developing nations also are characterized by organized welfare programming of only the most minimal nature (mean = 5.3). DMEs and ETAs, on the other hand, are characterized by considerably more favorable patterns of cultural homogeneity (means = 13.8, 11.0), and geologically, are more stable (means = 10.7, 13.7). Both economic development groupings also are characterized by very sophisticated public and private systems of nationally administered social welfare programs and services (means = 21.0, 18.0).

No doubt, patterns of higher cultural homogeneity and geological stability—combined with longer histories of political independence—have made it possible for DME nations to develop a fuller spectrum of nationally administered social programs. These patterns appear to have contributed, too, to the much more favorable political environment that continued to

TABLE 4-7   Percent Change in Standardized Indexes of Social Progress (ISP and INSP) 1969–79 by Mean Subindex Scores and Economic Development Groupings (N = 107)

Economic Development Groupings	Index of Social Progress	Education Subindex	Health Subindex	Women Subindex	Defense Subindex	Economic Subindex	Demographic Subindex	Geographic Subindex[a]	Political Stability Subindex	Political Participation Subindex	Cultural Diversity Subindex[a]	Welfare Effort Subindex[a]	Index of Net Social Progress[a]
Developed market economies (N = 24)	+0.6	+1.2	+0.6	−2.7	+34.2	−2.2	−1.1	NC	−29.3	+13.5	NC	NC	+0.6
Eastern trading area (N = 7)	−4.8	−5.0	−0.6	−4.7	−9.1	−17.1	−8.9		+16.5	−18.2			−5.0
Developing countries (N = 58)	+4.3	+7.7	−3.3	+5.3	−10.9	+19.4	+8.2		+11.0	−8.6			+2.0
Least developing countries (N = 18)	−8.1	−250.0	−15.2	−8.3	+3.5	−27.0	−16.7		−12.8	−5.7			−8.5

[a]Scores on these subindexes were treated as statistical constants for both time periods.

exist within DME nations over the decade. Certainly, social planners, welfare development specialists, and political leaders experience greater success in responding to the social needs of a more or less culturally homogeneous population (such as those found in the majority of Western and Northern European nations) than do their counterparts in nations characterized by considerable cultural diversity (the majority of developing nations and LDCs located in Western, Eastern, Middle and Southern Africa, the USSR, and in Southeast and Southwest Asia).

The Social Development Gap in "Relative" Terms

Another approach to examining disparities in adequacy of social provision found in the world's four economic development groups is reflected in Table 4–8. The table summarizes net changes on 32 ISP indicators for developing nations and the LDCs *as a percentage* of the 1970 and 1980 indicator values reported for DME nations in Table 4–1. That is, the table reflects changes that occurred within developing nations *relative* to changes that occurred within DME nations during the same time period. In this way, emphasis is placed less on the *actual* increases and decreases in social progress observed in developing nations (the rate of infant mortality in the LDCs dropped 5.8 percent between 1970 and 1980—Table 4–2) and more on the significance of these changes relative to changes that occurred on the same indicators in DME nations. In 1970, for example, the rate of infant mortality in the LDCs was nearly five times (476 percent) that found in DMEs; in 1980, LDC infant mortality rate was nearly seven times higher (672 percent) than that found in DME nations. Between 1970 and 1980, therefore, the gap in development between LDC and DME nations in relation to the rate of infant mortality *widened*.

Table 4–8 shows that the relative gap in social development between DME and developing nations widened on 13 indicators and narrowed on 19; for the LDCs the relative development gap widened on 17 indicators and narrowed on 15. These trends exist despite the fact that, in real terms, actual changes on the indicators show social progress on 18 of the 32 indicators for the LDCs and on 22 for the group of developing nations. Indeed, when examined from the perspective of the relative significance of changes in helping to bridge the development gap between rich and poor countries, Table 4–8 confirms that serious disparities in adequacy of social provision continue to persist, even grow, despite apparent movement forward on some indicators. Over the long term, even positive movement within developing nations toward achieving social development objectives will prove inadequate if development within the world's already highly advanced nations continues to occur at an equal or even at a somewhat less rapid pace than that found in the world's less advantaged nations.

TABLE 4–8   Net Changes on Selected Index of Social Progress (ISP) Indicators for Developing and Least Developing Countries as a Percentage of Developed Market Economy Nation Values in 1970 and 1980 (N = 107)

| | As Percent of Developed Market Economy Nation Score[b] | | | | | |
| | Developing Countries | | | Least Developing Countries | | |
Shortened Index Items[a]	1970	1980	1970–80	1970	1980	1970–80
Education Subindex[c]	48	52	+4	–2	–9	–7
School Enrollment Ratio (+)[d]	84	94	+10	33	48	+15
Pupil Teacher Ratio (–)	150	163	(+13)[e]	169	210	(+41)
Adult Illiteracy (–)	662	763	(+101)	1177	1395	(+218)
Percent GNP in Education (+)	74	75	+1	72	64	(–8)
Health Status Subindex	51	49	–2	–27	–24	–3
Rate Infant Mortality (–)	284	420	(+136)	476	672	(+196)
Population Per Physician (–)	938	857	–81	5175	5071	–104
Male Life Expectation (+)	78	77	(–1)	58	58	NC
Women Status Subindex	41	44	+3	–7	–7	NC
Percent Girls in Primary School (+)	74	84	+10	24	39	+15
Girls as Percent of Primary School (+)	88	90	+2	67	74	+7
Female Illiteracy (–)	1050	1207	(+157)	1726	2245	(+519)
Women Suffrage (+)	48	56	+8	32	43	+11
Suffrage Equality With Men (+)	47	57	+10	36	47	+11
Defense Effort Subindex	126	84	–42	156	120	–36
Percent GNP in Defense (–)	81	116	(+35)	63	78	(+15)
Economic Subindex	48	59	+11	45	34	–11
Economic Growth Rate (+)	91	134	+43	81	87	+6
P. C. Estimated Income (+)	17	17	NC	4	3	(–1)
Inflation Rate (–)	188	171	–17	82	88	(+6)

76

Demography Subindex	34	37	+3	20	17	−3
Population Size (−)	81	88	(+7)	20	21	(+1)
Birth Rate (−)	228	255	(+27)	259	303	(+44)
Death Rate (−)	139	120	−19	225	229	(+4)
Population Increase Rate (−)	245	338	(+93)	218	338	(+120)
Percent Population 15 Years (−)	164	160	−4	164	160	−4
Political Stability Subindex	121	191	+70	156	142	+36
Protest Demonstrations (−)	21	17	−4	2	6	(+4)
Riots (−)	47	24	−23	3	2	−1
Strikes (−)	53	36	−17	0	14	(+14)
Armed Attacks (−)	357	23	−334	13	16	(+3)
Deaths Domestic Violence (−)	4970	343	−4627	2830	1263	−1567
Political Participation Subindex	52	42	−10	23	19	−4
Years Since Independence (+)	46	50	+4	26	31	+5
Age Current Constitution (+)	28	29	+1	10	18	+8
Parliamentary System (+)	79	66	(−13)	52	38	(−14)
Political Party System (+)	67	50	(−17)	33	35	+2
Influence of Military (−)	700	1000	(+300)	1000	1600	(+600)
Elections Held (+)	38	36	(−2)	15	27	+12

a"Excludes the non-movable *Geography, Cultural Diversity* and *Welfare Effort* subindexes and "Per Capita Food Production Index" of the *Economic* subindex.

b"Base data for all three economic development groups are reported in Table 4–1. Percentage of DME indicator value was computed by dividing 1970 LDC indicator value by 1970 DME indicator value, and so on.

c"Based on standardized subindex scores reported in Table 4–5.

d"Plus and minus signs indicate the desired direction of movement toward increased levels of measurable social progress.

e"Brackets ( ) indicate those indicators for which the social development gap *widened* between the DME nations and the LDCs and other Developing nations.

REGIONAL CHANGES IN ADEQUACY OF SOCIAL PROVISION

In addition to assessing welfare trends occurring on the global level and those taking place within economic development groupings, the ISP also can be applied to welfare analysis at the level of specific geopolitical regions. This advantage of the ISP makes it an especially valuable social science tool for purposes of international comparative analysis. It also can contribute practical and timely social data for purposes of more rational planning and assistance actions on the part of international social development organizations (private and public philanthropic organizations, multinational social development bodies, and other organizations that seek to improve the level of living of people throughout the world).

ISP regional data are reported in Tables 4–9 and 4–10. In grouping nations into regions, this study makes use of the typology worked out by the United Nations for purposes of its data collection and statistical reporting (United Nations 1980a). Essentially, the United Nations divides the world's countries into seven major continental groupings—Africa (n = 35), North America (n = 2), South America (n = 22), Asia (n = 22), Oceania (n = 2), the Union of Soviet Socialist Republics (n = 1) and Europe (n = 23). Four of these continental groupings are subdivided into smaller geopolitical entities: five subregions within Africa, four subregions within South America, four subregions within Asia, and four subregions within Europe. (The reader is referred to the preceding chapter—Chart 3–3—for a complete listing of the individual nations that are included in each of these 24 regional and subregional groupings.)

The data contained in Table 4–9 show that the world regions with the most favorable ISP scores in 1980 are Oceania (mean = 185.0) and Europe (mean = 165.0). Within Europe, 1980 ISP scores are even more favorable for the 12 nations of Northern (mean = 180.8) and Western (mean = 178.2) Europe. ISP scores are the least favorable for the group of 35 African nations (mean = 51.9), but especially for those countries located in the Eastern (mean = 37.5), Middle (mean = 44.0) and Western (mean = 47.3) parts of the continent.

As expected, scores on each of the subindexes for these regions are uniformly low or uniformly high. Among the European nations, for example, the quality of educational achievement, health services, status of women, economic capacity, and so on, far exceed those found among the 28 nations that make up the East, Middle, and West African subgroupings. Indeed, the subindex scores for Europe are considerably higher than for all the nations of the world with the exception of the two Oceanic countries—Australia and New Zealand—that are characterized by higher 1980 scores on all but the Economic and Demographic subindexes.

TABLE 4–9   Mean Scores on the Indexes of Social Progress by Geographic Regions, Subindexes, and Modal Years (N = 107)

	Index of Social Progress	Education Subindex	Health Subindex	Women Subindex	Defense Subindex	Economic Subindex	Demographic Subindex	Geographic Subindex	Political Stability Subindex	Political Participation Subindex	Cultural Diversity Subindex	Welfare Effort Subindex	Index of Net Social Progress
Africa	57.5[a]	2.4	−0.3	1.3	11.6	7.2	4.0	10.4	11.0	5.0	1.7	3.7	56.2
(N = 35)	51.9[b]	2.5	−0.5	1.9	9.0	5.6	3.2		10.2	4.5			50.6
Western	50.8	0.3	−1.8	0.6	12.8	6.7	4.1	10.7	10.2	4.3	0.2	3.2	49.2
(N = 13)	47.3	1.0	−2.5	0.3	11.9	4.5	2.2		11.5	4.1			45.5
Eastern	57.0	2.2	0.2	0.4	14.1	6.7	3.1	11.6	11.4	5.9	0.8	1.1	54.5
(N = 11)	37.5	1.5	−2.9	1.18	5.6	4.6	2.8		8.3	3.6			35.0
Northern	73.0	7.6	4.5	0.7	5.0	9.3	4.3	7.3	11.7	3.5	13.0	6.5	74.7
(N = 6)	85.8	9.7	8.3	2.8	6.7	9.5	4.3		11.7	6.5			87.7
Middle	41.3	0.5	−6.3	2.8	10.5	6.0	4.8	8.8	11.5	5.0	−6.0	4.5	41.8
(N = 4)	44.0	−1.0	−2.3	2.8	12.0	5.5	4.5		12.0	2.8			44.5
Southern	121.0	9.0	7.0	20.0	13.0	12.0	7.0	18.0	11.0	12.0	−6.0	18.0	112.0
(N = 1)	98.0	3.0	7.0	21.0	9.0	9.0	7.0		−3.0	14.0			89.0
North America	124.0	21.5	18.5	18.5	4.0	20.0	14.5	−8.0	−6.5	18.5	8.5	14.5	141.0
(N = 2)	143.0	20.0	18.0	18.5	10.5	17.0	15.0		5.0	25.0			160.0

79

TABLE 4–9 Continued

	Index of Social Progress	Education Subindex	Health Subindex	Women Subindex	Defense Subindex	Economic Subindex	Demographic Subindex	Geographic Subindex	Political Stability Subindex	Political Participation Subindex	Cultural Diversity Subindex	Welfare Effort Subindex	Index of Net Social Progress
South America (N = 22)	112.0	10.6	12.5	12.1	13.5	7.0	7.5	6.2	9.7	10.4	14.9	7.5	115.0
	113.3	10.5	12.6	12.1	13.9	7.3	9.5		10.4	8.4			116.3
Tropical (N = 6)	107.0	10.8	11.8	12.0	13.0	6.0	5.5	4.8	11.0	8.8	13.2	10.0	111.3
	112.8	11.5	11.3	12.7	14.5	10.8	7.5		8.5	7.7			117.2
Middle (N = 7)	105.4	9.4	12.1	10.7	14.6	8.4	4.7	2.4	11.1	12.4	15.0	4.3	112.3
	106.1	9.0	12.7	10.6	16.6	9.0	7.4		10.7	8.9			113.1
Temperate (N = 4)	125.8	13.0	14.3	14.5	13.3	3.8	13.3	11.3	2.8	10.5	15.0	14.0	123.3
	119.8	12.3	14.5	14.5	9.5	-1.8	13.8		10.5	5.8			117.5
Caribbean (N = 5)	116.2	10.4	12.2	12.4	12.4	8.6	9.4	9.0	11.6	9.4	16.6	4.4	116.6
	118.8	10.0	12.4	11.6	13.0	7.8	11.2		12.0	10.8			119.0
Asia (N = 22)	96.7	9.4	13.1	10.0	5.9	9.9	4.6	4.4	7.5	10.8	12.5	4.9	102.1
	104.6	10.2	13.4	10.0	6.7	12.4	10.1		9.7	11.1			109.6
East (N = 2)	125.5	11.5	17.0	14.0	12.0	13.5	13.0	1.0	7.5	14.5	16.5	6.0	133.5
	132.0	12.5	17.5	14.0	11.5	15.0	14.0		10.5	14.0			140.0
Middle South (N = 5)	64.0	2.4	6.0	3.2	11.4	8.0	2.4	5.6	6.0	9.8	4.6	4.4	67.6
	65.6	4.4	6.2	2.8	8.4	7.6	4.0		6.2	11.4			69.0
South East (N = 8)	69.3	7.9	9.0	9.6	4.3	1.8	7.6	6.6	6.6	5.9	5.8	3.8	71.7
	76.1	7.8	8.9	9.1	1.9	9.6	7.3		11.5	6.3			81.3
West (N = 7)	69.2	9.9	11.9	4.0	-13.7	10.1	6.9	10.6	9.6	6.3	14.3	3.1	71.6
	86.1	10.6	12.0	5.0	-2.9	11.3	6.4		7.4	8.1			84.1

	(1)	(2)	(3)	(4)	(5)	(6)	(7)	(8)	(9)	(10)	(11)	(12)	(13)
Oceania (N = 2)[a]	175.5	16.0	18.0	26.0	11.0	12.5	16.0	13.5	11.5	15.0	12.5	23.5	171.0
Oceania (N = 2)[b]	185.0	18.0	18.0	25.0	14.0	13.5	18.5		11.5	17.5			181.0
USSR (N = 1)[a]	132.0	23.0	17.0	21.0	1.0	18.0	9.0	9.0	9.0	15.0	−5.0	16.0	132.0
USSR (N = 1)[b]	113.0	21.0	16.0	20.0	−6.0	13.0	8.0		6.0	16.0			113.0
Europe (N = 23)[a]	167.5	17.0	17.5	17.4	9.5	14.4	19.5	13.0	8.7	13.9	15.1	21.7	163.8
Europe (N = 23)[b]	165.0	16.3	17.6	16.8	10.8	14.1	18.7		6.4	14.6			161.3
Western (N = 6)[a]	177.2	18.0	18.1	17.0	10.7	14.3	19.2	13.2	9.7	17.7	14.0	25.3	173.2
Western (N = 6)[b]	178.2	16.2	18.3	16.0	12.0	14.8	20.0		9.3	19.0			174.2
Southern (N = 6)[a]	143.3	12.5	16.5	13.5	7.7	12.3	18.0	13.5	7.7	10.0	15.0	17.3	139.2
Southern (N = 6)[b]	137.3	13.3	16.3	13.2	6.7	12.0	17.3		0.8	12.0			133.2
Eastern (N = 5)[a]	164.4	17.4	16.8	17.2	8.6	18.2	20.6	15.0	8.6	9.0	13.6	20.2	159.4
Eastern (N = 5)[b]	163.6	16.8	17.0	16.6	12.6	16.0	18.4		11.2	7.0			158.2
Northern (N = 6)[a]	184.5	20.2	18.3	22.0	11.0	13.3	20.5	10.7	8.7	18.2	17.5	23.8	182.8
Northern (N = 6)[b]	180.8	19.2	18.5	21.3	12.0	13.8	18.8		5.2	19.0			179.2
All countries, continents and regions (N = 107)[a]	100.0	9.1	9.1	9.1	9.1	9.1	9.1	9.1	9.1	9.1	9.1	9.1	100.0
All countries, continents and regions (N = 107)[b]	100.0	9.1	9.1	9.1	9.1	9.1	9.1		9.1	9.1			100.0

[a] Scores for Modal Years 1968–70
[b] Scores for Modal Years 1978–80

Average ISP scores also are favorable—well above the world average ISP score of 100—for the two countries of the North American region (Canada and the United States; mean = 143.0) and for the two East Asian nations of Japan and Korea (mean = 132.0). Conversely, regional ISP scores for Middle South (mean = 65.6) and Southeast (mean = 76.1) Asia are very unfavorable. Again, values obtained on the ISP's various subindexes, especially the Cultural Diversity and Welfare Effort subindexes, correlate strongly with level of social progress that is observed within each of the groups of nations.

Between 1969–70 and 1979–80, several important shifts occurred in the adequacy of social provision found in several of the world's major regions (Table 4–10). ISP scores for the North American region, for example, increased by more than 15 percent over the decade; scores for the seven Southwest Asian nations increased by an average of 24 percent, however, and ISP values for the eight nations of Southeast Asia rose by about ten percent. Within Africa, the most dramatic ISP increases occurred within nations of the North Africa region (+18 percent). These rather dramatic shifts upward in the adequacy of social provision found among four of the world's 24 regions is striking indeed (the average ISP increase within these 23 nations over the decade was 16.9 percent, or nearly 2 percent annually). The magnitude of these ISP changes suggests, too, the enormous commitment that has characterized the governments of nations within these regions to improve both the range and quality of human services found within these regions (and, of course, within the individual nations that make up the region). These important advances in social progress are especially noticeable among the nations of Southeast Asia and North Africa, given the extraordinary high levels of human suffering and social deprivation that have characterized the peoples of these regions in recent years.

Increases in level of observed social progress were not found in all regions of the world. Instead, rather dramatic declines over earlier ISP scores were observed for the USSR (−14 percent) and for the Eastern (−34 percent) and Southern (−19 percent) regions of Africa. Indeed, ISP scores declined by an average of nearly 10 percent for all 35 African nation states.

The USSR

The decade of the 1970s marked a period of very sharp social decline in the Soviet Union. Its ISP score dropped by 14 percent (from 132 to 113) and seven of the eight moveable ISP subindexes for the region reflected losses in adequacy of social provision over prior levels of accomplishment: Education (−9 percent), Health Status (−6 percent), Women Status (−5 percent), Defense Effort (−700 percent!), Economic (−28 percent), Demographic (−11 percent), Political Stability (−33 percent). Increases were

TABLE 4–10   Percent Change in Mean Index of Social Progress (ISP) Scores between 1970 and 1980 by Geopolitical Regions and Subregions[a] (n = 107)

Region	(n)	Percent Change
Africa	(n = 35)	−9.7
Western	(n = 13)	−6.9
Eastern	(n = 11)	−34.2
Northern	(n = 6)	+17.5
Middle	(n = 4)	+6.5
Southern	(n = 1)	−19.0
North America	(n = 2)	+15.3
South America	(n = 22)	+1.2
Tropical	(n = 6)	+5.4
Middle	(n = 7)	+0.1
Temperate	(n = 4)	−4.8
Caribbean	(n = 5)	+2.2
Asia	(n = 22)	+8.2
East	(n = 2)	+5.2
Middle South	(n = 5)	+2.5
South East	(n = 8)	+9.8
South West	(n = 7)	+24.4
Oceania	(n = 2)	+5.4
USSR	(n = 1)	−14.4
Europe	(n = 23)	−1.5
Western	(n = 6)	+0.6
Southern	(n = 6)	−4.2
Eastern	(n = 5)	−0.5
Northern	(n = 6)	−2.0

[a]A listing of countries included within each geopolitical grouping appears in Chapter 3, Chart 3–3.

found only on the Political Participation subindex (+7 percent). This change is not regarded as significant, however.

The USSR is one of the most culturally diverse regions on earth (subindex mean = −5.0). Only the five nations of Middle and South Africa—Central African Empire, Chad, United Republic of Cameroon, Zaire, South Africa—contain populations that are more varied with respect to language, religion, and ethnic mixture (mean = −6.0). The USSR has a favorable geographic environment, however, and experiences comparatively few of the major natural disasters that impact on the earth. Its level of organized

Welfare Effort (mean = 16.0) is very substantial, which, in part, makes the losses on the Education, Health Status, and Demographic subindexes surprising.

The sharp increase in defense expenditures over the decade, combined with a worldwide economic recession, obviously has contributed to a general lowering of social provision in the Soviet Union. One consequence of these declines is the increase in incidence of politically induced strikes, protest demonstrations, etc., reflected on the Political Stability subindex. Obviously, the USSR used the period of the decade to enhance its military posture at a time when all but developing nations were attempting to reduce theirs (Tables 4–1, 4–2). Given the internal social turmoil within the Soviet Union during this period, its military buildup occurred at the expense of domestic social programming and political stability.

South Africa

Declines on the ISP within the South African region are the result of a somewhat different constellation of factors. Significant declines were observed on four of the movable subindexes: Education (− 67 percent), Defense Effort (− 31 percent), Economic (− 25 percent), and Political Stability (− 127 percent). Scores on the Health Status (mean = 7.0) and Demographic (mean = 7.0) subindexes remained constant over the decade and, though higher on average than those of other nations within Africa, were considerably lower than comparable average subindex scores for the group of DME nations (17.6 and 17.7, respectively) of which the Republic of South Africa is a part.

As within the USSR, political instability increased over the period of the decade. Not surprisingly, one of the several consequences of South Africa's continuing internal social problems—which are basically racial in nature—is the loss of social progress achieved during earlier decades of development; that is, level of Welfare Effort is the highest in Africa and is among the highest found anywhere in the world (mean = 18.0). The social gains observed on the Women Status (+ 5 percent) and Political Participation subindexes (+ 17 percent) were not sufficient to offset the more dramatic losses measured for South Africa on other components of the ISP.

East Africa

ISP losses in East Africa between 1970 and 1980 were especially dramatic (down by an average of 34 percent, from 57.0 in 1969–70 to 37.5 in 1979–80). These overall declines in levels of previously attained social progress are judged to be very serious inasmuch as seven, or two out of three, of the 11 nations in this subregion are classified officially by the United Nations as

LDCs (they are Burundi, Ethiopia, Malawi, Rwanda, Somalia, Uganda, and the United Republic of Tanzania). As Least Developing Countries, these nations have been targeted for priority social development assistance from the United Nations and other multilateral international organizations (the World Bank, OECD, and so on) with initiation of the First International Development Decade in the early 1960s.

ISP losses in East Africa were observed on seven of the eight moveable subindexes: Education (-32 percent), Health Status (-155 percent), Defense Effort (-60 percent), Economic (-31 percent), Demographic (-10 percent), Political Stability (-27 percent), and Political Participation (-39 percent). Very significant gains were made on the Women Status subindex, however ($+195$ percent). Though characterized by higher than average scores on the Geography subindex (mean = 11.6), East African nations, on the average, are culturally very diverse (subindex mean = 0.8) and have the lowest Welfare Effort average score of any region in the world (mean = 1.1). Also, with the exception of Zimbabwe, all other nations within East Africa are governed either directly (Burundi, Ethiopia, Rwanda, Somalia, and Uganda) or indirectly by military authorities—a factor that, of course, is related directly to political instability and lower levels of political participation currently observed within the region. The influence of the military over all aspects of governmental decision making within these nations would appear to account, too, for the rather sharp rise in defense expenditures throughout the region.

North Africa

Relative to the declines in social progress found in East Africa, social progress in North Africa has been steady and substantial. Between 1970 and 1980, average ISP scores increased within the region by 17.5 percent. Increases also were observed on six of the ISP's eight moveable subindexes: Education ($+28$ percent), Health Status ($+84$ percent), Women Status ($+300$ percent), Defense Effort ($+34$ percent), Economic ($+2$ percent), and Political Participation ($+86$ percent). The Demographic and Political Stability subindexes remained constant for both time periods (4.3 and 11.7, respectively).

The combination of stable levels of political participation, relatively low levels of political instability, and an only somewhat above average profile for military expenditures suggests that a general stabilizing force began to operate within the region over the past decade. Only three of these six nations are governed directly by military authorities (Algeria, Libya, and Sudan), although the government of Tunisia appears to be strongly influenced by military authorities. Egypt and Morocco also are continuing to invest heavily in their military and defense reserves. Algeria and Libya, as oil-exporting nations, of course, do have extraordinary economic and financial reserves; resources which, in time, may contribute further to the even more rapid social development of their neighbors within the region.

As the only LDC within the region, Sudan's social progress has been relatively steady. Average ISP scores increased from 49 to 60 (+23 percent) between 1970 and 1980 with the most significant gains occurring in the Education, Defense, and Political Participation subindexes. Unlike other nations in the region, however, Sudan lost ground on the Health Status, Economic, and Demographic subindexes (see Table 5–1). Sudan is governed by military forces and since 1970 has been beseiged by numerous internal armed attacks, attempted coups, and assaults from without.

Asia

Substantial ISP gains were observed in both Southwest (+24.4 percent) and Southeast (+9.8 percent) Asia. The particularly impressive social gains found among the seven nations of Southwest Asia—Iraq, Israel, Jordan, Lebanon, Syrian Arab Republic, Turkey, and PDR Yemen—are the result of sharp increases on the Women Status (+25 percent), Defense Effort (+79 percent), and Political Participation (+22 percent) subindexes. Significant social gains within the region also took place on the Education (+7 percent) and Economic (+12 percent) subindexes.

Long-term problems of regional political turmoil continued to characterize Southwest Asia throughout the decade, however. These problems have imposed severe hardships on people of the region, problems that are reflected in very unfavorable Political Stability subindex scores (between 1970 and 1980 subindex values dropped 23 percent from 9.6 to 7.4). The fact that the region has the lowest Welfare Effort subindex scores (mean = 3.1) for any region in Asia—indeed the second lowest for the entire world—suggests that persons living within these embattled nations have relatively few social services available to assist them with the multiplicity of human problems associated with war and internal civil strife.

The more modest average ISP gains reported for the eight nations of Southeast Asia—Burma, Democratic Kampuchea, Indonesia, Malaysia, Philippines, Singapore, Vietnam, Thailand—are accounted for primarily by major advances within the region on the Economic (+433 percent) and Political Stability (+74 percent) subindexes. These gains occurred mainly in Vietnam and Kampuchea, countries in which devastating wars ended during the decade. Increased Political Stability in Indonesia and Malaysia also contributed to changes observed on the Economic and Political Participation (+7 percent) subindexes.

Social progress on some subindexes notwithstanding, Southeast Asia continues to be one of the least socially developed regions in the world (mean = 76.1). Its problems were exacerbated further by losses over the decade on the Education (−1 percent), Health Status (−1 percent), Women Status (−8 percent), Defense Effort (−56 percent) and Demographic (−4 percent) subindexes. Within the region, only Malaysia and Singapore are governed directly by civilian leaders; all other nations of the region are governed either directly or indirectly by military authorities.

In sharp contrast to the average ISP scores achieved by other nations in the region, ISP scores for the East Asian nations of Japan and Korea are high indeed (mean = 132). In fact, the 1980 ISP score for Japan (157) is higher than that reported for eight of Japan's 23 economic counterparts included in the DME classification—including that attained by the United States for 1980 (ISP = 116). Progress within the relatively culturally homogeneous East Asian subregion (mean = 16.5)—the least culturally diverse region in Asia and, in the world, second only to that found in Northern Europe (mean = 17.5)—is reflected in very favorable gains on the Economic subindex as well as on the subindexes of Political Stability and Political Participation. Between 1970 and 1980 scores on the first two subindexes moved even higher over the already favorable ratings that existed at the beginning of the decade (+11 percent and +40 percent). Political Participation scores did drop slightly during the decade (−3 percent), however, largely because of continuing political dissension within Korea. Welfare Effort, Geography, Education, Health Status, Status of Women, and Defense Effort subindex scores are the most favorable within the East Asian region. Though the military persists as an influence in the civilian life of Korea, neither Japan nor Korea are ruled directly by military authorities.

North America

In contrast to previous investigations of "quality of life" around the world (McGranahan 1972; Morris 1979), in the present study the two nations of the North American region—Canada and the United States—did not emerge at or very near the top of the list of nations achieving the most favorable ISP scores. Three reasons account for this disparity in findings between present and earlier studies.

1. The level of social provision that exists in Northern, Western, and Eastern Europe and in Oceania is far superior to that found in North America, but particularly to that found in the United States. On the Welfare Effort subindex alone, for example, mean scores for each are considerably higher than those observed for North America (mean = 14.5), 23.8, 25.3, 20.2, and 23.5 respectively.

2. Problems of *Cultural Diversity*, particularly those that are grounded in chronic racial inequalities, are particularly prominent in North America

(especially in the United States) and have the effect of seriously lowering overall ISP averages for the region. Blacks in the United States, for example, continue to experience dramatically higher rates of infant mortality, unemployment, school dropout, illiteracy, and early death, than do white Americans (National Urban League 1977; Rudov and Santangelo 1979; Lane et al. 1983).

3.   North America is one of the regions most prone to natural disasters (mean subindex score = − 8.0!). Between 1947 and 1979, for example, of the 937 major natural disasters that occurred on the planet, 326, or 35 percent, took place in just one North American nation—the United States (Regulska 1980).[6] While the actual number of lives lost in these disasters was low, they did, nonetheless, bring about enormous damage to property and other valuable manmade and natural resources.

The North American region, nonetheless, is one of the most socially developed regions of the world. Between 1970 and 1980, average ISP scores even increased some 15 percent, thereby bringing the region into closer social proximity to its counterpart nations in Europe and Oceania. Substantial ISP increases over the decade occurred in the Defense Effort (+ 163 percent), Political Stability (+ 177 percent) and Political Participation (+ 39 percent) subindexes. Changes upward on the latter two subindexes reflect resolution of the political turmoil that existed in the United States during the late 1960s and early 1970s (racial strife, dissension over the American wars in Southeast Asia, the assassination of key political and civil rights leaders, and so on). Increases on the Defense Effort subindex within the United States reflect a general easing, even if for only a brief time period, of the tensions between the United States and the Soviet Union. During the same period of time, expenditures for domestic social welfare programs increased dramatically within the United States.

Problems of worldwide economic recession are reflected in regional losses on the Economic (− 15 percent) subindex. Slight shifts downward also were observed on the Education (− 7 percent) and Health Status (− 3 percent) subindexes. The governments of both nations remained under civilian control throughout the decade.

Overall, Canada outperformed the United States on the ISP (mean = 170 vs. 116); albeit, like the United States, Canada experienced serious so-

---

[6]In commenting on this finding, Regulska (1980) properly notes that more complete reporting practices, combined with the higher value attached to property damaged during natural disasters, may account for at least some of the disproportionate number and assessed destructive impact of natural disasters that occurred within the United States relative to other nations. Even so, given its size, geographic location, and variations in climate and topography, the United States on average does appear to experience more major natural disasters (floods, tornados, hurricanes) than does any other nation on the planet.

for the very negative impact of the high incidence of national disasters on the ISP score for the United States—that is, by utilizing the *ten*-subindex INSP—the average net social progress levels observed for the United States and Canada are more comparable (1980 mean INSP = 174 and 146, respectively). These scores rank Canada and the United States as 10.5 and 23 among the 107 nations included in the study, compared with world ranks of 12.5 and 42, respectively, when using the more inclusive ISP. (The rankings for all 107 nations studied are presented in the next chapter.)

South America

ISP changes over the decade in the four subregions of South America tended to be less dramatic than those found for other world regions (average change = + 1.2 percent). The most significant shifts (+ 5.4 percent) occurred within the six nations of Tropical South America—Bolivia, Brazil, Colombia, Ecuador, Peru, Venezuela—especially on the Economic (+ 80 percent), Defense Effort (+ 12 percent) and Demographic (+ 36 percent) subindexes. ISP shifts downward, however, were found in the Health Status (− 4 percent), Political Stability (− 23 percent), and Political Participation (− 13 percent) subindexes. These negative political changes took place primarily in Ecuador and Peru. Political Stability subindex scores, however, also fell in Brazil (− 27 percent) and Colombia (− 27 percent) but increased in Venezuela (+ 9 percent). Within the region the governments of Bolivia, Brazil, Ecuador, and Peru are either controlled or heavily influenced by military authorities.

Progress in adequacy of social provision also was observed in the five-nation Caribbean subregion (+ 2.2 percent). These shifts occurred mostly on the Demographic and Political Participation subindexes. ISP scores for the seven-nation Middle South America region tended to remain more or less stable over the decade (average ISP change = + 0.1 percent).

Average ISP scores for the four nations of Temperate South America—Argentina, Chile, Paraguay, Uruguay—moved downward over the decade (− 5.4 percent). Analysis of the subindexes shows that these losses resulted, in the main, from declines in the general economic well-being of these nations (− 147 percent), coupled with a dramatic increase in military expenditures (− 29 percent). Even so, levels of regional Political Stability increased substantially (+ 275 percent) over the decade but, as reported for other regions, at the cost of sharp reductions in the level of popular Political Participation (− 45 percent). As of 1980, all four governments of the region were either controlled or heavily influenced by military authorities.

DISCUSSION

As evidenced by the data presented in this chapter, the gap in social development that long has existed between the world's richest and poorest nations continues to exist. The dimensions of the gap changed considerably over the period of the last decade, however. Between 1970 and 1980, for example, significant gains were observed in the capacity of the majority of developing nations (60 percent) to provide more adequately for the basic social and material needs of their people. These gains in social progress are real and should be sustained as long as national and international commitments continue to assist less advantaged nations in solving their social development problems.

Social gains in the LDCs were less impressive than those that occurred among the group of developing nations. Only one in three of the LDCs registered ISP gains over the decade. For the majority of these nations, gains on the ISP must be regarded as tentative in nature given the very fragile socio-economic and political environments that characterize much of life within the LDCs. That ISP losses occurred for two out of three LDC nations is a source of real worry for the international community as a whole. In effect, the profound levels of human suffering and social deprivation that historically have characterized the LDCs became even more exacerbated over the decade. Only very dramatic international efforts will succeed in reversing the social stagnation found within these nations.

Significant social losses on the ISP also were found for the ETA nations. These countries experienced serious economic problems throughout the decade, which, in part at least, added to already existing problems of internal political instability. Declines in adequacy of social provision observed for these nations are not as serious as those found in the LDCs, or even in the minority of developing nations; nonetheless, any reversals will require significant internal actions on the part of ETA political leaders. ETA nations, like the DMEs, remain among the most socially advanced nations on the planet.

Overall, these finds can be regarded as a basis for cautious optimism among development specialists that international efforts aimed at improving the level of living throughout the world are succeeding. These gains are substantial and are occurring at a steady pace, especially within developing nations. Significant LDC losses on the ISP, however, serve as a reminder of the fragile nature of progress in achieving social development objectives over the short term. Clearly, nothing short of unequivocal worldwide commitment to international social justice will bring about the long-term improvements in social progress sought after by people everywhere.

5

National Social Progress

One of the most important features of the ISP is its ability to provide detailed information concerning changes in social development that take place within individual nations over time. These data are essential for purposes of social planning; they form, too, the basis for evaluating the effectiveness of alternative forms of social intervention. Nation-specific information also serves as a basis for comparing the relative successfulness of national governments in providing more adequately for the basic social needs of their people compared to efforts undertaken by the governments of other nations on behalf of their people. These data also are helpful to international social development organizations for use in formulating more rational social assistance priorities, especially in relation to those sectors of national life that are in need of external social intervention. Finally, nation-specific data of the type produced by the ISP can help international development specialists to understand better the complex interplay of social, political, economic, and cultural forces that influence so directly the great variation in patterns of social development found throughout the world.

This chapter presents ISP findings for individual nations at two points in time—1969–70 and 1979–80. National scores are reported for the study's two composite indexes (the ISP and the INSP)[1] and for each of the ISP's eleven subindexes. Nations are rank-ordered with respect to the adequacy of social provision found within their borders and in relation to that observed for other nations. Emphasis throughout the chapter is given to the identification of specific ISP changes that have taken place within individual nations and to the social factors that best account for these changes (shifts in the national economy, war, changing status of women and chil-

[1]The differences between these two indexes are discussed in Chapter 3.

91

dren, success and failure in containing long-term social problems such as population growth, and so on).

Nations for which dramatic ISP changes were observed—whether of a positive or negative nature—receive special attention in this chapter. Finally, nations are regrouped into "Zones of Social Vulnerability" that more adequately reflect the differential levels of social provision that are found among the world's nations. A concept developed in the present study, Zones of Social Vulnerability, group nations that are more or less socially comparable with one another without regard to particular political or economic systems, official economic development classifications, or geographic regions.

SOCIAL PROVISION: THE NATIONAL PERSPECTIVE

The major data of this chapter are presented in Table 5–1. This table contains an alphabetical listing of the study's 107 nations grouped by economic development classification, that is, DME, ETA, DC, and LDC. Subindex and composite index scores for both modal years are reported in the table, as are average index and subindex scores for each economic development grouping. Presenting summmary data in this way allows the reader to make more reasonable comparisons between ISP scores for individual nations and those of the larger economic grouping of which the country is a part (for instance, changes in social provision observed for Japan, given the high level of development with which Japan began the decade, can be compared with changes taking place in other DME nations—a more appropriate basis of comparison than with changes occurring in the LDCs).

Table 5–1 reflects the enormous variations that exist in level of social provision observed for nations within the same economic development classification. Among DME nations, for example, 1980 ISP scores range from a high of 201 for Denmark to a low of 92 for Israel, a range of some 109 ISP points! Hungary achieved the most favorable 1980 ISP score for ETA nations (169), with Albania (108) scoring just below the USSR (113) for the grouping's least favorable score (range = 61). Table 5–2 reports the "most favorable" and "least favorable" ISP scores for countries grouped in each of the study's economic development classifications for 1969–70 and 1979–80.

Table 5–3 lists all nations alphabetically and reports their ISP and INSP scores for both 1969–70 and 1979–80. World rankings for individual countries—based only on the 107 nations included in the study—appear in parentheses to the right of each score. This table makes explicit the finding suggested by the data summarized in Table 5–1 that—although related to level of economic development—level of social development (that is, adequacy of social provision) varies considerably both within and between na-

TABLE 5–1 Scores on the Index of Social Progress (ISP) and Index of Net Social Progress (INSP) by Economic Development Level, Country, Subindex and Modal Year (N = 107)

	Index of Social Progress (Vulnerability Zones)	Education Subindex	Health Subindex	Women Subindex	Defense Subindex	Economic Subindex	Demographic Subindex	Geographic Subindex	Political Stability Subindex	Political Participation Subindex	Cultural Diversity Subindex	Welfare Effort Subindex	Index of Net Social Progress (Vulnerability Zones)
Developed Market Economies (N = 24)	160.4[a]	16.1	17.5	18.3	7.3	13.9	17.9	10.7	7.5	15.5	13.8	21.0	158.8
	161.4[b]	16.3	17.6	17.8	9.8	13.6	17.7		5.3	17.6			159.8
Austria	186(1)	18	17	20	15	12	20	12	11	15	18	28	184(1)
	192(1)	18	18	19	16	15	20		12	16			189(1)
Australia	173(2)	16	18	25	9	16	16	14	11	14	12	22	168(2)
	184(1)	18	18	24	13	16	18		11	18			179(1)
Belgium	175(1)	19	18	17	11	15	20	13	11	18	7	25	171(2)
	178(1)	19	18	16	11	16	20		12	21			174(2)
Canada	157(2)	23	18	17	12	18	17	5	9	16	5	16	161(2)
	170(2)	21	18	17	15	16	18		12	27			174(2)
Denmark	198(1)	22	19	21	12	14	21	16	11	14	19	28	191(1)
	201(1)	20	19	21	13	15	20		12	18			194(1)
Finland	169(2)	20	17	22	15	10	21	5	12	12	17	18	173(2)
	174(2)	18	18	21	16	13	20		12	14			178(1)
France	172(2)	18	18	15	8	16	18	14	7	18	14	26	168(2)
	165(2)	18	18	14	9	15	19		1	16			161(2)

TABLE 5-1   Continued

	Index of Social Progress (Vulnerability Zones)	Education Subindex	Health Subindex	Women Subindex	Defense Subindex	Economic Subindex	Demographic Subindex	Geographic Subindex	Political Stability Subindex	Political Participation Subindex	Cultural Diversity Subindex	Welfare Effort Subindex	Index of Net Social Progress (Vulnerability Zones)
FDR Germany	179(1)	17	18	20	9	14	18	13	6	16	19	29	175(1)
	174(2)	6	18	19	11	14	20		9	16			170(2)
Greece	136(3)	10	18	14	6	11	20	12	11	0	19	16	133(3)
	146(3)	10	18	14	4	12	18		9	15			144(3)
Ireland	185(1)	16	18	20	15	11	21	16	11	13	19	25	178(1)
	183(1)	17	18	20	15	11	16		11	15			176(1)
Israel	87(5)	18	18	13	-50	18	13	14	11	12	11	7	81(5)
	92(5)	19	19	13	-32	11	11		5	14			86(5)
Italy	160(2)	17	18	14	11	12	19	15	-5	14	20	26	155(2)
	158(2)	17	18	14	13	9	19		-8	16			152(2)
Japan	149(3)	15	18	14	16	16	17	1	4	16	20	12	157(2)
	157(2)	16	19	14	17	14	17		11	16			165(2)
Netherlands	187(1)	20	19	21	9	14	19	13	12	20	15	25	182(1)
	190(1)	20	19	20	11	15	19		10	23			186(1)
New Zealand	178(1)	16	18	27	13	9	16	13	12	16	13	25	174(2)
	186(1)	18	18	26	15	11	19		12	17			183(1)
Norway	186(1)	21	19	23	9	15	20	6	12	18	19	24	189(1)
	193(1)	21	19	22	11	18	20		12	20			196(1)
Portugal	131(3)	7	16	10	1	10	19	13	8	14	20	13	127(3)
	146(3)	14	15	12	11	11	17		9	10			142(3)
South Africa	121(4)	9	7	20	13	12	7	18	11	12	-6	18	112(4)
	98(5)	3	7	21	9	9	7		-3	14			89(5)

	C1	C2	C3	C4	C5	C6	C7	C8	C9	C10	C11	C12	C13
Spain	156(2)	10	18	19	13	9	18	15	9	13	12	21	150(2)
	129(3)	11	18	17	15	13	17		−29	18			122(4)
Sweden	198(1)	23	19	26	9	19	21	6	12	20	19	23	201(1)
	189(1)	19	19	25	11	16	21		12	15			192(1)
Switzerland	164(2)	16	19	9	12	15	20	14	11	19	11	19	159(2)
	170(2)	16	19	8	14	14	22		12	22			165(2)
United Kingdom	171(2)	18	18	20	6	11	19	15	−6	32	12	25	165(2)
	145(3)	18	18	19	7	10	16		−28	32			139(3)
United States	91(5)	20	19	20	−4	22	12	−21	−22	21	12	13	121(4)
	116(4)	19	18	20	6	18	12		−2	23			146(3)
Yugoslavia	140(3)	16	15	13	5	14	18	14	11	10	5	19	136(3)
	137(3)	14	16	12	5	15	18		12	7			133(3)
Eastern Trading Area (N = 7)	155.9	17.9	16.4	16.9	7.7	18.1	18.0	13.7	9.1	9.9	11.0	18.0	151.9
	148.4	17.0	16.3	16.1	7.0	15.0	16.4		10.6	8.1			144.3
Albania	173(3)	15	14	11	10	18	14	12	12	9	14	9	134(3)
	108(4)	14	13	10	−8	12	15		12	6			106(4)
Bulgaria	167(2)	17	18	13	10	21	23	14	12	9	11	20	163(2)
	155(2)	17	17	12	12	13	20		12	8			151(2)
Czecho-slovakia	151(2)	17	17	20	6	19	21	14	−3	7	10	24	147(3)
	163(2)	20	17	19	10	13	18		11	7			158(2)
Hungary	173(2)	18	16	16	11	16	22	17	11	9	16	22	166(2)
	169(2)	17	17	16	14	14	19		12	6			161(2)
Poland	168(2)	18	17	20	6	17	19	15	11	10	17	18	163(2)
	168(2)	14	17	21	12	20	17		11	7			163(2)
Rumania	163(2)	17	16	17	10	18	18	15	12	10	14	17	158(2)
	163(2)	16	17	15	15	20	18		10	7			158(2)
USSR	132(3)	23	17	21	1	18	9	9	9	15	−5	16	132(3)
	113(4)	21	16	20	−6	13	8		6	16			113(4)

TABLE 5–1 Continued

	Index of Social Progress (Vulnerability Zones)	Education Subindex	Health Subindex	Women Subindex	Defense Subindex	Economic Subindex	Demographic Subindex	Geographic Subindex	Political Stability Subindex	Political Participation Subindex	Cultural Diversity Subindex	Welfare Effort Subindex	Index of Net Social Progress (Vulnerability Zones)
Developing Countries (N = 58)	85.3	7.8	9.0	7.5	9.2	6.7	6.1	7.6	9.1	8.1	9.0	5.3	86.9
	89.0	8.4	8.7	7.9	8.2	8.0	6.6		10.1	7.4			88.6
Algeria	87(5)	9	7	3	12	7	3	7	12	0	14	13	89(5)
	96(5)	12	7	5	14	7	2		12	2			97(5)
Argentina	116(4)	14	14	17	13	6	17	14	−11	5	14	12	110(4)
	124(4)	14	14	16	14	−2	15		6	6			119(4)
Bolivia	84(5)	11	11	6	15	3	5	7	11	1	4	8	85(5)
	92(5)	11	8	6	14	11	9		12	1			93(5)
Brazil	123(4)	13	13	17	12	2	6	6	11	9	19	16	127(3)
	137(3)	11	11	15	17	15	6		8	12			141(3)
Burma	80(5)	5	8	14	4	11	9	7	11	−2	9	3	81(5)
	70(6)	1	1	13	8	5	6		11	3			71(6)
Cameroon	62(6)	4	−2	9	13	6	6	9	12	10	−9	4	62(6)
	65(6)	4	0	10	15	7	5		12	7			66(6)
Chile	135(3)	12	13	15	13	4	12	4	9	15	17	20	140(3)
	90(5)	13	14	16	−6	−18	13		12	4			95(5)
Colombia	117(4)	8	11	11	15	8	5	7	11	13	19	11	120(4)
	130(3)	11	12	13	17	10	8		8	14			133(3)

96

Costa Rica	138(3)	19	14	13	15	9	6	10	11	16	19	6	138(3)
	152(2)	17	16	13	18	12	12		12	18			152(2)
Cuba	140(3)	21	16	18	3	11	13	12	11	5	19	11	138(3)
	141(3)	23	17	16	1	5	16		12	8			139(3)
Dom. Republic	113(4)	5	14	13	12	9	3	10	11	12	19	5	112(4)
	118(4)	4	11	13	11	11	8		12	14			117(4)
Ecuador	108(4)	10	10	15	13	10	5	1	11	11	13	10	116(4)
	105(4)	12	11	16	14	12	6		9	1			113(4)
Egypt	72(6)	8	8	3	-11	7	6	6	12	9	19	5	75(5)
	81(5)	9	9	2	-8	11	8		10	11			84(5)
El Salvador	115(4)	8	13	10	11	8	6	14	11	13	16	6	110(4)
	109(4)	5	12	9	15	11	8		11	3			104(4)
Ghana	58(6)	5	7	5	12	8	5	13	10	-2	-7	1	54(6)
	39(7)	6	0	5	16	-2	1		9	-2			36(7)
Guatemala	66(6)	3	8	7	16	8	4	-13	11	13	6	2	88(5)
	72(6)	2	8	6	17	11	6		12	15			94(5)
Honduras	86(5)	8	11	9	13	8	3	-2	11	10	17	1	100(4)
	80(5)	8	12	9	15	3	5		12	1			92(5)
India	46(7)	3	4	7	11	4	-11	6	2	14	0	6	49(7)
	53(6)	3	3	6	11	6	-9		4	17			56(6)
Indonesia	28(7)	4	1	9	10	-24	-1	5	11	7	3	2	32(7)
	71(6)	7	2	10	10	11	2		12	6			75(5)
Iran	66(6)	4	7	1	4	13	4	-6	11	12	7	9	81(5)
	69(6)	10	9	3	-10	13	9		12	12			83(5)
Iraq	64(6)	12	13	-4	-11	10	5	9	11	0	13	5	63(6)
	66(6)	9	12	1	-8	10	3		11	1			65(6)
Ivory Coast	68(6)	4	0	3	15	10	5	13	11	8	-5	5	64(6)
	73(6)	5	0	3	19	13	0		12	7			69(6)

TABLE 5–1 Continued

	Index of Social Progress (Vulnerability Zones)	Education Subindex	Health Subindex	Women Subindex	Defense Subindex	Economic Subindex	Demographic Subindex	Geographic Subindex	Political Stability Subindex	Political Participation Subindex	Cultural Diversity Subindex	Welfare Effort Subindex	Index of Net Social Progress (Vulnerability Zones)
Jamaica	130(3)	10	16	13	17	11	10	11	12	10	18	3	128(3)
	132(3)	13	15	12	17	8	12		12	11			130(3)
Jordan	42(7)	4	14	4	-34	7	3	7	11	4	19	3	44(7)
	54(6)	6	13	4	-32	11	7		12	4			56(6)
Kampuchea	49(7)	9	3	2	4	-16	12	3	12	2	13	6	56(6)
	49(7)	4	5	1	-10	-1	11		12	5			55(6)
Kenya	68(6)	6	10	1	15	12	4	7	9	8	-5	1	70(6)
	56(6)	8	6	6	8	7	5		12	3			58(6)
Korea, South	102(4)	8	16	14	8	11	9	1	11	13	13	0	110(4)
	107(4)	9	16	14	6	16	11		10	12			115(4)
Lebanon	112(4)	14	15	9	11	9	13	9	4	12	10	5	112(4)
	93(5)	11	16	8	11	9	9		-9	13			93(5)
Liberia	69(6)	-2	4	1	16	10	8	9	12	15	-2	-1	69(6)
	65(6)	0	1	2	17	8	4		12	16			65(6)
Libya	49(7)	11	-4	-2	-5	13	4	5	12	-2	16	1	52(6)
	86(5)	15	12	9	3	6	3		12	4			90(5)
Madagascar	83(5)	-2	5	9	14	7	3	14	12	8	7	6	78(5)
	79(5)	3	2	10	13	2	3		12	7			74(6)
Malaysia	81(5)	9	12	7	10	9	6	7	11	11	-5	4	32(5)
	92(5)	12	15	8	6	14	8		12	12			95(5)

Mauritania	63(6)	5	−3	−2	15	3	6	2	12	8	14	5	70(6)
	27(7)	1	−3	−2	−12	4	2		12	4			34(7)
Mexico	120(4)	7	13	14	16	11	5	11	11	13	14	5	118(4)
	121(4)	12	14	15	18	8	5		6	13			120(4)
Morocco	72(6)	6	3	−2	11	9	3	7	10	7	10	9	74(6)
	73(6)	7	11	−2	2	5	2		12	11			76(5)
Nicaragua	83(5)	6	11	9	15	7	2	−9	11	10	17	3	101(4)
	87(5)	6	11	9	15	10	5		11	8			105(4)
Nigeria	3(8)	1	5	0	−1	1	1	13	−6	−3	−9	1	−1(8)
	33(7)	4	3	0	4	7	1		12	−2			28(7)
Pakistan	40(7)	−4	9	−1	9	8	2	8	−5	2	7	3	41(7)
	31(7)	−1	7	−3	6	6	3		−5	1			32(7)
Panama	128(3)	15	15	13	16	8	7	6	12	12	16	7	131(3)
	122(4)	13	16	13	18	8	11		11	4			125(3)
Paraguay	115(4)	10	14	9	13	8	6	9	12	9	17	8	115(4)
	125(3)	8	14	9	16	12	9		12	12			125(3)
Peru	82(5)	10	10	11	10	1	6	0	11	6	6	9	91(5)
	76(5)	10	10	13	9	6	8		2	4			85(5)
Philippines	98(5)	13	9	14	15	8	4	7	9	12	1	4	100(4)
	91(5)	9	12	13	13	12	5		10	5			93(5)
Senegal	75(5)	0	5	2	14	9	5	14	9	8	3	6	70(6)
	68(6)	−1	2	1	14	7	3		12	8			63(6)
Sierra Leone	80(5)	0	0	−1	16	7	8	17	12	19	0	1	72(6)
	62(6)	1	0	−2	17	4	4		11	8			54(6)
Singapore	106(4)	13	18	6	6	12	15	9	12	7	5	4	106(4)
	107(4)	10	17	4	3	16	16		12	10			107(4)
Sri Lanka	119(4)	10	14	15	16	10	11	11	11	11	5	5	118(4)
	118(4)	9	14	13	18	8	12		8	14			117(4)

TABLE 5-1 Continued

	Index of Social Progress (Vulnerability Zones)	Education Subindex	Health Subindex	Women Subindex	Defense Subindex	Economic Subindex	Demographic Subindex	Geographic Subindex	Political Stability Subindex	Political Participation Subindex	Cultural Diversity Subindex	Welfare Effort Subindex	Index of Net Social Progress (Vulnerability Zones)
Syria	71(6)	8	13	1	-7	12	4	14	12	0	14	1	66(6)
	115(4)	11	13	2	18	19	6		12	5			110(4)
Thailand	104(4)	9	12	14	11	12	6	8	11	8	11	1	105(4)
	99(5)	11	11	14	10	12	7		11	4			100(4)
Togo	41(7)	-3	-3	1	15	8	1	9	12	-2	0	2	41(7)
	46(7)	6	-4	5	13	-1	2		12	1			46(7)
Trinidad/ Tobago	123(4)	13	15	14	17	8	14	10	12	10	8	3	123(4)
	126(3)	12	16	13	19	9	13		12	11			125(3)
Tunisia	109(4)	13	8	3	14	8	6	12	12	9	18	7	106(4)
	119(4)	11	7	4	16	19	9		12	6			116(4)
Turkey	99(5)	9	5	12	7	7	7	11	7	13	16	5	98(5)
	112(4)	13	6	12	6	11	8		9	15			110(4)
Uruguay	137(3)	16	16	17	14	-3	18	18	1	13	12	16	128(3)
	140(3)	14	16	17	14	1	18		12	1			131(3)
Venezuela	128(3)	13	16	12	13	12	6	8	11	13	18	4	129(3)
	137(3)	14	16	13	16	11	8		12	14			138(3)
R. Vietnam	8(8)	1	9	11	-26	2	10	7	-24	2	9	6	10(8)
	53(6)	8	8	10	-25	8	3		12	5			54(6)
Zaïre	43(7)	8	-5	2	10	5	4	10	11	2	-7	4	42(7)
	52(6)	6	-1	3	10	6	4		12	5			51(6)

Zambia	73(6)	7	8	1	16	6	2	11	11	10	-1	2	71(6)
	37(7)	9	-4	2	-5	7	2		12	4			35(7)
Zimbabwe	80(5)	9	11	3	14	8	4	7	11	10	6	-4	82(5)
	33(7)	6	5	1	-12	7	3		2	12			35(7)
Least Developing Countries (N = 18)	44.4	-0.4	-4.6	-1.2	11.4	6.3	3.6	10.2	11.7	3.5	2.4	2.1	43.4
	40.8	-1.4	-3.9	-1.3	11.8	4.6	3.0		10.2	3.3			39.7
Benin	44(7)	1	-1	0	13	6	4	6	12	-2	2	4	47(7)
	42(7)	0	-2	0	15	3	1		12	1			45(7)
Burundi	36(7)	0	-11	-3	15	6	1	13	12	-1	4	1	32(7)
	24(8)	-3	-8	-4	8	3	-1		12	1			20(8)
C. African Empire	35(7)	-2	-7	2	11	9	4	4	12	-2	0	5	40(7)
	45(7)	-3	3	-2	14	2	5		12	0			50(6)
Chad	25(7)	-8	-11	-2	8	4	5	12	11	10	-8	5	23(8)
	14(8)	-11	-11	-4	9	7	4		12	-1			11(8)
Ethiopia	36(7)	-7	-8	-3	13	7	3	16	11	10	-5	-1	30(7)
	-12(8)	-6	-14	-5	8	3	1		-10	2			-19(8)
Guinea	43(7)	0	-3	0	7	6	3	10	12	4	-1	6	43(7)
	57(6)	2	-5	-2	14	7	3		12	10			56(6)
Haiti	75(5)	3	0	4	13	4	7	2	12	10	19	0	82(5)
	77(5)	-2	3	4	17	6	7		12	10			84(5)
Malawi	44(7)	1	-5	-1	17	6	2	8	12	7	-4	1	45(7)
	37(7)	-5	-8	-1	15	9	2		12	7			38(7)
Mali	46(7)	1	-5	1	13	8	2	10	12	-2	2	5	45(7)
	35(7)	-1	-9	-1	9	3	3		10	4			34(7)
Nepal	49(7)	-1	-4	-6	17	5	6	9	11	10	4	-1	49(7)
	57(6)	1	-2	-5	17	5	5		12	13			57(6)

TABLE 5-1 Continued

	Index of Social Progress (Vulnerability Zones)	Education Subindex	Health Subindex	Women Subindex	Defense Subindex	Economic Subindex	Demographic Subindex	Geographic Subindex	Political Stability Subindex	Political Participation Subindex	Cultural Diversity Subindex	Welfare Effort Subindex	Index of Net Social Progress (Vulnerability Zones)
Niger	34(7)	−5	−11	−2	16	6	2	6	12	8	2	2	38(7)
	34(7)	−2	−1	−3	7	0	2		12	−2			37(7)
PDR Yemen	39(7)	4	5	−7	−12	8	3	10	11	3	17	−4	37(7)
	71(6)	5	5	−5	17	8	1		12	5			69(6)
Rwanda	61(6)	0	−8	3	14	4	2	16	12	10	9	2	55(6)
	59(6)	−3	−5	4	15	5	4		12	0			53(6)
Somalia	58(6)	4	−1	−5	13	5	4	10	12	−1	19	1	57(6)
	50(6)	3	0	−3	0	2	4		12	2			49(7)
Sudan	49(7)	−1	5	−1	9	12	4	7	12	−2	1	4	52(6)
	60(6)	4	4	−1	13	9	2		12	5			63(6)
Tanzania	43(7)	0	−1	0	11	8	3	14	12	7	−13	2	37(7)
	29(7)	2	−5	3	1	6	4		11	4			23(8)
Uganda	45(7)	6	2	−1	13	5	6	12	11	−3	−8	1	42(7)
	21(8)	2	−1	0	11	0	4		4	−2			19(8)
Upper Volta	37(7)	−3	−18	0	15	5	3	18	12	−3	3	5	28(7)
	34(7)	−8	−14	−2	12	5	3		12	0			25(7)

ᵃScores for Modal Years 1969–70
ᵇScores for Modal Years 1979–80

TABLE 5-2 Nations with the Most Favorable and Least Favorable ISP Scores by Economic Development Classification and by Year
(N = 107)

	1969–70				1979–80			
	Most Favorable ISP		Least Favorable ISP		Most Favorable ISP		Least Favorable ISP	
Developed Market Economies	Denmark	(198)	Israel	(87)	Denmark	(201)	Israel	(92)
	Sweden	(198)	United States	(91)	Norway	(193)	South Africa	(98)
	Netherlands	(187)			Austria	(192)		
	Norway	(186)			Netherlands	(190)		
	Austria	(186)			Sweden	(189)		
	Ireland	(185)						
Eastern Trading Area	Hungary	(173)	U.S.S.R.	(132)	Hungary	(169)	Albania	(108)
	Poland	(168)	Albania	(137)	Poland	(168)	U.S.S.R.	(113)
	Bulgaria	(167)						
Developing Countries	Cuba	(140)	Nigeria	(3)	Costa Rica	(152)	Mauritania	(27)
	Costa Rica	(138)	Vietnam	(8)	Cuba	(141)	Pakistan	(31)
	Uruguay	(137)	Pakistan	(40)	Uruguay	(140)	Nigeria	(33)
	Chile	(135)	Togo	(41)	Venezuela	(137)	Zimbabwe	(33)
	Jamaica	(130)	Jordan	(42)	Brazil	(137)	Zambia	(37)

TABLE 5–2   Continued

	1969–70		1979–80	
	Most Favorable ISP	Least Favorable ISP	Most Favorable ISP	Least Favorable ISP
Least Developing Countries	Haiti (75) Rwanda (61) Somalia (58)	Chad (25) Niger (37) Upper Volta (37) PDR Yemen (39)	Haiti (77) PDR Yemen (71) Sudan (60) Rwanda (59) Nepal (57) Guinea (57)	Ethiopia (−12) Chad (14) Uganda (21) Burundi (24)

tions grouped by economic development classification. Examination of the 1980 ISP world rankings shows, for example, that not all DME nations are among the highest ranked nations with respect to adequacy of social provision. Indeed, Israel (rank = 55.3), South Africa (rank = 52), Spain (rank = 33), and the United States (rank = 42)[2] are social "laggards" when compared with the very high levels of social provision found in the majority of DME nations. They are social laggards, too, when compared with the majority of ETA nations that have developed a fuller spectrum of social programs designed to respond effectively to the basic social and material needs of their populations, for instance, Hungary (rank = 14), Poland (rank = 15), Rumania (rank = 17.5), and so on.

Surprising, too, at least to this investigator, is the high level of social provision observed for many DCs, especially those located in selected areas of Asia and Latin America. For example, Costa Rica (rank = 22), Cuba (rank = 26), Uruguay (rank = 27), Venezuela (rank = 28.3), Brazil (rank = 28.3), Jamaica (rank = 31), among others, all have 1980 ISP scores that place them in the upper one-third of the world's nations with respect to adequacy of social provision. Many of these nations began the decade with high levels of social provision that continued to advance over much of the ten-year period.

Table 5–3 also makes clear that not all of the world's least socially developing nations are officially classified as such by the United Nations. For example, Pakistan (rank = 101), Zimbabwe (rank = 99.5), Nigeria (rank = 99.5), Zambia (rank = 94.5), and many DCs have substantially lower 1970 and 1980 ISP scores than those found for some officially designated LDCs (Haiti, P.D.R. Yemen, Sudan, Rwanda). That these DCs have ISP scores that consistently place them in the bottom one-fourth of the world's least socially developed nations would suggest that these countries, too, should be singled out for preferential international social and economic assistance. Certainly, the level of human suffering and social deprivation that exists in many of the world's poorest DCs does not vary much from that found among the officially designated LDCs.

SOCIAL "LEADERS" AND "SOCIALLY LEAST DEVELOPING" NATIONS

In any study of this type certain countries out-perform others in achieving international development objectives and emerge as social leaders in the

---

[2]When the very unfavorable *Geographic* subindex scores for the United States (-21) are controlled for, that is, by using the INSP rather than the ISP, its world ranking increases from 54 to 38 in 1970 and from 42 to 23 in 1980. INSP scores for all of the study's countries are reported in Tables 5–1 and 5–3.

TABLE 5–3   Alphabetical Listing of Countries with Index of Social Progress (ISP) and Index of Net Social Progress (INSP) Scores and Rank by Year (N = 107)

ISP 1969–70 (Rank)	ISP 1979–80 (Rank)	Country	INSP 1969–70 (Rank)	INSP 1979–80 (Rank)
137 (27.5)	108 (47)	Albania	134 (28)	106 (49)
87 (56.6)	96 (53)	Algeria	89 (58)	97 (53)
116 (42)	124 (36)	Argentina	110 (47.3)	119 (39)
186 (4.5)	192 (3)	Austria	184 (4)	189 (4)
173 (10.5)	184 (7)	Australia	168 (11.5)	179 (7)
175 (9)	178 (9)	Belgium	171 (10)	174 (10.5)
44 (89.5)	42 (92)	Benin[a]	47 (88)	45 (92)
84 (58)	92 (55.3)	Bolivia	85 (60)	93 (57.3)
123 (36.5)	137 (28.3)	Brazil	127 (35.5)	141 (26)
167 (16)	155 (21)	Bulgaria	163 (15.5)	151 (22)
80 (63.3)	70 (72)	Burma	81 (64.3)	71 (71)
36 (99.5)	24 (104)	Burundi[a]	32 (101.5)	20 (104)
62 (79)	65 (76.5)	Cameroon	62 (79)	66 (74)
157 (20)	170 (12.5)	Canada	161 (17)	174 (10.5)
35 (102)	45 (91)	Cen. African Empire[a]	40 (97)	50 (89)
25 (105)	14 (106)	Chad[a]	23 (105)	11 (106)
135 (30)	90 (59)	Chile	140 (24)	95 (54.5)
117 (41)	130 (32)	Columbia	120 (39)	133 (30.5)
138 (26)	152 (22)	Costa Rica	138 (25.5)	152 (20.5)
140 (23)	141 (26)	Cuba	138 (25.5)	139 (27.5)
151 (22)	163 (17.5)	Czechoslovakia	147 (23)	158 (18.5)
49 (83.2)	49 (89)	Democratic Kampuchea	56 (81)	55 (84)
198 (1.5)	201 (1)	Denmark	191 (2)	194 (2)
113 (45)	118 (40.5)	Dom. Republic	112 (44.3)	117 (40.5)

Ecuador	113	(44.5)	116	(42)	105	(50)	108	(48)
Egypt	84	(65.5)	75	(68)	81	(62)	72	(69.5)
El Salvador	104	(51)	110	(47.3)	109	(46)	115	(43.5)
Ethiopia[a]	−19	(107)	30	(103)	−12	(107)	36	(100.5)
Finland	178	(8)	173	(9)	174	(10.5)	169	(14)
France	161	(16.5)	168	(11.5)	165	(16)	172	(12)
Germany, F.D.R.	170	(12)	175	(7)	174	(10.5)	179	(7)
Ghana	36	(95)	54	(83)	39	(93)	58	(81.5)
Greece	144	(24)	133	(29)	146	(23.5)	136	(29)
Guatemala	94	(56)	88	(59)	72	(69)	66	(75.5)
Guinea[a]	56	(81.3)	43	(92)	57	(81.5)	43	(92.3)
Haiti[a]	84	(65.5)	82	(62.5)	77	(65)	75	(66.5)
Honduras	92	(60)	100	(54.5)	80	(63)	88	(55)
Hungary	161	(16.5)	166	(13)	169	(14)	173	(10.5)
India	56	(81.3)	49	(86.5)	53	(85.5)	46	(87.5)
Indonesia	75	(69)	32	(101.5)	71	(70.5)	28	(104)
Iran	83	(67)	81	(64.3)	69	(73)	66	(75.5)
Iraq	65	(75.5)	63	(78)	66	(75)	64	(76)
Ireland	176	(9)	178	(6)	183	(8)	185	(6)
Israel	86	(63)	81	(64.3)	92	(55.3)	87	(56.5)
Italy	152	(20.5)	155	(21)	158	(19)	160	(19)
Ivory Coast	69	(72.5)	64	(77)	73	(67.5)	68	(73.5)
Jamaica	130	(33)	128	(33.5)	132	(31)	130	(33)
Japan	165	(13.5)	157	(20)	157	(20)	149	(23)
Jordan	56	(81.3)	44	(91)	54	(84)	42	(95)
Kenya	58	(79)	70	(72.3)	56	(83)	68	(73.5)
Korea, South	115	(43)	110	(47.3)	107	(48.5)	102	(51)
Lebanon	93	(57.3)	112	(44.3)	93	(54)	112	(46)
Liberia	65	(75.5)	69	(75)	65	(76.5)	69	(72)
Libya	90	(61)	52	(84.5)	86	(61)	49	(83.2)

TABLE 5–3 Continued

ISP 1969–70 (Rank)	ISP 1979–80 (Rank)	Country	INSP 1969–70 (Rank)	INSP 1979–80 (Rank)
83 (59.5)	79 (64)	Madagascar	78 (67)	74 (70)
81 (62)	92 (55.3)	Malaysia	83 (61)	95 (54.5)
46 (87.5)	35 (96)	Mali[a]	45 (89.5)	34 (98.5)
44 (90.5)	37 (94.5)	Malawi[a]	45 (89.5)	38 (93)
63 (78)	27 (103)	Mauritania	70 (72.3)	34 (98.5)
120 (39)	121 (38)	Mexico	118 (40.5)	120 (38)
72 (69.5)	73 (67.5)	Morocco	74 (69)	76 (68)
49 (83.2)	57 (81.5)	Nepal[a]	49 (86.5)	57 (80)
187 (3)	190 (4)	Netherlands	182 (5)	186 (5)
178 (8)	186 (6)	New Zealand	174 (8)	183 (6)
83 (59.5)	87 (60)	Nicaragua	101 (53)	105 (50)
34 (103)	34 (97.5)	Niger[a]	38 (98)	37 (94)
3 (107)	33 (99.5)	Nigeria	-1 (107)	28 (101)
186 (4.5)	193 (2)	Norway	189 (3)	196 (1)
40 (97)	31 (101)	Pakistan	41 (95.5)	32 (100)
128 (34.5)	122 (37)	Panama	131 (31)	125 (34.3)
115 (43.5)	125 (35)	Paraguay	115 (43)	125 (34.3)
82 (61)	76 (66)	Peru	91 (57)	85 (64)
98 (53)	91 (58)	Philippines	100 (54.5)	93 (57.3)
168 (15)	168 (15)	Poland	163 (15.5)	163 (15)
131 (32)	146 (23.5)	Portugal	127 (35.5)	142 (25)
163 (18)	163 (17.5)	Romania	158 (19)	158 (18.5)
61 (80)	59 (80)	Rwanda[a]	55 (82)	53 (87)
75 (66.5)	68 (74)	Senegal	70 (72.3)	63 (77.5)
80 (63.3)	62 (78)	Sierra Leone	72 (70)	54 (85.5)
106 (49)	107 (48.5)	Singapore	106 (50.5)	107 (48)

Somalia[a]	58	(81.5)	50	(88)	57	(80)	49	(90)
South Africa	121	(38)	98	(52)	112	(44.3)	89	(62)
Spain	156	(21)	129	(33)	150	(22)	122	(37)
Sri Lanka	119	(40)	118	(40.5)	118	(40.5)	117	(40.5)
Sudan[a]	49	(83.2)	60	(79)	52	(84.5)	63	(77.5)
Sweden	198	(1.5)	189	(5)	201	(1)	192	(3)
Switzerland	164	(17)	170	(12.5)	159	(18)	165	(13.5)
Syria	71	(71)	115	(43)	66	(76)	110	(46.5)
Tanzania[a]	43	(92.3)	29	(102)	37	(99.5)	23	(103)
Thailand	104	(50)	99	(51)	105	(52)	100	(52)
Togo	41	(96)	46	(90)	41	(95.5)	46	(91)
Trinidad/Tobago	123	(36.5)	126	(34)	123	(37)	125	(3)
Tunisia	109	(47)	119	(39)	106	(50.5)	116	(42)
Turkey	99	(52)	112	(45)	98	(56)	110	(46.5)
Uganda[a]	45	(89)	21	(105)	42	(93.5)	19	(105)
United Kingdom	171	(13)	145	(25)	165	(14)	139	(27.5)
United States	91	(54)	116	(42)	121	(38)	146	(23)
Upper Volta[a]	37	(99)	34	(97.5)	28	(104)	25	(102)
Uruguay	137	(27.5)	140	(27)	128	(33.5)	131	(32)
USSR	132	(31)	113	(44)	132	(30)	113	(44.5)
Venezuela	128	(34.5)	137	(28.3)	129	(32)	138	(29)
Vietnam	8	(106)	53	(85.5)	10	(106)	54	(85.5)
Yemen, PDR[a]	39	(98)	71	(70.5)	37	(99.5)	69	(72.5)
Yugoslavia	140	(24.5)	137	(28.3)	136	(27)	133	(30.5)
Zaïre	43	(92.3)	52	(87)	42	(93.5)	51	(88)
Zambia	73	(68)	37	(94.5)	71	(71)	35	(96.5)
Zimbabwe	80	(63.3)	33	(99.5)	82	(62.5)	35	(96.5)

[a]Indicates countries classified by the United Nations (1971; 1975) as "Least Developing Countries."

world community of nations. Other nations are characterized by such a morass of social needs and problems that little or no movement toward realizing social development objectives seems to take place within them. Such was the case when the ISP was applied over the ten-year period to the study's 107 nations.

Table 5–4 identifies world social leaders and least socially developed nations for both 1970 and 1980. In examining the table the reader should note immediately that in 1970 eight out of ten (80 percent) of the world's socially leading nations are in Europe, whereas in 1980 nine out of eleven (82 percent) of these countries are in Europe. The only non-European nations on this list are Australia and New Zealand, both of which, of course, share extensive social histories that are rooted in Europe.

Typically, the world's socially leading nations are comparatively small in population (median = 8.2 million persons), geographically stable (subindex average = 11.5), culturally homogenous (subindex average = 15.5), and have long histories of political independence (the average age of current constitutions within these countries is 80 years). Social leader countries also have achieved a high level of economic cooperation through the establishment of common markets and similar European-based trade and exchange agreements. Socially leading nations also are very politically stable (subindex average = 11.4), and commit relatively few of their national resources to defense expenditures (Defense Effort subindex average = 13.2).

In sharp contrast to the predominately white, Protestant, monolinguistic, relatively small "social leader" nations, the "least socially developed" nations listed in Table 5–4 are predominantly black, religiously diverse and linguistically fragmented (Cultural Diversity subindex = − 1.2). With the exception of Pakistan and Indonesia, all are located in Africa. More than half of them are officially designated as LDCs.

Least socially developing nations also are economically impoverished and have only the most fragile economic and trade agreements with nations located in other parts of the world. Their average population size was approximately 21.5 million persons in 1980. As a group these nations are relatively young, with the exception of Ethiopia, having achieved independence as autonomous nation states, on average, only around 1960. These nations are characterized by social programs of only a minimal nature which, when available, provide inadequately for the needs of their people in relation to sickness and accidents, work injury, early death, disability, and survivorship (Welfare Effort subindex mean = 2.1).

Though somewhat politically stable on the average (mean = 7.2), the level of popular political participation in socially least developing nations is very low (mean = 0.8). With the exception of Zimbabwe, civilian affairs in these nations are influenced either directly or indirectly by military rather than civilian authorities. Defense expenditures within these countries also

TABLE 5–4   Index of Social Progress (ISP) Scores for World Social Leaders and Least Socially Developed Nations, 1970 and 1980

World Social Leaders				Least Socially Developed Nations			
1969–70	(ISP)	1979–80	(ISP)	1969–70	(ISP)	1979–80	(ISP)
Denmark	(198)	Denmark	(201)	Nigeria	(3)	Ethiopia[a]	(−12)
Sweden	(198)	Norway	(193)	Vietnam	(8)	Chad[a]	(14)
Netherlands	(187)	Austria	(192)	Chad[a]	(25)	Uganda[a]	(21)
Austria	(186)	Netherlands	(190)	Indonesia	(28)	Pakistan	(31)
Norway	(186)	Sweden	(189)	Niger[a]	(34)	Nigeria	(33)
Ireland	(185)	New Zealand	(186)	Ethiopia[a]	(36)	Zimbabwe	(33)
New Zealand	(178)	Australia	(184)	Upper Volta[a]	(37)	Upper Volta[a]	(34)
Belgium	(175)	Ireland	(183)	PDR Yemen[a]	(39)	Niger[a]	(34)
FDR Germany	(174)	Belgium	(178)	Pakistan	(40)	Tanzania[a]	(29)
Australia	(173)	Finland	(174)	Togo	(41)	Burundi[a]	(24)
		FDR Germany	(174)				

[a]Indicates nations officially designated by the United Nations as "Least Developing Countries" (United Nations 1971, 1975).

are well above average (mean = 6.1) and are continuing to increase (SIPRI 1981).

Between 1970 and 1980, six out of ten nations remained on the list of socially developed nations for both modal time periods: Ethiopia, Chad, Pakistan, Nigeria, Upper Volta, and Niger. Uganda, Zimbabwe, and Tanzania were added to the list in 1980 due in large measure to a combination of severe economic and political problems that occurred within those countries during the decade.

The nations that experienced the largest net gains and net losses in adequacy of social provision between 1970 and 1980 are identified in Table 5–5. As seen in this table, the nations listed in both categories all are either DCs or LDCs. Though significant ISP shifts occurred for many DME and ETA nations over the decade, overall changes in level of social provision observed in these comparatively rich countries were less dramatic than those found in the world's less socially advanced nations.

Of particular note are the very significant increases in ISP scores observed for Nigeria (+1000 percent) and Vietnam (+563 percent). Certainly, Nigeria's entry into the group of oil-exporting nations contributed to the dramatic, hopefully long-lasting, social changes found in that nation. The end of the 30-year war in Southeast Asia permitted Vietnam to devote more of its scarce resources to social development, rather than to military purposes. Even within a comparatively short period of time, very significant progress has been observed in both of these nations now that resources have become available to them to respond to the basic social and material needs of their populations.

Progress in Indonesia also has been impressive. These gains have been brought about by the high level of Political Stability (subindex = 12) that characterized the nation over the decade, albeit popular Political Participation (subindex = 6) has continued to be low. Indonesia also experienced a period of rapid Economic expansion (+146 percent) over the decade, which favorably influenced development in other sectors of Indonesian life, especially in Education (+75 percent), Health Care (+100 percent), Women Status (+11 percent), and so on.

The People's Democratic Republic of Yemen was the only LDC to experience substantial gains on the ISP between 1970 and 1980. The country began the decade with a new constitution and, despite many internal political upheavals, was able to register ISP increases in the areas of Defense Effort (+242 percent), Political Stability (+9 percent), and Political Participation (+67 percent), among others. ISP gains in PDR Yemen must be regarded as quite fragile, however, especially given the country's economic fragility and rapidly increasing population (−67 percent).

The most significant percentage of social losses on the ISP occurred for six nations, two of which, Ethiopia and Uganda, are officially designated as

TABLE 5–5   Countries with the Largest Percentage Gains and Losses on the
ISP, 1970–80 (N = 107)

	ISP 1969/70	ISP 1979/80	Net ISP Change 1970–80	Percentage Change
Countries with Largest Percentage Increases on the ISP				
Nigeria	3	33	30	+1000
Vietnam	8	53	45	+563
Indonesia	28	71	43	+154
PDR Yemen*	39	81	42	+82
Libya	49	86	37	+76
Syria	71	115	44	+62
Countries with Largest Percentage Decreases on the ISP				
Ethiopia[a]	36	−12	−48	−133
Zimbabwe	80	33	−47	−59
Uganda[a]	45	21	−24	−53
Zambia	73	37	−36	−49
Ghana	58	39	−19	−33
Chile	135	90	−45	−33

[a]Indicates nations officially designated by the United Nations as "Least Developing Countries" (United Nations 1971, 1975).

LDCs. Ethiopia lost ground on all eight of the ISP subindexes. The severe social decline observed in this nation is related to the country's serious economic problems, severe difficulties brought on by drought and famine, political instability throughout the country, and a continuing civil war in Eritrea and Ogaden. Over the period of the decade, these massive social problems resulted in the deaths of hundreds of thousands of Ethiopians. The country's very significant cultural diversity and meager welfare programs and services have contributed to its social problems as well. Despite Ethiopia's profound human needs, it has not received the level of social and economic assistance that is required to reverse its massive social problems.

The situation in Uganda between 1970 and 1980 was not unlike that found in Ethiopia. Scores on all eight subindexes were lower for Uganda in 1980 than in 1970, with the most significant losses occurring on the Economic (−57 percent) and Political Stability (−191 percent) subindexes. Uganda's score on the Cultural Diversity subindex (−8 percent) is among the least favorable found in the world; its social welfare programs also are basically non-existent (Welfare Effort subindex = 1). Engaged in protracted national and international conflicts during much of the decade, as many as one million Ugandans may have died as a result of civil strife and human rights violations. With the forced removal of Idi Amin from the office of President For Life in April, 1979, constitutional government was returned to the country in December 1980, although military authorities continue to carry an important role in the nation's civilian affairs.

Now a country governed by its black majority, Zimbabwe also experienced significant social losses over much of the decade. Losses were found on all but the Political Participation subindex ($+20$ percent), with the most significant losses registered on the Defense Effort (-186 percent) and Political Stability (-82 percent) subindexes. Like most of southern Africa, Zimbabwe is culturally diverse (subindex score $= 6$), a factor that for decades has impeded rather than promoted national social development. Zimbabwe, along with the PDR of Yemen, has the least favorable Welfare Effort scores (-4) observed anywhere in the world. Though reluctant to recognize the new black majority government of Zimbabwe in 1979, in recent years Western nations have made major financial commitments to assist the country in achieving its development objectives. The prospects for Zimbabwe's immediate future remain cautiously optimistic, however.

Social losses observed for Zambia, Ghana, and Chile were less severe than those found in Ethiopia, Uganda, and Zimbabwe, but were quite serious even so. The only South American country placed on the list of LDCs, Chile has been a world center of internal and regional political conflict throughout much of the decade. In 1973, Chile's history of 46 years of constitutional government came to an end with a successful coup by Chilean military leaders. Since that time, the government's systematic violations of human rights have been denounced by all major international bodies. Defense expenditures escalated dramatically within Chile over the decade (subindex scores dropped from $+13$ to -6, a drop of 146 percent) and level of Political Participation dropped by some 73 percent (from 15 to 4).

For the last several years Chile's economy has been at the point of near collapse (subindex scores dropped 550 percent, from a high of $+4$ in 1970 to a low of -18 in 1980). Problems of inflation, currency devaluation, and sharp declines in national productivity also plague Chile. These problems exist despite Chile's favorable Cultural Diversity subindex score (17) and its high level of Welfare Effort (subindex $= 20$). Though shifts toward a more participatory form of popular governance are beginning, Chile has yet to regain the level of social progress with which it began the decade.

ZONES OF SOCIAL VULNERABILITY

For analytical purposes ISP scores were collapsed and divided into eight regions referred to as Zones of Social Vulnerability. These zones group nations by comparable social development criteria rather than by either economic development classifications or by geo-political region. Zones take into account all of the social, economic, political, and national geographic factors that form the ISP. Nations located in Zone 1 are characterized by the highest levels of social provision, and those in Zone 8 by the lowest. Thus, a new mix emerges of nations that are more or less comparable to one another with respect to social development criteria. Tables 5–6 through 5–8 report the major patterns that result from the rank ordering of nations into vulnerability zones.

Note in Table 5–6 that vulnerability zones are *not* equally distributed among nations grouped in the four economic development classifications. Although in both 1969–70 and 1979–80 only DME nations are found in Zone 1, other zones reflect a more heterogeneous mixture of nations, including those DME countries that are not found in Zone 1. Note, too, that ETA nations are grouped into Zones 2 and 3 in 1969–70 but into Zones 2 and 4 in 1979–80. Similarly in 1969–70, developing nations are found only in Zones 3 and lower; by 1979–80, however, one country—Costa Rica—moved into the more favorable Zone 2. For both time periods all the LDCs are found in Zones 5 through 8 with four LDCs actually dropping down into Zone 8 over the decade—Burundi, Chad, Uganda, and Ethiopia. The two DCs found in Zone 8 in 1969–70 moved into higher zones by 1979–80, Nigeria into Zone 7, and Vietnam into Zone 6.

Interest in the vulnerability zone concept, of course, extends beyond a simple ranking of nations in terms of a new concept. It helps to spot *major* changes that occur in the adequacy of social provision found within nations over time and also helps to assess the desirability of those changes. Thus, nations that move from lower to higher zones (those closer to Zone 1) can be thought of as having made significant progress in providing more adequately for the basic social needs of their people; those that move to lower zones (those closer to Zone 8) are assessed as having lost social gains that were realized during earlier decades of development. Movement of more than one zone in either direction during a decade is regarded as being quite unusual and generally reflects very major social development shifts within a nation. These changes, of course, can be of either a positive or negative nature, depending on the direction of the movement.

Zonal positions for all 107 nations included in this study are reported in Table 5–7. The table also shows zonal shifts that took place within these nations over the decade. Table 5–8 summarizes zonal movement for the 107 nations by economic development classification.

Between 1970 and 1980 zonal changes were observed for 43 (41 percent) of the 107 nations (Table 5–8). These shifts were about equally divided between those nations that increased their level of social provision and those that experienced significant social losses over the decade, (21 and 20 percent, respectively). Four of five zonal changes occurred in DCs and LDCs, however; the majority of these changes (56 percent) were shifts into more favorable vulnerability zones.

TABLE 5-6   Distribution of countries by Zones of Social Vulnerability, Economic Development Groupings and Year (N = 107)

Collapsed ISP Score Ranges	1969–70					1979–80				
	DME (%)	ETA(%)	DC(%)	LDC (%)	Row Percentage	DME (%)	ETA(%)	DC(%)	LDC (%)	Row Percentage
Zone 1 (175–225)	9(38)	–	–	–	9(8)	9(38)	–	–	–	9(8)
Zone 2 (150–174)	8(33)	5(71)	–	–	13(12)	7(29)	5(71)	1(2)	–	13(12)
Zone 3 (125–149)	4(17)	2(29)	7(12)	–	13(12)	5(21)	–	8(14)	–	13(12)
Zone 4 (100–124)	1(4)	–	15(26)	–	16(15)	1(4)	2(21)	12(21)	–	15(14)
Zone 5 (75–99)	2(8)	–	13(22)	2(11)	17(16)	2(8)	–	13(22)	1(6)	16(15)
Zone 6 (50–74)	–	–	13(22)	1(6)	14(13)	–	–	16(28)	6(33)	22(21)
Zone 7 (25–49)	–	–	8(14)	15(83)	23(21)	–	–	8(14)	7(39)	15(14)
Zone 8 (–25–24)	–	–	2(3)	–	2(2)	–	–	–	4(22)	4(4)
All Zones	24(100)	7(100)	58(100)	18(100)	107(100)	24(100)	7(100)	58(100)	18(100)	107(100)

TABLE 5–7   Country Groupings by Zones of Social Vulnerability and Year (N = 107)

1969	1979								Totals
	Zone 1	Zone 2	Zone 3	Zone 4	Zone 5	Zone 6	Zone 7	Zone 8	
Zone 1 $\bar{X}$ = (175–225)ᵃ	Austria Belgium Denmark Ireland Netherlands Norway Sweden New Zealand	FDR Germany →1							N = 9 8.4%
Zone 2 $\bar{X}$ = (150–174)	Australia ←1	Canada Bulgaria Czechoslovakia Finland France Hungary Italy Poland Rumania Switzerland →1	Spain United Kingdom						N = 13 12.1%
Zone 3 $\bar{X}$ = (125–149)	Costa Rica Japan ←1		Cuba Jamaica Uruguay Venezuela Greece Portugal Yugoslavia →1	Panama Albania USSR →1	Chile →2				N = 13 12.1%

TABLE 5–7   Continued

1969	1979								
	Zone 1	Zone 2	Zone 3	Zone 4	Zone 5	Zone 6	Zone 7	Zone 8	Totals
Zone 4 $\bar{X} = (100\text{–}124)$			Trinidad/ Tobago Brazil Colombia Paraguay ←1	Tunisia Dominican Republic El Salvador Mexico Argentina Ecuador Sri Lanka South Korea Singapore	South Africa Lebanon Thailand				N = 16 15.0%
Zone 5 $\bar{X} = (75\text{–}99)$			1	United States Turkey ←1	Algeria Madagascar Haiti[b] Honduras Nicaragua Bolivia Peru Israel Malaysia Philippines 1	Senegal Sierra Leone Burma	Zimbabwe		N = 16 15.0%
Zone 6 $\bar{X} = (50\text{–}74)$				Syria	Egypt	Cameroon Ivory Coast Kenya →1	Ghana Mauritania Zambia →2		N = 15 14.0%

								Zone total
Zone 7 $\bar{X} = (25\text{–}49)$			Liberia Morocco Rwanda[b] Somalia[b] Guatemala Iran Iraq	Libya	Zäire Guinea[b] Sudan[b] India Indonesia Jordan Nepal[b] PDR Yemen[b]	Central African Empire[b] Benin[b] Malawi[b] Mali[b] Niger[b] Togo Tanzania[b] Upper Volta[b] Kampuchea Pakistan	Burundi[b] Chad[b] Uganda[b] Ethiopia[b]	N = 23 21.5%
(arrows)		←2	←1	→1	2← 1←		→1	
Zone 8 $\bar{X} = (-25\ -\ -24)$					Vietnam	Nigeria		N = 2 1.9%
(arrows)					2←	←1		
All zones	N = 9 8.4%	N = 13 12.1%	N = 13 12.1%	N = 15 14.0%	N = 16 15.0%	N = 22 20.1%	N = 15 14.0%	N = 4 3.7%	N = 107 100%

[a] Indicates range of Index of Social Progress scores (ISP) used to define each vulnerability zone.

[b] Countries officially classified by the United Nations (1975) as "Least Developing Countries" (LDCs).

[c] Arrows indicate shifts in zones of vulnerability between 1969 and 1979, for instance, FDR Germany moved down one zone, from Zone 1 in 1969 to Zone 2 in 1979.

TABLE 5–8   Country Shifts in Zones of Social Vulnerability by Economic
Development Classification, 1970–80 (N = 107)

Development Classification	Zone of Social Vulnerability Changes			Totals (%)
	Advances(%)	Declines(%)	Unchanged(%)	
Developed Market Economies	3 (13)	4 (17)	17 (71)	24 (100)
Eastern Trading Area	–	2 (29)	5 (71)	7 (100)
Developing Countries	15 (26)	11 (19)	32 (55)	58 (100)
Least Developing Countries	4 (22)	4 (22)	10 (56)	18 (100)
All nations	22 (21)	21 (20)	64 (60)	107 (100)

Between 1970 and 1980 no ETA nation advanced into a more favorable vulnerability zone. Two ETA nations experienced significant social
losses over the decade, however, and moved into less favorable zones; Albania and the U.S.S.R. both moved from Zone 3 to Zone 4. Among DME
nations, three nations shifted into higher vulnerability zones, Australia
(from Zone 2 to Zone 1), Japan (from Zone 3 to Zone 2), and the United
States (from Zone 5 to Zone 4). Significant social losses took place in four
DME nations, however, with the result that they are found in less favorable
vulnerability zones at the end of the decade than at its beginning: FDR Germany (from Zone 1 to Zone 2), Spain and the United Kingdom (both from
Zone 2 to Zone 3), and South Africa (from Zone 4 to Zone 5). With the
exception of FDR Germany, which suffered only a three percent drop in its
1970–80 ISP score (from 179 to 174), all other DME and ETA nations
shifted into less favorable vulnerability zones as a result of net ISP losses of
at least 14 percent over the decade (see Table 5–1 for nation-specific composite and subindex scores).

All four of the LDCs for which zonal advances occurred shifted from
Zone 7 to Zone 6—Guinea, Sudan, Nepal, and PDR Yemen. Though still
quite low, ISP scores observed for these nations increased by 33 percent, 22
percent, 16 percent, and 82 percent respectively, between 1970 and 1980.
Much of the improvement observed to have taken place within these nations is accounted for by significant increases on the Education, Political Sta-

bility, and Political Participation subindexes. Sharp increases in the Defense subindex, especially for PDR Yemen, also resulted in more favorable ISP scores and a higher zone of social vulnerability classification.

Within the larger group of DCs, very significant zonal shifts took place in Syria (from Zone 6 to Zone 4), Libya (from Zone 7 to Zone 5), and Vietnam (From Zone 8 to Zone 6). In each of these nations major advances were observed on the Education subindex and selected political data. Important economic gains in Syria and, as stated earlier, an ending of the war in Southeast Asia, explain the substantial gains registered by these nations. Even more impressive social gains might have occurred over the decade in Libya were it not for that country's severe economic problems which, to a large extent, were brought about by Libya's military interventions into other countries of the region and in other parts of Africa.

The average ISP losses already discussed for Ethiopia, Zimbabwe, and Uganda are reflected in the significant zonal shifts downward for these countries shown in Table 5–7 (from Zone 7 to Zone 8 for Ethiopia and Uganda and from Zone 5 to Zone 7 for Zimbabwe).

As an analytical tool, the Zones of Social Vulnerability concept offers yet another perspective from which changes in national social development over time can be examined. When used in conjunction with the ISP and its component subindexes, reference to these zones allows for a quicker assessment of the social *significance* of development changes observed for particular nations. The concept also represents a dynamic approach to characterizing development within groupings of nations that are more or less similar to one another with respect to adequacy of social provision. Using this concept, for example, the specific social development classification of a given nation can advance or decline *in direct relation to social changes that occur within that nation.* In this way, the taxonomic problems encountered in using static approaches to classifying groups of more or less similar nations can be avoided (for example, the "economic development" classification scheme currently in use by the United Nations and other international organizations).

Overall, social progress within nations between 1970 and 1980 has been considerably uneven. Some nations have succeeded in achieving significant social gains during the decade, while others have made gains of only a modest nature. Declines in level of social development also were common, however, especially for those poorest nations on earth that could little afford to lose the meager social gains that had taken a decade to accomplish.

The worldwide economic recession of the 1970s, rampant international human rights violations, increased political instability, and a general shift toward militarism (especially among Third and Fourth World nations) were among the most alarming social phenomena observed during the decade. Gains in population control, modest improvements in the status of women, and increased access to primary school education and health services for larger segments of the world's population were among the decade's major social accomplishments. The social agenda before the world's nations remains a heavy one, then, and will continue to pose many difficult challenges to international social development leaders for decades yet to come.

6

Summary of Major Findings

A number of significant social development trends have emerged from application of the Index of Social Progress (ISP) to 107 nations at two time intervals, 1969–70 to 1979–80. Several of these trends require the urgent attention of world welfare planners and social development specialists.

DEVELOPED MARKET ECONOMIES (DMEs)

During the ten-year period 1970–80, increases in levels of National Social Progress—as measured by the ISP—were most dramatic among the world's already developed nations, but especially among those nations located in Northern and Western Europe and in North America. The ISP provides demonstrable evidence that the so-called rich countries of the world (Developed Market Economies, DMEs) have continued their success in achieving development objectives in a variety of social, economic, and political sectors. More particularly, since 1969, DMEs succeeded in three areas:

1. DMEs achieved further reductions in population growth trends. Population growth rates were down by more than 27 percent from an average population increase of 1.1 percent in 1969 to only 0.8 percent in 1979.

2. DMEs are providing a more diverse spectrum of effective health, education, and welfare services for their populations. For example, while length of overall male life expectation remained relatively unchanged during the period, the rate of infant mortality declined by 33 percent, from 27.7 per 1,000 live-born in 1969 to 18.5 per 1,000 live-born in 1979. Similarly, the supply of trained health care personnel in DMEs rose during the period, so that each physician served a population 13 percent smaller, from

0.8 thousand persons per physician in 1969 to 0.7 in 1979. Rates of adult illiteracy, for both men and women, also dropped over the decade, from 7.3 percent to 6.2 percent. The majority of DME nations continued to expand programs of welfare provision designed to minimize the most serious social and economic problems associated with poverty, hunger, illness, disability, early death, and survivorship.

    3. DMEs significantly improved their ability to maintain desired levels of political participation and political stability. No DME nation was dominated by military forces in the late 1970s, and all had functioning political party and parliamentary systems of popular governance. The vast majority of adults in DME nations continued to participate in local and national political elections as well. Similarly, the civil unrest that characterized several DMEs during the late 1960s and early 1970s—including the United States—dropped sharply in 1979.

    The status of women and children in DME nations improved steadily between 1969 and 1979. For example, the percentage of age-eligible girls enrolled in primary education programs remained at historically high levels, and similarly, the level of adult female illiteracy dropped by more than 28 percent during the decade, from 5.3 percent in 1969 to 3.8 percent in 1979.

    DME economic progress, though less impressive than in earlier decades, continued throughout the 1970s; real growth continued in the economies of most nations. While DME economic growth rates were down from an average of 4.7 percent in 1969 to 3.8 percent in 1979, per capita income levels during the same time period, not controlling for reduced purchasing power brought about by inflation, rose 219 percent, from an average of $1,961 in 1969 to $6,259 in 1979. Rates of inflation, though unusually high for most DMEs (mean = 11.9 percent), were considerably lower than inflationary patterns found in the world's DCs (mean = 20.3 percent).[1]

    Overall, between 1970 and 1980, of the 24 DME nations, 15 (63 percent) realized social development gains in their capacity to provide for the basic social and material needs of their populations (for example, Australia, +6 percent; Canada, +8 percent; Greece, +7 percent; Israel, +6 percent; Japan, +5 percent; Portugal, +12 percent; United States, +28 percent). Between 1970 and 1980, however, declines in level of social provision were observed in nine (38 percent) DME nations (France, −4 percent; F.D.R. Germany, −3 percent; Ireland −1 percent; Italy, −1 percent; South Africa, −19 percent; Spain, −17 percent; Sweden, −5 percent; United Kingdom, −15 percent; Yugoslavia, −2 percent). In each case significant net

---

[1]For comparative purposes, the reader is referred to Table 4–1 which reports changes in per capita income levels and inflation rates for all nations by economic development groupings.

losses on the ISP for DME nations resulted from increased internal political instability: rioting, political strikes, armed attacks, and the like. For South Africa, substantial losses on the Defense (− 31 percent) and Economic (− 33 percent) subindexes contributed to significantly lower ISP scores as well.

EASTERN TRADING AREA NATIONS (ETAs)

Of the seven centrally planned (Eastern Trading Area, ETA) countries included in this study, the composite ISP scores for only one, Czechoslovakia, increased (+ 8 percent) between 1970 and 1980. The ISP scores for four ETAs were significantly lower at the end of the decade than at its beginning (Albania, − 21 percent; Bulgaria, − 7 percent; Hungary, − 2 percent; and the USSR, − 14 percent). Further, no shifts in level of attained social progress were found for Poland or Romania during this period. Overall ETA scores on the ISP declined an average of 4.8 percent between 1970 and 1980.

In the main, the lack of significant social progress in ETA nations during the past decade resulted from sharp increases in defense expenditures (+ 11.9 percent), reduced levels of political participation (− 18.2 percent), and a declining, increasingly more fragile economic situation within these centrally planned economies (− 17.1 percent). An increase in population growth rates (+ 11.1 percent) also was a significant factor contributing to losses on the ISP for three (43 percent) of the seven ETAs. Even with these losses, however, average ETA scores on the ISP continued to compare favorably with those of DME nations for both 1970 (156 versus 160 for DMEs) and 1980 (148 vs. 161). Both ETA and DME nations continue to be the most socially and economically advantaged nations anywhere in the world, despite the reality that the combined populations of these 31 nations made up only 39 percent of the world's total inhabitants in 1980.

DEVELOPING COUNTRIES (DCs): SOCIAL GAINS

Of the 58 DCs included in this study, ISP gains were observed for 35 (60 percent). Of these countries, very substantial ISP gains (larger than five percent) were observed for 23 (40 percent). ISP changes of this magnitude reflect what is apparently a fundamental improvement in the capacity of many DCs to provide more adequately for the basic social, economic, and political needs of their people.

For the group (n = 58), significant progress in achieving social development objectives is evidenced by: (1) increases in the proportion of age-eligible children enrolled in primary schools (+ 4.8 percent); (2) decreases in adult illiteracy (-2.1 percent); (3) reductions in overall rates of infant mortality (-1.3 percent); (4) decreases in the number of people served per physician (-20.0 percent); (5) increases in suffrage for women ($+41.4$ percent); (6) increases in rates of economic growth ($+18.6$ percent) and per capita income levels ($+221.7$ percent); and (7) decreases in previously high levels of political instability (subindex average $= +11.0$ percent).

In addition, certain DCs significantly increased the diversity and comprehensiveness of their nationally organized and administered programs of social welfare provision during the ten-year period of the study. A greater number of DCs, for example, now have national programs designed to assist their populations with recurrent social problems arising from unemployment, illness, disability, early death, retirement, and survivorship. The proportion of DC populations now covered by national social welfare programs increased consistently between 1970 and 1980.

On the negative side, the rate of inflation in DCs increased by 121 percent between 1970 and 1980. However, this increase was less than the DME rate ($+143$ percent) and was considerably lower than the average increase that took place among the world's least developing nations ($+163$ percent).

Population growth continued to be a major problem confronting DCs ($+11.2$ percent), despite an average decline of 6 percent in the birth rate. The increase in average population size resulted primarily from the success of a variety of public health measures that reduced the crude death rate in DCs by 20 percent (from 14.2 per 1,000 persons to 11.4 per 1,000 persons) between 1970 and 1980.

The DCs with the most substantial gains on the composite ISP between 1970 and 1980 were: Indonesia, $+154$ percent; Jordan, $+29$ percent; Libya, $+76$ percent; Nigeria, $+1000$ percent; Syria, $+62$ percent; Vietnam, $+563$ percent; and Zaire, $+21$ percent. The reader should note, however, that while the increases in ISP scores for these nations were substantial (compared with an average increase among developing nations of only 4.3 percent in 1980 over 1970), the average ISP score for all 58 DCs was only 85.3 in 1970 and 89.0 in 1980. These scores compare very unfavorably with the much higher average ISP scores attained by DME nations during the same time period (160.4 and 161.4, respectively). Despite the much lower percentage of increase in average ISP scores for DME nations ($+0.4$ percent), even a proportionately smaller upward change in DME scores has the effect of further widening the already very great social development gap that exists between DMEs and DCs.

These gains on the part of some of the DCs must be regarded as tentative, for the present time at least. ISP gains are not likely to be long-lasting should recurrent problems of inflation, political instability, population growth, or present-day economic and military exploitation of developing nations by DME and ETA countries persist.

DEVELOPING COUNTRIES (DCs): SOCIAL LOSSES

Between 1970 and 1980, significant negative changes in adequacy of national social provision were found for 22 of the 58 developing nations; ISP scores for 21 DCs actually declined over the decade. These data confirm that a high degree of social deterioration existed within nearly two out of every five (38 percent) DCs during the last decade.

DCs with the highest ISP losses between 1970 and 1980 include: Chile, − 33 percent; Ghana, − 33 percent; Mauritania, − 57 percent; Pakistan, − 23 percent; Sierra Leone, − 23 percent; Zambia, − 49 percent; and Zimbabwe, − 59 percent. Substantial ISP losses also occurred for: Burma, − 13 percent; Kenya, − 18 percent; South Korea, − 19 percent; and Lebanon, − 17 percent.

One of the most alarming trends that occurred in DCs during the decade was their rapid move toward increased militarism and the suppression of internationally guaranteed individual freedoms. Between 1970 and 1980, the "official" percentage of DC GNP allocated to defense expenditures increased from 3.5 percent to 4.3 percent, an overall increase of 23 percent. Defense expenditures in DME nations dropped by 14 percent during the same time period. Within ETA nations, defense expenditures increased, but at a rate of only half as much (+ 12 percent) as that of DCs.

Although the level of political stability in DCs increased appreciably between 1970 and 1980 (subindex mean = 11.0 percent), the level of political participation declined overall by a subindex average of 8.6 percent. A large part of this change was due to the sharp decline in the number of DCs with functioning parliamentary systems of government (− 17.4 percent), multiple political parties (− 16.7 percent), frequency of regularly scheduled popular elections (− 20.0 percent), along with an increase in the number of DC governments under either direct or indirect influence of military authorities (+ 42.9 percent). Between 1970 and 1980, for example, the number of DCs with either military or quasi-military governments increased from 22 (40 percent) to 39 (67 percent), an overall increase of 77 percent in one decade!

Clearly, during the last decade, the majority of DCs attempted to achieve increased political stability within their boundaries at the expense of internationally guaranteed freedoms and political participation for their citizens. This trend—when combined with the dramatically increased expenditures for defense (including expenditures for nuclear weapons on the part of several DCs)—must be considered an alarming one. At a minimum, the allocation of scarce national (and international) resources for fundamentally antihumanistic purposes represents a profound drain on the meager human and material resources presently available to DCs for solidifying the fragile social development gains realized in other areas of national life.

LEAST DEVELOPING COUNTRIES (LDCs)

Between 1970 and 1980, 12 (67 percent) of the world's 18 most impoverished nations (Least Developing Countries, LDCs) made little or no progress in ameliorating the profound social problems existing within their societies. Indeed, during the decade, 11 (61 percent) of the LDCs actually lost social gains achieved during earlier years of progress. LDC scores on the ISP dropped an average of 8.1 percent during the period of the inquiry, the single largest percentage drop for any group of nations studied.

These deplorable shifts downward in level of LDC social development occurred principally because of: (1) continuing sharp increases in the rate of population growth (+13 percent); (2) very high rates of economic inflation (+163 percent); (3) high levels of internal political instability, as manifested by increases in the number of political protest demonstrations (+200 percent), strikes (+20 percent), armed attacks (+270 percent), and deaths from domestic violence (+34 percent); and (4) decreases in levels of popular political participation (subindex mean change = −8.5 percent).

Losses in these areas of the ISP were substantial enough to overshadow impressive gains made by some LDCs in raising the level of primary school enrollment (+36 percent), lowering the rate of infant mortality (−5.8 percent), reducing levels of adult female illiteracy (−6.8 percent), and providing for greater equality of suffrage among men and women (average increase = 64 percent). During the period, per capita income levels within LDC nations increased by 124 percent, from $76 to $172 per annum. In terms of after-inflation purchasing power, however, this increase is meager given the extraordinarily high, and growing, per capita income levels of DME (1979 mean = $6,259; +219 percent) and ETA (mean = $3,355; +60 percent) nations.

The LDCs with the greatest ISP losses between 1970 and 1980 were: Burundi, −33 percent; Chad, −44 percent; Ethiopia, −133 percent; Malawi, −16 percent; Mali, −24 percent; Somalia, −14 percent; Tanzania, −33 percent; Uganda, −53 percent; Upper Volta, −8 percent. The six LDCs with gains on the ISP during the period were: Central African Republic, +29 percent; Guinea, +33 percent; Haiti, +3 percent; Nepal, +16 percent; PDR Yemen, +82 percent; and Sudan, +22 percent.

Overall, then, two out of three (66 percent) of LDCs did not succeed in achieving gains on the ISP over the ten-year period beginning in 1969. This trend must be considered ominous, given the high level of human suffering and deprivation that has long existed, and continues to exist, in countries frequently referred to as "the poorest of the poor." International social welfare authorities and social development specialists the world over must recommit their energies to providing much needed long-term social, economic, and technological assistance to LDCs in helping them to reduce the deplorable level of deprivation experienced by their populations.

THE SOCIAL DEVELOPMENT "GAP"

The gap in social development that long has characterized the world's richest and poorest nations continued to exist over the ten-year period covered by this study. Though beginning to close for some DCs, the gap widened for most countries of the world and especially for the LDCs. Further, this research confirms that the gap in adequacy of social provision among the world's nations is not a unidimensional problem that exists only in relation to (1) the world's rich and poor nations; rather, it is one that also persists between (2) the DMEs and ETAs, and those DCs for which 1970–80 ISP losses were observed, between (3) DME and ETA nations, and between (4) DCs and LDCs. Yet another gap exists (5) in the considerable variation that characterizes ISP scores for nations grouped within the same economic development classification (1980 ISP scores for DME nations range from a high of 201 for Denmark to a low of 92 for Israel).

The five-fold gap in social development uncovered in this study should be a source of major concern to social development specialists around the world. Certainly, the degree of social progress found to have taken place in many DCs can serve as a reasonable basis for believing in the success of international efforts directed toward helping those nations provide more adequately for the basic social and material needs of their people. The social development gains observed for these countries are impressive and should continue, at least for the short term.

For many nations, though, progress in achieving social development objectives over the decade has been less impressive; the prognosis for future development within these countries remains precarious. Indeed, between 1970 and 1980, ISP scores declined for 46 (43 percent) and remained constant for 4 (4 percent) of the study's 107 countries. Declines in social development were especially critical within the LDCs, nations that, as a group, have received preferential international social and economic assistance since the early 1960s. Within the majority of LDCs, the level of human suffering and social deprivation had grown more severe at the end of the decade than at its beginning.

Significant social losses over the decade for the majority of ETA nations (57 percent) and for two in five (38 percent) DME countries also is a source of concern compared to the social development gains observed for most of the world's "rich" countries (52 percent). Certainly, social declines within ETA and DME nations pose different assistance problems for development specialists than do declines in DCs and LDCs; these problems, nonetheless, require serious international attention. Recurrent gaps in social development within economic development groupings ultimately constitute social inequalities for which workable solutions may prove to be as elusive as those required to reduce the more familiar social inequities that exist between economic development groupings (for instance, the special development needs of Southern Europe in relation to those of Northern and Western Europe).

7

Problems of Progress in a Critical Decade

The social and economic gap that long has been evident between the world's most advantaged (Developed Market Economies and Eastern Trading Area) and most disadvantaged (Developing and Least Developing) nations persisted over the ten-year period, 1970–80. Indeed, despite significant welfare gains on the part of some Third World nations, the gap between the rich and the majority of the world's poorest countries actually widened. This failure on the part of the world community to help developing nations to provide more adequately for the basic human needs of their populations—who make up 60 percent of the world's total population—resulted from a variety of factors:

1. Continuing population growth pressure within developing nations. In most cases, this had the effect of offsetting any modest social gains that had already been achieved by these countries in the past only as a result of strict discipline and extraordinary national hardship.

2. The differential rates of economic growth that are characteristic of rich and poor nations, given the very unfavorable economic base from which most DCs and LDCs begin.

3. Recurrent, and increasingly more serious, problems of inflation, inequitable rates of monetary exchange, economic protectionism. These factors and related international economic forces are impacting more adversely on the fragile economies of developing countries than on the economies of DMEs and ETAs.

4. Current trends toward increased militarism of the developing world.

5. Violations of basic human rights and freedoms in the majority of developing nations.

6. Nuclearization of the developing world.

7. The steady erosion and, in time, eventual collapse of the extended family as the basic social welfare "institution" in the majority of the world's developing nations.

8. Indifference—indeed callousness—of the majority of First World (DME) and Second World (ETA) nations to the very special social development requirements of Third World (DCs) and Fourth World (LDCs).

9. The continued social, economic, military, and political exploitation of the developing world by both DME and ETA nations in their pursuit of narrow ideological self-interests.

POPULATION GROWTH PRESSURES

Population growth pressures around the world continue to be enormous. Between 1970 and 1980, for example, the world's total population increased from 3.5 to 4.3 billion persons, an overall increase of 23 percent. Eighty percent of this increase, however, occurred in the world's DC and LDC nations, a growth pattern equivalent in numbers of people to 46 Ugandas, eight Pakistans, or one India being created every ten years!

Even though modest gains have been realized in slowing the rate of population growth in some countries, particularly in the DME nations, rates for the world as a whole are far from being under control. The time required to double the world's population[1] now stands at 32 years compared with the 200 years required in A.D. 1650 to double the world's then estimated population of 500 million persons (Ehrlich and Ehrlich 1972). Given the current rate of population increase, the United Nations estimates that there will be a world population of between 6.5 and 7.0 billion persons by the year 2000 and perhaps as many as 10 to 12 billion persons by the year 2050 (United Nations 1979e). Much of this increase is expected to continue to occur in the world's DC and LDC nations which, on average, have a current population doubling time of only 26 years, compared with 87 years for DME nations and 69 years for the ETAs.

The social, political, and economic problems that can be anticipated as the world's population reaches 10 billion persons, or even eight billion, are staggering. This is especially so given present-day international difficulties

---

[1]Population "doubling time" is computed by dividing 69.31 by the annual population growth rate; thus, the time required to double the 1981 population of Italy is 231 years—that is, 69.31/0.3 percent = 231 years (see Ehrlich and Ehrlich 1972, for a fuller discussion of the origins of this formula).

encountered in assuring even the most minimal level of living for the 4.3 billion persons that currently inhabit the earth.

Imagine, for example, the magnitude of the social problems that a DC such as India must resolve should its current annual 1.8 percent population growth rate swell its 1980 population of 680 million persons to nearly one billion persons by the year 2000. At the same time as her population base continues to expand, average per capita income in India for the year 2000 is expected to fall far below her 1979 average of only $140. By the year 2000, China's 1980 population of 950 million persons is expected to increase to 1.2 billion; that of the United States, by contrast, is expected to increase from 220 million persons in 1980 to 253 million by the end of the century. The pattern of increased population size combined with decreased per capita resources is expected to repeat itself again and again throughout the remainder of the century in the majority of developing nations located in Asia, South America, and Africa.

Clearly, rich and poor countries alike share a major common interest in containing further sharp increases in national and international population growth rates. For rich countries, the problem will become more urgent as the proportion of the world's population residing in socially advanced countries dwindles from 39 percent in 1980 to only 20 percent by the year 2000. For developing nations, however, the population problem is more acute and the urgency over growing numbers exists now. World population control continues to warrant priority attention on the international social agenda. Reasonable solutions to the problem must be found soon, especially if the modest social and economic gains that have been hard-won by many developing countries are not to be eroded by increases in the number of persons residing within their borders who must be fed, clothed, sheltered, and educated, or for whom other human services must be provided. For the world community to not act cooperatively in containing population growth would be folly indeed! To act too late will mean that countless numbers of persons in as yet unborn generations will be forced to suffer a level of deprivation not previously experienced on the planet.

DIFFERENTIAL RATES OF ECONOMIC EXPANSION

Between 1970 and 1980 actual gains were observed on three of the four Economic subindex indicators for the DCs (rate of economic growth, +19 percent; per capita income, +222 percent; per capita food production, +0.4 percent). Within the LDCs economic improvement occurred on two of the subindex's indicators (economic growth rate, +13 percent; and per capita income, + 124 percent). These gains are real and do reflect substantial improvements in the economic capacities of many DC and LDC nations. They are especially impressive given the average loss of 19 percent in the economic growth rate observed for DME nations over the same time period (down from 4.7 percent in 1970 to 3.8 percent in 1980).

Examination of the actual gains (and losses) observed on selected economic indicators alone, however, does not provide a complete picture of the economic changes that are occurring within and between nations organized by various economic groupings. More particularly, by placing the emphasis only on actual economic changes, one can easily miss the more fundamental economic shifts that are taking place in the economic capacity of nations *relative to one another*. This study shows, for example, that, while real advances are occurring along significant dimensions of economic activity within some DC and LDC nations (Table 4–2), these advances are *not* sufficient to close the gap in economic development that historically has characterized the distance between the world's rich (DME and ETA) and poor (DC and LDC) nations (see Table 4–8). Indeed, when DC and LDC nation economic changes are examined relative to economic changes within DME nations, the gap in economic development can be seen to have widened even more over the period of the decade. These more fundamental changes in the *relative* economic capacity of DME nations make clear the more advantaged economic position of DME nations compared to the DCs and LDCs. This is the case despite whatever the annual rate of economic expansion within DME nations might be during a limited period of time, even if the DME economic growth rate is less favorable than that observed for the world's DC and LDC nations.

The simple reality is that no matter how hard DC and LDC nations strive to achieve social and economic parity with DME nations, its realization is not likely to occur easily because of: (1) the enormity of the economic and social gap that separates DME, LDC, and DC nations from one another *at the outset* and continues to do so; (2) the existence of an international social, political and economic system which, ultimately, better serves the economic interests of the world's most socially advanced nations than those of developing countries (see Hogendorn and Brown 1979); and (3) the inability of less developed countries to achieve sufficient control over the global social, economic, and political forces that—as this and other analyses have shown—are necessary to bring a new international social order into being (Singh 1977; Hogendorn and Brown 1979).

Given current international political and economic realities, the world's developing nations can hope to achieve significant gains in providing for only the minimal needs of their populations. Without extraordinary international assistance—such as that given to Japan and Germany following

World War II—most developing nations cannot reasonably hope to achieve economic equality with socially advantaged nations, at least not by using the calculus for national economic growth promulgated by the world's most economically advanced nations (limited industrialization, entry into the global free market economic system, variable rates of exchange that are tied to DME currencies, variable prices for commodities, grains, and other developing nation goods and raw materials). Dramatic shifts forward in raising the *relative* level of economic development are likely to occur within developing nations only when the further development of their national economies is either influenced significantly by DME nations or, at a minimum, economic expansion of DC economies is within the direct vested economic interests of DME nations.

Economic and social parity among all of the world's nations will require dramatic changes in the existing international economic order (see Sauvant and Hasenpflug 1977; Makler 1982). International economic changes of this magnitude will not be possible, however, until the chronic disparity in development between the world's rich and poor nations becomes too dysfunctional to retain. These changes are inevitable over the long term, however, especially as the number of people residing in developing countries continues to increase and DME and ETA control diminishes over the world's scarce and dwindling natural resources—many of which are located within developing nations (for example, petroleum, copper, chromium, and tin). Very significant economic and social adjustments of the type forced on DME and ETA nations by the world's oil-exporting countries— the majority of which are developing nations—may become more frequent in the decades just ahead.

Whether as a result of choice or of confrontation, however, the level of living for all the world's people must improve in both actual and relative terms or all will be forced to endure a level of deprivation that no group of rational people would seek.

GLOBAL MILITARISM

One of the most alarming trends of the past decade has been the dramatic increase in the number of countries that are governed either directly or indirectly by military authorities. In all, political decision-making in 65 (61 percent) of the 107 nations included in this study now is significantly influenced by military authorities, compared with only 33 (31 percent) of the study's countries in 1970—an increase of nearly 100 percent in just one decade!

In a recent study reported by the New York-based Freedom House—an organization that annually examines changes in "political rights"[2] and "civil liberties"[3] in 162 nations—the "status of freedom" throughout the world in 1981 was as follows:

Not Free: 1,911.9 million (42.5 percent) of the world's population, of whom 1,910.1 million live in 58 countries (35.8 percent of the world's nations), and 1.8 million reside in 4 (11.2 percent) political territories controlled by these nations.

Partly Free: 970.9 million (21.6 percent), of whom 962 million live in 53 nations (32.7 percent), and 8.9 million reside in 23 (41.1 percent) related territories.

Free: 1,613 million (35.9 percent), of whom 1,607.6 million inhabit 51 countries (31.4 percent), and 5.4 million live in 29 (51.8 percent) related territories.

According to Freedom House, the *percentage* of the world's population living in "partly free" and "not free" nations declined slightly, from 68 percent in 1973 to 64 percent in 1981. The *absolute number* of persons living in "partly free" and "not free" nations during the period, however, increased by 25 percent, from 2,303 million in 1973 to 2,882 million in 1981. At the same time, both the percentage and absolute numbers of persons residing in nations assessed to be "free" rose by 12 percent and 57 percent respectively (from 1,029 million persons to 1,613 million persons) (Dolmatch 1981, 125).

These patterns confirm the more general political findings reported in the present study, albeit the Freedom House study includes a substantially larger number of countries, including smaller political dependencies and territories of larger, politically autonomous nation states, while the present study includes only countries that are politically autonomous nation-states. The present study also shows that patterns of increased militarism are more characteristic of some economic development groupings than others. Table 4–3 of Chapter 4, for example, shows that military forms of government are most prevalent in the LDCs (94 percent) and DCs (67 percent). All seven of the Eastern Trading Area nations are judged to be heavily "influenced" by military authorities as well. However, in only two DME nations—Yugoslavia and Portugal—are civilian political affairs judged to be substantially under the direct influence of military authorities.

---

[2]Political rights have to do with the nature and distribution of political decision making within societies. Among the criteria used to rate nations along this dimension of "freedom" are: political party structure, open elections, decentralization of political power, and so on.

[3]Civil liberties include a free and open press and the rights to assemble, to express divergent political opinions, to privacy, to "due process" in criminal proceedings, and so on.

The trend toward increased global militarism is a strong one and is likely to continue until at least the end of the present century. Six factors account for it:

1. The nation-building requirements of countries that only recently have gained independence as autonomous nation-states, often only as a result of protracted civil or regional wars (for example, Chad, 1960; Mali, 1960).

2. The relative scarcity, in the majority of the world's developing and least developing countries, of national and man-made resources that are required to satisfy the basic needs of escalating numbers of people within these countries (that is, for the full spectrum of social, economic, health, education, housing, and other human services).

3. The perception of political leaders in many developing nations of the need for strong, absolute, and centralized control over all of the resources available to a nation to assist it both in meeting basic human needs and in moving toward the realization of broader national development objectives (for example, the development of national infrastructures, new economic systems, cities, employment, and so on).

4. The continuing desperate socioeconomic struggle that characterizes life for the majority of persons living in developing and least developing nations.

5. The continuing unrest within these countries, often centuries-long in duration, that stems directly from regional and subregional differences in history, tradition, customs, language, and religion, manifested as well in opposing views concerning both the ends and means of nationhood and national development objectives (in Iran, Lebanon, Tanzania, and the like).

6. The political, economic and military needs of the world's "superpowers"—mainly, but not exclusively, the United States and the USSR—for new economic markets and for comparatively "safe" territories on which their own ideological and military battles can be fought (Cuba, Angola, Vietnam, El Salvador, Nicaragua, Afghanistan, and so on).

One of the most direct consequences of increases in worldwide militarism is the sharp rise in defense expenditures that occurred over the decade, expenditures that were incurred almost always at the cost of spending for national social programs. During the fiscal year 1982, for example, global spending on military armaments alone exceeded $400 billion—60 percent of which was spent by the United States and the USSR (SIPRI 1983). Increasingly, though, DCs and the LDCs are committing a larger share of their Gross National Products to military expenditures, a cost which even the most affluent of these nations can little afford to bear. The majority of arms purchased by the DCs and LDCs, of course, are supplied by the Soviet Union, the United States, or NATO agreement allies of the United States (most notably France, Great Britain, and Germany). Understandably, both the United States and the Soviet Union are perceived throughout DC and LDC nations with considerable trepidation, not infrequently because of their international role as "arms dealers" to the world.

A second consequence stemming from increased global militarism is the incidence of worldwide political instability and, with it, the increased frequency of internal civil wars and intra-regional military conflicts. According to the Washington-based Center for Defense Information, as of spring 1983, 45 nations were engaged in "wars" of some type (CDI 1983). These conflicts have been intense, always bloody, and some have spanned a period of ten or more years. Since the inception of these conflicts a minimum of between 1 million and 5 million persons have been killed. The majority of these wars are being fought in DC or LDC nations[4] and most are supported, often financed, directly by either the United States or the USSR. "The main ideological thread woven through almost all these diverse conflicts," according to retired Admiral Eugene Carroll, Deputy Director of the CDI, "is nationalism, not communism versus democracy."

The world's most violent conflicts are taking place in DC and LDC nations. Among them are the following:

Kampuchea (49/49)[5]—a civil war started in 1970 in which between 1 million and 4 million persons already have died.
East Timor (n/a)—guerrilla war began in 1975 with between 100,000 and 250,000 deaths.
Afghanistan (n/a)—war began in 1978 with a minimum of 100,000 deaths.
Iraq (64/66)–*Iran* (66/69)—war began in 1980 with at least 100,000 deaths for both sides.
Lebanon (112/93)—civil war began in 1975 with more than 85,000 deaths.
China (n/a)–*Vietnam* (8/53)—war began in 1979 with about 50,000 deaths.
Guatemala (66/72)—guerrilla war began in 1967 with a minimum of 30,000–40,000 dead.
El Salvador (115/109)—civil war began in 1977 with an unknown death toll, but at least 30,000 to date.
Ethiopia (36/−12)—guerrilla war with Eritrea began in 1962 with fatalities of at least 30,000.

Yet another major social problem created by increased global militarism is the displacement from their homelands of persons, who, if they were

---

[4]Exceptions include Northern Ireland, with the civil disturbance between Protestant Irish paramilitary groups and Catholic Irish guerrillas; Spain, with the northern Basque guerrilla war; and Italy, home of the Red Brigade and other far-left revolutionary groups.

[5]ISP scores for 1970–80; n/a means ISP scores are not available for these countries.

to remain, would be subjected to acts of personal violence, terrorism, or death. These political refugees numbered approximately 10 to 12 million persons in 1980, nearly all of whom were forced to leave their homelands through involuntary expulsion (for instance, Asian-born citizens of the United Kingdom living in Uganda; Palestinians living in Jordan and Lebanon), as a result of discrimination (Jewish citizens of the USSR; the Falashas of Ethiopia), or because of the threat of genocide (the ethnic Chinese of Vietnam). International political refugees swelled in numbers by more than 20 percent between 1978 and 1980 alone because of the conflicts in Ethiopia, Indochina, and Afghanistan. The worst situation of the decade existed in Somalia, which received more than 700,000 political refugees as a result of the Ethiopia-Eritrean civil war.[6]

Finally, a survey reported by the *World Press Review* predicted that more than 1 million Africans would die in the winter of 1980–81 in a famine caused by wars and severe drought that had destroyed large quantities of livestock and crops throughout the decade (*WPR* 1980a). In fact, several hundreds of thousands of Africans in Uganda, Somalia, and Djibuti did die that winter as a result of famines and starvation brought on by war and war-related problems.

That "war is not healthy for people and other living things" requires no elaboration for the readers of this volume. Certainly, humanistically oriented persons can find no sympathy for those elements found in every society (terrorists, neo-Nazis, Ku Klux Klan, the Red Brigade, and the like) that advocate depriving others of the very rights, entitlements, and protections of society that they seek for themselves, for instance, the right to assemble in public, to express opposing points of view, to be free of excessive governmental interference. Authoritarianism, however, especially in the form of military dictatorships and military-dominated civilian governments, appears to have gained a strong foothold throughout the world over the past decade. Within many of the world's nations political participation is at its lowest possible level and political oppression appears never to have been more widely distributed or as intense as it is.

The national and international forces that sustain the move toward global militarism are complex and deep-seated; they will not be easily dislodged. In all likelihood, the current trend toward global political authoritarianism will continue until such time as the countries involved achieve a national level of living that will permit more open expression of dissenting opinions and contrary viewpoints. The trend will continue, too, until such time as world superpowers no longer require developing and least developing nations to join with them as political allies in pursuing their narrow

---

[6]See United Nations High Commissioner for Refugees (Brissimi 1980) for a fuller discussion of the issues surrounding political refugees.

ideological interests in exchange for meager amounts of social and economic development assistance. The even greater tragedy in all of these
short-sighted international machinations, of course, is that the DCs and
LDCs require substantial long-term support from *both* groups of super-
power nations in order to reduce the profound social, political, and economic problems that threaten world political stability for rich and poor nations alike. Given the essentially protectionist posture that predominated
among the world's most socially advanced nations during the period 1970–
80, development assistance—at the level required to allow the majority of
developing nations to make major leaps in their adequacy of social provision—is not likely to be forthcoming, at least not in the foreseeable future.

HUMAN RIGHTS VIOLATIONS

A social phenomenon that is closely related to increases in militarism
throughout the world is the wide-spread violation of basic human rights
observed over the decade. These violations have been extensive and have
involved literally hundreds of millions of persons located on every continent of the planet.

Human rights violations observed over the decade have included, but
have not been limited to, the following:

1. Discrimination on the basis of: *Religion* (Christians vs. Moslems of
Lebanon; Hindus vs. Moslems in India; Bahais vs. Moslems of Iran, and so
on); *Sex* (in relation to the women of Japan, India, most Arab states in the
Middle East and in major parts of Africa); *Race* (for example, whites vs.
blacks in the United States and South Africa; ethnic Chinese of Vietnam,
and so on); *Ethnicity* (Sinhalese vs. Tamils of Sri Lanka; ethnic Chinese, In-
dians, and Malays of Malaysia, and the like); *Language* (French vs. English-
speaking in Canada; Dutch-speaking Flemish vs. French-speaking Walloons
in Belgium, among others); *Culture* (Turks vs. Greeks of Cyprus; Jews vs.
Palestinian Arabs of Israel; Christians vs. Moslems of Eritrea in Ethiopia);
Political Ideology (in Angola, Argentina, Uganda, Cambodia, Brazil, as well
as approximately 60 other nations).

2. Illegal detention (Poland; Iranian seizure of U.S. hostages; Cuba;
Iraq; Argentina; the USSR; Chile; South Africa, among others).

3. Execution without trial (El Salvador, Chile, Nicaragua, Argentina, Democratic Kampuchea, in addition to about 20 other DC and LDC
nations).

4. Denial of the right to leave a country (the USSR and other War-
saw Pact nations; Iran; Syria; Argentina, among others).

5.   Confiscation of private property.
6.   Imposition of martial law (the Philippines, Poland, South Korea).
7.   Torture, including officially sanctioned torture by medical practitioners in at least 50 of the world's nations (Treen 1983).
8.   Child labor, exploitation, abandonment, prostitution (exists widely in areas of Latin America, Asia, and Africa).
9.   Genocide (Tutsis vs. Hutus of Burundi; ousted Pol Pot Regime in Cambodia)
10.   Slavery (Mauritania).

Serious violations of basic human rights continue to be found in virtually every nation of the world. These violations are most insidious when they are practiced systematically by the societal institutions on which all persons residing within a nation must depend (access to programs of basic and advanced education, employment, housing, health services, social services, political decision-making and so on). They are also most serious in countries in which national leaders provide either explicit or implicit support to the denial of human rights to one or another group of persons for whom they share responsibility (for instance, the persecution of Bahais and other non-Moslems in Iran; Israeli persecution of Arab Israelis and other Arabs living in Israeli-occupied Arab territories).

The human rights agenda before the world community is a long one indeed; it is also an old one. Success in achieving international justice and social equality for the entire world's population still lies many generations into the future. Until such time as human values are substituted for political values, or for the even more transitory economic values, however, progress in this area will not be realized.

GLOBAL NUCLEARIZATION

As of early 1980, membership in the Nuclear Club numbered 13 (*WPR* 1980b). Five nations are confirmed members of the club—the United States, the USSR, France, Great Britain, and China. Eight are probable members: Iraq, South Korea, Taiwan, Argentina, Brazil, Israel, South Africa, and Pakistan. Further, Nigeria, along with other DCs, is well-advanced in its research and development efforts to become an autonomous nuclear state (*WPR* 1981).

The spread of nuclear capability around the world is one of the most awesome problems to emerge during the past decade. It is a factor that has contributed directly to the international race to develop even more lethal weapons and, in large measure, is responsible for the political instability reported in this study for many DME nations. The spread of nuclear arms also has contributed to the sense of desperation felt throughout the world concerning the capacity, perhaps eventual willingness, of people to work toward peaceful resolutions of the myriad social, political, and economic problems that confront mankind. This capacity has exacerbated as well the sense of despondency felt by many social development specialists concerning the very limited time available to mankind to redress global social inequalities before the occurrence of a nuclear cataclysm between rich and poor nations (see United Nations 1978a; Falk 1971).

The prospects for nuclear terrorism during the 1980s and 1990s are troublesome. Not only can isolated groups of political fanatics be expected to promote their social causes through nuclear terrorism but, in time, autocratic governments that control nuclear weapons can be expected as well to engage in acts of international terrorism aimed at maintaining their despotic rules. Sadly, as the capacity to produce nuclear weapons continues to spread to even larger numbers of nations, the strategic deterrence once associated with relatively few nations possessing such capability, if indeed such a deterrence ever did exist, will erode entirely. Simultaneously, the risks of global nuclear accidents of the worst magnitude will increase.

Certainly, no reasonable set of solutions that seek to remedy the world's social problems can exclude careful consideration of alternative ways which, in time, could lead to the complete elimination of all nuclear weapons from the planet.

EROSION OF THE EXTENDED FAMILY

The extended family has performed critical social welfare functions since the earliest beginnings of humankind. Consisting of parents, children, older siblings, grandparents, aunts, uncles, cousins, and other blood and non-blood relatives, these family units have delivered the newborn, nursed the sick, educated the young, selected mates for their young adult men and women, cared for the disabled and aged, and buried the dead. The extended family also has functioned as the central reservoir and promulgator of community history, values, traditions, standards, and culture. Historically, the extended family has been the center of major financial and economic transactions within the local community as well.

For good reasons, virtually every society has identified the family as its basic social unit, that is, as the foundation upon which all other societal institutions rested. It is with the intention of maintaining and strengthening family life that every nation has developed a complex system of civil and family law.

Contemporary forms of social and economic development, however, have tended to de-emphasize the significance of the extended family as a basic social institution worthy of support and strengthening. In most cases, this has occurred accidentally, that is, as one of the many unintended social consequences associated with industrialization, urbanization, the shift to a monetary form of economic exchange and wealth redistribution, as well as from the external events of history and cross-cultural exposure.

Often, though, assaults on the structure of the extended family have been more intentional, for example, persons seeking the relative anonymity of urban life and, with it, release from the sometimes oppressive social, financial, and emotional responsibilities associated with participation in the extended family. The more serious attacks on the integrity of the extended family, however, have resulted from governmental policies that have contributed systematically to a weakening of family structures rather than to their strengthening, for instance, national policies that encourage large numbers of able-bodied workers to leave their spouses, children, aged parents, and other dependent family members to seek employment in other parts of the nation (South Africa, Nigeria) or, increasingly, in other areas of the world (India, Pakistan, Algeria). While serving an apparent short-term economic need of nations to export surplus labor in exchange for scarce foreign currencies, for many countries, the long-term *social* costs associated with these policies have been greater than the economic benefits received (problems created by crowded urban living conditions, the abandonment of older and other dependent persons in rural villages, increased public financial dependency, the need for publicly financed social services that perform functions previously carried by the extended family, increases in rates of juvenile delinquency, alcoholism, sexual promiscuity, desertion, divorce, and other forms of family breakdown). Similar problems are associated with the now substantial numbers of young persons from developing nations that have pursued advanced educations in DME and ETA countries who, on their return—should they return at all—feel estranged from their own national cultures, families, and so on.

Other assaults on the integrity of the extended family have come from international development assistance organizations as well. Originating in countries where the extended family has all but disappeared, many of the economic and social development programs of these organizations assign high priority to smaller, more atomized family units and give low priority to initiatives that involve the "more cumbersome" extended family. The majority of imported programs for urban housing development and redevelopment in developing nations, for example, make it all but impossible for the extended family to remain together. Similarly, internationally imported systems of education, health care, social insurance, finance, and so on, place emphasis on individual autonomy, almost invariably at the expense of the individual's responsibilities to persons outside of the smaller "nuclear" family. Though well-intentioned and functional within the context of the social structure of DME or ETA nations, these culture-specific approaches to "development" in DC and LDC nations may ultimately result in a weakening of one of the most valuable natural human resources available to developing nations.

Obviously, developing nations that are seeking to advance their economic development without equal concern for the social costs associated with this development, especially in relation to the extended family, are shortsighted indeed. And yet, during the past decade one finds a steady erosion of the extended family in nearly every region of the world, almost always because of the economic advantages that are associated with smaller, mobile family units that can be more easily relocated to wherever their labor or skills are most needed. Unfortunately, though, relatively few DC or LDC nations have been able to set aside the financial resources needed to create the public systems of social provision required to replace those functions previously performed by the larger, but less mobile, family units (day care, basic education, spacious housing in livable surroundings, services for disabled, aged, or otherwise economically non-productive family members, and so on).

One of the great social tragedies of the second half of the twentieth century may well be the unintended near collapse of the extended family everywhere *without* the concurrent emergence of alternative forms of social institutions that can at least approximate the spectrum of human services carried for millennia by the family. This may occur as a result of inadequate anticipatory social planning alone. At a minimum, development requires an integrated approach to social and economic planning, one that carefully assesses the social impact of economic development on the basic institutions that make up the very foundation of local and national social life. If newer forms of the family need to be developed, and they may well be needed for the majority of the world's developing nations, then these new family structures should emerge from the social experiences of developing nations themselves and not, as often has been the case, follow from either inadequate social planning or be one of the many unintended consequences stemming from efforts to advance economic development.

8

Since 1980

Scientists Move Up Doomsday

The "doomsday clock" was created by a group of nuclear scientists to show graphically how close they believe the world is to a nuclear holocaust. Last week the monthly *Bulletin of the Atomic Scientists*, on the advice of 47 scientists (including 18 Nobel prizewinners), set the clock forward one minute, at three minutes before midnight. That is the closest in 30 years.

Time
January 1984

And thus began 1984!

During the three-year period since the statistical portion of this study ended, the major social events that have shaped the world have continued to be characterized by political turmoil and economic insecurity. The devastating civil and regional wars identified in the previous chapter have persisted; several have escalated in intensity and now threaten the peace and security of other nations in these regions as well. Further, new conflicts have emerged during this period, at least two of which—those in Central America and Lebanon—contain within them the prospects for war on a more global scale.

The Central American nations of Honduras, El Salvador, Nicaragua, and Costa Rica, for example, are now engaged in several ruthless, bloody, civil and regional wars. These hostilities have spread to nations in the Caribbean and to areas of South America; in the process, the political instability that has existed within these regions for more than a decade has become exacerbated. Hostilities in Central and South America are contributing, too, to even more serious military confrontations between major Eastern and Western nations, prompting, in late 1983, an invasion and military defeat of the tiny Cuban-prone island nation of Grenada (1983 population—108,000) by the United States. Based on a variety of international evidence, a great many nations in Central and South America appear to be on the brink of social, economic, and political collapse. Many observers fear that the fragile democratic forms of government currently found in several of these nations cannot long survive the assaults occurring both within and outside their borders. Ultimately, dramatic new international initiatives will be required to restore stability to countries in these regions. Certainly, the tens of thousands of Central Americans who have died in conflicts over the past three years, or as a result of political oppression within their nations, provide evidence of the profound social deterioration that is taking place within the region.

Peace in the Middle East continues to be an elusive goal. Israel now occupies major parts of Lebanon, and Syria and Israel are locked in bitter confrontations with one another. In September 1983, several hundred Palestinian refugees living in Beirut were slaughtered by a Lebanese opposition group during the Israeli military occupation. This action led to considerable international criticism of Israel's military activities and rather quickly resulted in the loss of support from several of her most important allies. The incident also resulted in an early-morning suicide raid, October 23, 1983, on the international peace-keeping force in Lebanon. In this raid, at least 241 American Marines and 58 French soldiers died while they were sleeping, during a terrorist action alleged to have been organized by pro-Iranian forces operating from within Lebanon.

The continuing war between Iran and Iraq poses yet another source of global insecurity that originates in the Middle East. After fighting intermittently for nearly a year over the sovereignty of the disputed Shatt al-Arab waterway that divides the two nations, in September 1980, Iran and Iraq entered into open warfare when Iraqi bombers attacked 10 Iranian airfields, including Teheran airport. The Iranian government responded by bombing two Iraqi airbases. Since, then, fighting between the two nations has continued, especially in the areas of Abadan and Iran's oil-rich province of Khuzistan. Casualties from these and related conflicts number more than 40,000 dead and at least 100,000 wounded or captured from 1980 to the end of 1982 (Lane et al. 1983, 508). The fighting also has had a devastating impact on the economies of these major oil-exporting nations, a problem that intermittently threatens the steady flow of oil through the Iranian-controlled Persian Gulf to other parts of the world. Because of the deadlock nature of the conflict, neither the Islamic government of Ayatollah Ruhollah Khomeini nor the Marxist government of President Saddam Hussein At-Takriti remain securely in power. Systematic oppression of opposition political and religious minorities within these countries has escalated to historically high levels. Estimates even suggest that Iran's persecution of its minorities has been greater since that country's popular "religious" revolution in 1979 than during the 35 years of autocratic role by the Shah.

Political turmoil also is in evidence in other parts of the world as well. In April 1982, Argentina and the United Kingdom engaged in a war over possession of the Falkland (Malvinas) Islands with the result that the already precarious government of Argentina's President Leopoldo Galtieri was forced to resign following that country's defeat. With an inflation rate approaching 165 percent in 1982 (Lane et al. 1983, 475), and an outstanding estimated foreign debt of more than $43 billion at the end of 1982 (*Time* 1983, 43), Argentina has fallen into an even more debilitating economic situation than that which existed before the war. In 1983 payments on foreign debts were suspended by the country's military government. Violations of constitutionally guaranteed human rights are known to be widespread in the country.

Civilian governments in Liberia (1980), the Central African Empire (1981), Guatemala (1982), and Bangladesh (1982) have fallen under the direct control of military authorities since 1980. Similarly, the fledgling civilian government of Nigerian President Alhaji Shehu Shegari—brought to power by peaceful means following 13 years of military rule—collapsed following a relatively peaceful military coup at the end of 1983. In all cases, the civilian governments of these countries had been widely criticized for problems of corruption and economic irresponsibility, and for administrative ineptness. The violence that accompanied the military overthrow of several of these governments, however, resulted in the deaths of hundreds of thousands of persons. In most countries, civil law and constitutionally guaranteed human rights have been suspended. Whether these nations will fare better under military rule in the distant future remains to be seen. Certainly, for the foreseeable future, popular participation in the political decisions that will affect the daily lives of persons residing in these nations has come to a standstill.

In Uganda, four separate civilian governments have been formed since the ouster of Idi Amin from that country in 1979. All, however, have collapsed. Rated as one of the world's least socially advanced nations in this study (with a 1980 rank of 105 out of 107 nations), Uganda continues to remain in a state of social and economic chaos. With 90 percent of her labor force in agriculture, Uganda continues to experience extraordinarily high levels of inflation. The country is financially bankrupt and experiences severe difficulty in repaying a 1981 external public debt[1] in excess of $540

---

[1]"External public debt outstanding and disbursed" represents the amount of public and publicly guaranteed loans that have been disbursed, net of repayments of principal and write-offs at year-end. In estimating external public debt as a percentage of GNP, GNP was

million. The amount is equivalent to 5.2 percent of Uganda's GNP (World Bank 1983, 178). Reports of political terrorism, not unlike those that occurred under Idi Amin, have once again begun to appear.

On yet another front in Africa, the Republic of South Africa has continued its violation of international agreements to work toward the elimination of apartheid within her borders. In an effort to halt regional opposition to South Africa's racist practices, in 1981 the country's military forces invaded Angola and Mozambique to stamp out the terrorist activities of the Southwest African People's Organization (SWAPO) originating from within the borders of those countries. International efforts failed to establish a demilitarized zone between the borders of these nations. In defiance of agreements with the United Nations to move Namibia—a protective territory in Southwest Africa, approximately twice the size of California—toward independence, in January 1983, South Africa dissolved the Namibian National Assembly and resumed direct military control over the territory. International economic pressures have been directed at forcing South Africa to eliminate its 35-year-old apartheid laws, but these are unevenly applied and appear to be having little impact on improving the political and economic standing of the country's majority black and Asian populations. Between 1960 and 1981, South Africa spent more than $21 billion on defense (Sivard 1983), a figure well in excess of an estimated 15 percent of her total public expenditures for the period. The bulk of these military expenditures, of course, were committed to suppressing antigovernment activities originating both from within the country and from opposition antigovernment and "liberation groups" that operate from countries that border South Africa.

In North Africa, efforts on the part of Libya and Chad to unite in 1981 were thwarted by a block of European and African nations that feared the potential impact of such a union on the security of other African states. Believed to be responsible for much of the political instability in Africa and elsewhere, Marxist-dominated Libya recently has begun to experience serious economic problems as a consequence of falling oil prices resulting from a surplus in petroleum products on world markets. Enforced military conscription and rigorous currency controls also are contributing to considerable dissension within Libya, especially in response to efforts by the country's leader, Colonel Muammar Al-Qaddafi, to repress antigovernment activities initiated by the country's political minorities.

Tensions between Libya, Sudan, and Chad also have escalated in part because of the large numbers of political refugees that have entered the

converted from national currencies to dollars at the average official exchange rate for the year in question. The summary measures are weighted by GNP in current dollars. (World Bank 1983, 208)

Sudan from Chad, estimated at several hundred thousand by the end of 1982 (Lane 1983, 561). Along with Libya, the historically impoverished nations of Chad and the Sudan are experiencing even more severe economic hardships arising from double-digit inflation, unfavorable borrowing rates, and declining world markets for their largely unprocessed products, as well as from an extraordinarily high volume of 1981 external public indebtedness, amounting to $201 million for Chad and $4,807 million for the Sudan. These levels of external public indebtedness amounted to 50.9 percent and 59.3 percent of the total GNP for Chad and the Sudan, respectively, in 1981 (World Bank 1983, 178). Because of the serious political and economic problems that exist in these nations, the already highly unfavorable Index of Social Progress (ISP) ratings observed for these LDCs in 1980 (106 for Chad and 79 for the Sudan out of 107 nations) have assuredly slipped still further.

The Soviet Union has continued its military occupation of Afghanistan begun in December 1979. Since then, tens of thousands of dissenting Afghanis have been brutally killed by the Soviet and Afghani government forces; at least three million other Afghani civilians have been forced to flee their homeland in search of political asylum in Iran and Pakistan. The willingness of Afghanistan's Islamic neighbors to offer safe haven to so many refugees over such a short period of time, however, has intensified considerably the economic problems experienced by both Iran and Pakistan. Pakistan's military government of President Mohammed Zia ul-Haq, in particular, is experiencing intense economic pressures due, in part, to an outstanding external public debt in Pakistan of $8,814 million (World Bank 1983, 178). International economic and military aid to assist Pakistan, both with its own development needs and with meeting even the most basic needs of the Afghani refugees, has not been adequate. Political opposition against the Pakistani government is considerable, and is growing. Global pressures to force Soviet withdrawal from Afghanistan have not been effective, despite severe international criticism of the occupation and serious economic problems, related to the occupation, within the Soviet Union itself. Afghanistan and Pakistan are already deeply impoverished nations, and the social situation in both can be expected to deteriorate further should guerrilla warfare, economic failures, expenditures for military and defense, political oppression, civil unrest, and related social problems continue to persist.

POLITICAL REFUGEES: THE CONTINUING ANGUISH

Despite the enormity of the problems posed by the presence of at least 2.6 million Afghani political refugees, Pakistan is not alone in receiving, processing, and supporting a large number of persons crossing national borders

TABLE 8–1   World Refugees by Region of Political Asylum, 1982

Regions	Estimated Numbers	Percent of Total
Africa	2,251,600	22.4
Asia	954,700	9.5
Europe	613,200	6.1
Latin America	268,700–388,700	3.9
North America	1,187,000	11.8
Middle East	4,637,200	46.2
Total all regions	10,032,000	100.0

Source: United States Committee for Refugees as cited in Lane, et al. 1983, 561.

because of religious, racial, or political persecution taking place within their own countries. Table 8–1 lists the region of asylum for more than 10 million persons officially designated as political refugees by the United Nation's High Commissioner for Refugees (Lane et al. 1983, 561).

Approximately the same number of refugees were identified in 1980, albeit with some differences in the countries of origin. Apart from the Afghani refugees, which make up about 27 percent of the world's total refugee population, substantial numbers of Palestinian refugees are continuing to receive political asylum in countries widely dispersed throughout the Middle East. The Palestinians and Afghanis, taken together, account for nearly half (46 percent) of all the world's current political refugees. The majority of the 2.3 million refugees receiving asylum in Africa have fled from the continuing conflicts in Ethiopia, Uganda, Chad, Angola, Zambia, Rwanda, and Zaire. Similarly, the bitter wars and conflicts occurring in Central America have resulted in at least 400,000 persons fleeing from their countries in search of safe haven in other parts of the world. Refugees from the several wars and conflicts that still persist in areas of Indochina have declined in numbers since 1980. Nevertheless, permanent resettlement awaits nearly one million refugees from Vietnam, Cambodia, the Philippines, Tibet, Indonesia, and elsewhere in Asia.

The personal anguish experienced by the world's political refugees is especially compelling. Forced to leave their homelands under threat of persecution or extermination, refugees often arrive receiving nations ill, injured, and without personal means of support. Typically, they are either alone or accompanied by only a few family members that were able to escape. Often uneducated, unskilled, and not conversant in the language of the receiving nation, refugees find themselves without citizenship and without legal rights. They may also be met with considerable hostility from among members of the local population, or even with exploitation by their fellow countrymen who preceded them. Most refugees anticipate returning to their homelands once the dispute has been settled; relatively few actually do so, however, and often those who are able, return only to find that their land and wealth has been confiscated or destroyed and the family members left behind have died or been killed.

The situation of massive numbers of political refugees on the global scale poses serious problems for rich and poor countries alike. Clearly, tens of millions of refugees cannot be constantly transported to countries located continents away from their homelands, and relatively few nations possess the financial wherewithal to offer indefinite financial support to what amounts to the equivalent of several small nations of people. In the end, the difficult and inclusive needs of refugees and receiving nations alike can only be met through the resolution of those basic social, economic, and political problems that force people to seek refugee status in the first place. These more fundamental problems will not be solved until such time as the nations of the world community perceive their larger strategic interests to be better served through peace and elimination of those forces that produce or sustain social inequality for people anywhere.

THE SHIFT TOWARD INCREASED MILITARISM AND NUCLEARIZATION

Since 1980 a sharp increase has taken place in the level of global expenditures for military and military-related activities. Ruth Sivard of the Washington-based World Priorities, Inc., estimates that global outlays for defense spending exceeded $660 billion in 1982, an amount some 10 percent higher than that spent by the world's nations in 1981 and more than 20 times greater—measured in constant dollars—than that spent by nations in the years preceding World War II (Sivard 1983). Further, today more than 25 million men and women are under arms.

Nations with cumulative military expenditures exceeding $10 billion during the period 1960–81 are identified in Table 8–2 and grouped by economic development classification as well. Table 8–3 shows patterns of governmental spending for defense contrasted with that for social programs for the years 1972 and 1980. Nations in this table are grouped by per capita income levels. The reader should note, however, that the data contained in Table 8–3 probably substantially underestimate national expenditures for defense and social programs in large countries (World Bank 1983, 212).

TABLE 8–2   Nations with Cumulative Military Expenditures Exceeding $10 Billion 1960–81 by Development Grouping (in $ billions) (N = 43)

Developed Market Economies (DME)

United States	$1,820	Netherlands	44	Norway	14
West Germany	239	Australia	38	Portugal	11
France	224	Sweden	37		
United Kingdom	213	Belgium	32		
		Spain	31		
Italy	82	South Africa	21		
Japan	77	Greece	19		
Canada	53	Switzerland	18		
Israel	52	Denmark	14		

(DME subtotal = $3,039 billion)

Eastern Trading Area (ETA)

USSR	$1,320	Yugoslavia	23
Poland	47	Rumania	15
East Germany	43	Hungary	11
Czechoslovakia	31		

(ETA subtotal = $1,490 billion)

Developing Countries (DC)

China	$290	Taiwan	20
Saudi Arabia	93	Vietnam	18
Iran	60	Nigeria	17
India	51	Argentina	16
Egypt	33	North Korea	15
Turkey	26	Pakistan	14
Brazil	24	Indonesia	14
South Korea	23	Syria	13
Iraq	22		

(DC subtotal = $749 billion)

Total $5,278 billion

Source: Sivard 1983.

Even so, the general pattern of expenditures for defense, as contrasted with those for social programs, is clear enough when the data reported in the two tables are examined together.

Without question, national governments, but especially the governments of poorer countries are, over time, continuing to commit relatively larger amounts of their total national wealth to military and defense activities. Relatively smaller amounts of national wealth are being used to provide for the basic social and material needs of the populations of a great many of

TABLE 8–3　Defense and Social Expenditures for Nations Grouped by Per Capita Income Level, 1972 and 1980 (N = 121)

| | Defense Expenditure as Percentage of: | | | | Central Government Expenditure Per Capita (1975 dollars) | | | | | | |
| | GNP | | Central Government Expenditure | | Defense | | Education | | Health | |
	1972	1980	1972	1980	1972	1980	1972	1980	1972	1980
Low-Income										
Economies (N = 34)	3.6	3.5	19.5	16.9	5	7	3	6	1	1
China and India	n/a	4.0	n/a	16.7	n/a	8	n/a	6	n/a	n/a
Other low-income	3.6	2.5	19.5	18.9	5	7	3	3	1	1
Middle-Income										
Economies (N = 60)	3.1	3.0	13.9	14.2	26	28	20	27	8	10
Oil Exporters	3.0	2.1	17.5	10.8	33	23	25	32	8	9
Oil Importers	3.1	3.4	12.5	16.8	23	32	17	22	9	11
Industrial Market										
Economies (N = 19)	5.0	3.6	21.3	12.2	281	254	77	111	141	240
East European Non-Market Economies (N = 8)	n/a	n/a	n/a	n/a	n/a	n/a	n/a	n/a	n/a	n/a

Source: World Bank 1983, 198–99.

the world's nations. The global consequences of a world armed to destroy itself is all the more shocking when one realizes that the cost of a single new nuclear submarine equals the annual education budget of 23 developing nations with 160 million school-age children (Sivard 1983). Similarly, during each minute of every day a sum equal to $1.3 million is spent on military activity. During this same period of time, 30 children will die for want of food and inexpensive vaccines!

The present military posture of the world's nations is a dreadful one. Neither the interests of governments nor those of individual persons are being served by the wanton waste of global resources that are desperately needed by many of the world's nations to eliminate, or at least substantially reduce, the complex social and economic problems that contribute directly to the causes of war and political instability: hunger, illiteracy, overpopulation, sickness, landlessness, oppression, and the like. With guarantees of adequate social provision for people everywhere—assurances that will be possible only through the redirection of global military expenditures to international social and economic development—situations can be averted such as those that led to the 1983 expulsion of more than 2 million Ghanians from Nigeria within a two-week period (LeMoyne 1983). A renewed commitment to global social development will minimize as well the occurrence of tragic incidents such as the February 1983 massacre of Moslem workers from Bangladesh living in Assam, India. Believing that these immigrants were depriving them of land, jobs, and political rights, local Hindus sought to force the Moslems to leave the country. In the brutal fighting that ensued as many as 3,000 Moslems were slaughtered, the majority of whom were either old, women, or children (Lane 1983, 879). Political hostilities brought about as a result of local and regional economic problems such as these are unnecessary and can be stopped. Sadly, these and related acts of brutality between and among impoverished people continue to be both stimulated and supported by global moves toward increased militarism.

As indicated by the chapter's opening quotation, the "nuclear menace" continues to be with us and has grown even more dangerous than it was just three years earlier. The 1980 *World Press Review* survey of global nuclear capability reported earlier in this volume, for example, identified 14 nations as either already possessing, or close to possessing military nuclear capability (*WPR* 1980b, 1981). By contrast, and as summarized in Table 8–4, in a 1983 survey reported by *Newsweek* (Beck et al. 1983) the number of nations already possessing, or close to possessing, military nuclear capacity, has increased from 14 nations to 31! Assuming both surveys to be reasonable estimates of the spread of military nuclear weapons capability throughout the world, this finding confirms that six nations are definite members of the

TABLE 8–4   Global Membership in the "Nuclear Club," 1980 and 1983
Estimates

1980[a]	1983[b]
Countries that have Built and Tested Nuclear Devices	
United States	United States
Soviet Union	Soviet Union
Britain	Britain
France	France
China	China
	India

Countries Believed Capable of Building Nuclear Weapons

Argentina	Argentina
Iraq	Canada
South Korea	West Germany
Israel	Israel
Taiwan	Italy
Brazil	Japan
Pakistan	Pakistan
South Africa	South Africa
	Sweden
	Switzerland

Countries Expected To Be Able To Build Nuclear Weapons By 1993

Nigeria	Australia	Iraq
	Austria	Libya
	Belgium	South Korea
	Brazil	Netherlands
	Denmark	Norway
	Egypt	Spain
	Finland	Taiwan
		Yugoslavia

[a]*World Press Review* (WPR) 1980b, 1981
[b]Beck et al. 1983, 56

"nuclear club," ten are "probable" members of the club, and an additional 15 nations can be expected to be autonomous club members by the end of the current decade or, at a minimum, by the middle of the next one.

Altogether, 19 DMEs, 2 ETAs, and 10 DCs possess, or can be expected to possess, nuclear capability sufficient to destroy all of civilization by the year 1995. Understandably, millions of persons the world over have begun to join together in more concerted efforts to halt the further deployment of military nuclear weapons. These efforts have included massive political demonstrations in Europe, North America, and elsewhere in direct response to the deployment of additional nuclear missiles in Europe. They have occurred, too, in response to the nuclear accident that occurred at the Three Mile Island nuclear energy plant in the United States and in response to near-nuclear-accidents in other parts of the world.

Concern over the proliferation of nuclear weapons has become sufficiently great so as to prompt major national religious bodies and world church leaders to condemn the use of nuclear weapons in any form for any reason at any point in time (*Chronicle of Higher Education* 1983). Even so, the proliferation of nuclear weapons continues unabated and, even now, the world's major military powers are engaged in competition over the control of outer space for military purposes.

Can the planet much longer endure such blatant and dangerous assaults on logic, reason, and mankind's own desire to survive this century? The current inclination of the leaders of the nuclear powers to talk and act as if they are prepared to use such weapons certainly shakes the confidence of even the most optimistic among us!

FINANCING WELFARE: AN EMERGING CRISIS

Continuing worldwide problems of economic recession, slow growth, high rates of inflation and unemployment, and declining markets have combined to produce severe strains on the economies of even the world's richest nations. At the present time, for example, some 30 million workers are jobless in Europe, a number that is expected to continue to swell until at least the middle of the decade (Zanker 1983, 82; *WPR* 1982, 37). Within developing nations, the rate of joblessness is even higher, with mid-1983 unemployment levels as high as the 30 percent in Chile and 80 percent in Djibouti not being unusual!

Per capita income levels are down in many parts of the world as well. Sadly, too, restrictive trade practices that limit the importation of unprocessed raw materials—the bulk of which are exported by the developing and least developing countries—once again are in force in many Developed Market Economy and Eastern Trading Area nations.

Within the Soviet Union and her East European Trading partners, current economic problems are now almost as serious as those that existed immediately following World War II. Shortages in food and raw material are especially common and, within several of these nations, antigovernment demonstrations have taken place in response to them (for example, in Poland and Romania). Thus far, corrective efforts on the part of several of these centrally planned nations, including those taken in the Soviet Union, have not proven effective. The massive military expenditures on the part of the Soviet government and her allies—estimated to amount to approximately 10 percent to 12 percent of the country's 1982 GNP (Sivard 1983)—

contribute substantially to the internal economic problems of these countries. Certainly the resources that are committed to military uses, as is true for all nations of the world, are not currently available to ETA nations to finance domestic social and economic programs.

Because of the now-chronic nature of national and international economic problems, many governments are seeking to restrict public expenditures for domestic social programs. Indeed, since 1980, even those nations identified in this volume as social leaders have sought to reduce the level of public social supports available to their citizens. In Belgium, for example, unemployment benefits were cut significantly to persons who were not heads of household. The government also proposed taxing social benefits for the first time. In France, in an effort to rescue the government-backed unemployment insurance program from financial collapse, President Francois Mitterand—one of the few Socialists in power in Europe—cut unemployment benefits to all jobless workers. Under the new scheme, French workers now get 80 percent of their salaries when first unemployed, rather than 90 percent. Similarly in the Netherlands, ten different categories of social benefits have been cut drastically. In doing so, the government expects to save $324 million alone by scaling down yearly increases in old-age benefits and civil service pay.

Governmental efforts to correct systemic economic problems by forcing individual citizens to carry a larger share of the financial burden have not always gone unopposed. In Denmark, for example, angry dock workers closed the Danish ports in spontaneous strikes to protest cuts in social benefits to part-time workers. The protests notwithstanding, the mandated cuts in benefits were implemented with an explanation by Danish Social Welfare Minister Palle Simonsen to the effect that "unlike the 1930s, no one is faced with the problem of mere survival, but rather of adjusting themselves to a lower level of consumption." Within one month of his election, Italian Premier Amin Tore Fanfani called for a $1 billion cut in government contributions to old-age insurance and a $1.5 billion reduction in upper-scale pension benefits. Changes in medical benefits, including a $1.05 tax on prescriptions led to strikes by Italian health workers.

Reports of spreading homelessness among a growing population of Europeans (Tennison 1983) and North Americans (Alter et al. 1984) have appeared regularly in the popular press. So, too, have reports of increases in the rates of crime, marital instability, and even suicide among the growing numbers of unemployed workers.

The present governments of Britain and the United States, both determined to minimize the role of their national governments in financing domestic social programs, have taken the posture that social assistance is the responsibility of private organizations, or at most a responsibility shared by private individuals and organizations with local government authorities.

Within the United States, the even more politically conservative view of President Ronald Reagan is that social problems such as poverty, involuntary unemployment, homelessness, and so on, are relatively rare. Mr. Reagan's attitude toward the role of government in meeting the needs of people who find themselves in socially compromised positions—not unlike the view he expressed to national leaders attending the 1981 Cancún summit on international development strategies (Sancton 1981)—would appear to be that "the poor should pull themselves up by their own bootstraps." The reality that the poor possess neither boots nor bootstraps with which to "pull themselves up" seems not to have occurred to the American President. In any event, this author has never met anyone who is capable of lifting himself from any spot while standing in such a humiliating position.

The annual report of the United Nation's Children's Fund (UNICEF) makes all too vividly clear the global social consequences that accrue to the world's poor when rich nations fail to respond decisively to human problems that are well within their capacity to solve. In its report, UNICEF's Executive Director, James Grant, estimates that approximately 15 million children residing in the world's poor nations died in 1983 from diseases for which treatments are readily available to children living in more developed nations (Grant 1983). Grant estimates these deaths to be equivalent in number to the entire population under five years old in the United States. The number also is equivalent to the combined under-five-years population of Britain, France, Italy, Spain, and West Germany. In commenting with reporters on UNICEF's concerns, Grant went on to say that for every child who died, ". . . another had been left blind or deaf or crippled or retarded." Grant was especially critical of the short-sighted, often piecemeal, approaches taken by the majority of rich nations to reduce financial support of international assistance programs because of domestic economic problems. Said Grant:

> To wait for recession to step aside and allow economic development to resume its slow walk toward social improvement is to accept that tens of thousands of children will continue to die each day and that millions more will live on in hunger and ill-health—a state of affairs which can and does undermine the very process of economic development itself. (Usher 1983)

Certainly, the economic problems facing governments are real and they must be solved. Realistic solutions to these problems, however, can only be found by individual citizens and governments working together. In the process, citizens may need to temporarily reduce their demands on government so that longer-term economic problems can be solved. Only then will governments be able to restore, and hopefully expand further, social benefits needed by their citizens. The notion, however, that current global, or even national, economic problems can be solved by denying already impoverished people the minimal social benefits that they are currently receiving must be rejected as a ridiculous one indeed. Solutions to social problems that exist in the economic structure of nations must be found in those segments of societies whose level of personal prosperity remains relatively unaffected by whatever social, economic, or political forces go on about them. In a crisis situation, the role of government—even more so than during noncrisis periods—must be to assure an equitable distribution of the nation's total resources so that at least the most basic human needs of all of its citizens are provided for. The function of government can never be one that at any time seeks to impoverish further people who are already poor! An appropriate balance between the needs of rich and poor persons within nations, as well as within the larger global community of nations, can be struck without exacerbating the current serious "crisis in welfare" that has been widely commented upon by both informed observers (*Economist* 1982; Gottlieb 1982; Arenson 1982; Nordheimer 1983) and welfare specialists (OECD 1981; Anner 1982).

9

The Need for Global Action Now

> A new international development strategy must be built upon rec-
> ognition of new economic realities. All nations have a strong mutuality
> of interests. All will suffer if development is delayed. Even though not
> universally reccognized, interdependence is a part of global reality. . . .
> Prosperity and stability in the North can no longer exist with poverty
> and instability in the South. The nations of the world will move toward
> development, equity, and justice together or not at all.
>
> *The Stanley Foundation* 1979, 7

Readers who are discouraged by the complexity of what appears to be un-
solvable international dilemmas should use their discomfort to propel
themselves into positive action. Yes, the global social, economic, and political
problems identified in this volume are many and they are complex. They
are persistent as well and will not respond to short-term or poorly conceived
remedies. Nor will they yield to fragmented approaches to development
that assign greater priority to economic and military objectives and relatively less importance to the achievement of global provision for the basic
social and material needs of profoundly impoverished people.

As early as 1969, U Thant, then Secretary-General of the United Nations, was painfully aware of the profoundly serious global consequences of
these chronic, international, social inequalities for the future of mankind.
In addressing the General Assembly on the need for newer, more dramatic
approaches to international social assistance, U Thant commented:

> I do not wish to seem overdramatic, but I can only conclude from
> the information that is available to me as Secretary-General, that the
> members of the United Nations have perhaps 10 years left in which to

subordinate their ancient quarrels and launch a global partnership to curb the arms race, to improve the human environment, to defuse the population explosion, and to supply the required momentum to development efforts. If such a global partnership is not forged within the next decade, then I very much fear that the problems I have mentioned will have reached such staggering proportions that they will be beyond our capacity to control.

Fortunately, the Secretary-General's deeply felt concerns over the immediacy of the catastrophe confronting mankind have not yet materialized. Even so, the sources of these worries continue to be with us and, in many respects, the world social situation is more precarious today than it was when U Thant spoke in 1969. Indeed, current global problems are recognized to be so severe today that, in his closing remarks to the 1983 General Assembly, Assembly President Jorge Illueca of Panama felt compelled to tell the Assembly, "I fear that despite our best efforts, the state of the world has steadily and sharply deteriorated" (*Time* 1984).

A SOCIAL AGENDA FOR MANKIND

The need for collective global action to halt the gap in development that continues to widen between the world's rich and poor nations has never been clearer than it is today. The time is now for the world's most powerful nations to take courageous actions that will promote global social justice for all nations. In doing so, the rich and powerful nations of the world need not act out of an exclusively humanitarian concern for the welfare of the world's poor, but rather, and more pragmatically, out of concern for promoting their own self-interests as well (Reed 1968; Myrdal 1970; Falk 1981; Schumacher 1973; Tinbergen 1976; Leontieff 1977; Mische and Mische 1977; Ehrlich and Ehrlich 1977; Laslo 1977; Boudreau 1980; Pentland 1981; Falk et al. 1982).

In essence, the following six-point plan of global action must be instituted soon if international social, political, and economic catastrophes of the worst sort are to be averted by the end of the present century.[1]

1.   Social reform in the context of international social development must begin with recognition that the most fundamental problems confronting mankind are political and social in nature. They are not problems of

---

[1]The author's more complete plan for reshaping the international social order will appear as *A Social Agenda for Mankind* (in preparation).

resource supply or resource scarcity though, indeed, very real and very serious limitations do exist with respect to the availability of material resources as well.

2. Global social reform will require from each of us, acting both alone and as members of larger social units, acceptance of our shared responsibility to be our "brother's keeper." The world simply has become too small and too interdependent for any of us to turn our back on the profound suffering experienced by our neighbors in many areas of the world. To do so, in the end, will bankrupt as morally and, ultimately, the tragic deprivations experienced by many of our neighbors, in time, can be expected to spread to our homes as well.

3. Global reform will require a speedier and more complete implementation of the basic economic reforms contained in various approaches that seek to establish a "New International Economic Order" (see Falk 1982; Hogendorn and Brown 1979; Leontieff 1977; Makler 1982; Sauvant and Hasenpflug 1977; Singh 1977). At a minimum, the strategies adopted must emphasize (a) global cooperation rather than competition; (b) global sharing rather than squandering; and (c) more generous and better sustained international subsidies and programs of international development assistance to the world's developing and least developing nations.

Ideally, such strategies would be carried out on a multilateral rather than bilateral basis. They would be built, too, on a greatly expanded system of internationally financed and administered loans, grants, and programs of technical assistance from already economically developed or resource-rich nations to the world's poorest countries and regions.

4. Global social reform will require, too, a significant shift from provincial nationalistic attitudes and postures to those that place increased emphasis on regionalism and internationalism.

Necessarily, to effect a change of this magnitude, existing international institutions will need to be strengthened and new international organizations will need to be developed. Within the next decade, for example, more effective global institutions will be needed to:

(a) promote global peace and cooperation;
(b) promote, monitor, and control the use of nuclear energy for peaceful purposes;
(c) oversee international efforts at arms control, arms reduction and military de-escalation;
(d) promote and protect the internationally guaranteed human rights of individual citizens everywhere from the tyranny of despotic or oppressive governments;
(e) manage the global economy, especially in relation to the flow of development and other resources between the world's rich and poor nations;

(f) promote access on the part of all the nations of the world to the bountiful resources that exist in the earth's seas and oceans and in outer space;

(g) implement a coherent and effective food policy for feeding all the world's hungry;

(h) halt the high rates of population growth found in many areas of the world; and

(i) manage problems related to preservation and conservation of the world's physical environment.

To carry out such far-reaching objectives will require careful planning on the part of significantly strengthened global organizations and institutions. Though the time may not yet be ready for all of these organizations to emerge in the immediate future, we should not fail to recognize the need for global institutions to manage problems that are essentially global in nature (problems of the world economy, environmental destruction, war and peace, nuclear armament and disarmament, assuring an adequate standard of living for people everywhere in the world, and so on). While ambitious, any global strategy to impact successfully on the world's most troublesome social, political, and economic problems must have real teeth, must place emphasis on national sovereignty, and must promote the three social objectives on which thoughtful people throughout the world agree: war prevention, economic security, and social justice.

5. A new, more dramatic, approach to global social development must be embarked upon. To be successful, such an approach must emphasize:

(a) people working for and on behalf of themselves and for one another within the context of their own history, traditions, values, and national social objectives;

(b) nations, but especially developing and least developing countries, must decide for themselves what their needs are and how the satisfaction of those needs should best be pursued;

(c) the international community, but especially already economically advanced nations, must perceive their role vis-à-vis developing nations to be that of a "partner," not as that of a decision maker or planner acting on behalf of what they perceive to be in the best interests of developing nations;

(d) an invigorated strategy leading to *social* development must emphasize the accomplishment of *social* objectives, not the realization of narrow economic or military goals. The simple reality is that, over the decade, many developing nations have slipped more deeply into poverty as a result of their efforts to emulate patterns of development found in the more economically advanced nations of the East and the West. For some countries, including several LDCs, the rapid shift toward a wage economy, urbanization, industrialization, and a national economy based on international exportation have conflicted both with their traditional values and with their only recently articulated national social objectives. For many of these countries, other forms of economic development would be more appropriate; always, though, such development must take place within a context that is consistent with both their national social purposes and their traditional social values (preservation of the extended family, rural patterns of population density, low- to mid-level technological innovation, decentralized forms of governance, and the like);

(e)   regionalism among developing nations should be strongly encouraged as a basis of developing programs of mutual aid, self-help, and regional cooperation;

(f)   to be effective on a global level, however, national social development must take place within the context of a larger, more fully integrated, plan of world social development. To achieve its objectives, the global social development strategy must:

    (1)   encompass development planning for all nations—developed and developing, rich and poor, market economies and those that are centrally planned;

    (2)   differentiate between the specialized development needs and objectives of individual nations and groups of nations;

    (3)   specify specific objectives that are to be completed within specifically designated time intervals;

    (4)   include a mechanism for on-going review and revision of planning efforts once implemented;

    (5)   include a mechanism for continuous reporting to the world's nations concerning the extent of progress in achieving world social development goals;

    (6)   contain the mechanisms necessary to generate the financial and human resources needed to finance development worldwide.

6.   To be effective, the new strategy for global social development also must:

(a)   foster maximum self reliance within each nation for planning and implementing its own program of national social development;

(b)   foster mutual participation and cooperation among all the world's nations in a coequal partnership focused on improving the adequacy of social provision for people everywhere;

(c)   advance creative, innovative, and flexible solutions to matters of subnational, national, regional, and global social development;

(d)   emphasize working for the benefit of all of mankind, while advocating and advancing the right of each nation to develop its own approach to social development that does not do harm to others.

PROBLEMS AND PROSPECTS

The prospects for achieving the needed global social transformations that will make possible an acceptable standard of living for people everywhere in the world, while not without frustrations, are nonetheless within our collective grasp. Certainly, not to embark on what is recognized to be a necessary, even if difficult, journey would be inexcusable. Inaction under any guise, given the inhumane conditions under which so many of the world's people live, would simply by morally corrupt. Continued resistance to global social justice from the world's affluent nations will doom hundreds of millions of people to yet another generation of suffering and social deprivation. It will also commit the world's most powerful nations to search for increasingly more militant means for co-existing in a world that each year will pose ever greater threats to their own peace, economic security, and high standard of living. In the end, neither rich nor poor nations will be advantaged by such a hostile, and ultimately hopeless, survival strategy. Failure to realize the objectives of what is recognized to be a far-reaching strategy for global social change will result in a hopelessly polarized world by the year 2000. The development gap between rich and poor nations will continue to widen with the result that, by the end of the present century, the world will have become vastly overpopulated, overly urbanized, and increasingly less safe, with poverty, starvation, and the dangers of war and destruction increasing daily.

Commenting on the positive prospects for the world community to solve its pressing social dilemmas, and thereby survive beyond this century, Willy Brandt, acting in his capacity as chairman of the Independent Commission on International Development Issues, reminds us:

> One should not give up hope that problems created by men can also be solved by men.
> This calls for understanding, commitment and solidarity—between peoples and nations. But they can come about only with a feeling for realities and a grasp of intertwined interests, even if these are not identical. It also calls for courage, for a vision of the future without which no great task has ever been completed. Such endeavours must be guided by mutual respect, open-mindedness and honesty, with a willingness not only to offer criticism but also to listen to it. (Brandt 1980, 10)

Certainly, the global social situation is not now so out of control that it will not respond to intelligent and meaningful corrective actions undertaken by private citizens and governments working together. Attention to the many global issues that constitute "the social agenda for mankind" before us, however, requires that each one of us recognize the profound nature of the desperate situation in which millions of our brothers and sisters live out their daily lives. Deprived of food, adequate shelter, basic education, health, and income, and denied freedom from political oppression, these people are without hope and without the promise of a better future for themselves or their progeny.

To significantly alter global social inequalities will require that each of us, acting as responsible citizens within our own nations *and* as citizens of the world community, accept personal responsibility for engaging in effective actions that will improve the adequacy of national, regional, and global social provision. Only when each of us demonstrates a willingness to act, can we be certain of achieving the global transformations needed to promote social justice throughout the world. Failure on our part to act quickly, decisively, and purposefully on these great moral issues will deprive ourselves, our own children, and all the peoples of the world of the promise of renewal that they and succeeding generations have a right to expect from us. Global changes on the magnitude suggested by the findings reported in this volume are within our power to accomplish. To realize them, though, we must commit ourselves to the task! The time is now; the course is a just one; and the means for its accomplishment are within our reach.

Appendix A

Indicator Sources and Operational Definitions

This appendix contains information concerning the source and operational definitions of the 44 indicators that form the Index of Social Progress (ISP). Readers interested in obtaining more detailed information concerning one or another set of indicators should consult the primary data source identified for the indicator(s).*

1. EDUCATION SUBINDEX

School Enrollment Ratio, First Level (+)

Based on total male and female enrollment of students of all ages in primary school. Although primary school age is generally considered to be 6–11 years, variations according to country in the ages and duration of schooling are reflected in the ratios given.

Source: UNESCO 1972, Table 2–7, 99–119; UNESCO 1980, Table 3–2, 153–215.

Pupil/Teacher Ratio, First Level (−)

Based on UNESCO estimates that take into account the number of trained educators relative to the number of students enrolled in primary school programs.

---

*Signs indicate directionality of indicators, that is, a positive sign (+) indicates that *more* of factor "X" is more desirable than less of factor "X"; similarly, a negative sign (−) indicates that *less* of factor "X" is more desirable.

Source: UNESCO 1973, Table 3–2, 130–58; UNESCO 1977, Table 4–2, 194–212; UNESCO 1980, Table 3–4, 233–59.

Percent Adult Illiteracy (−)

Adult illiteracy is the percentage of persons aged 15 years and over who cannot read and write.

Source: UNESCO 1978, Table 1–3, 42–51; UNESCO 1980. Data supplemented by United Nations 1971a, Table A–10, and by Bacheller 1980, 504–710. Estimates for missing data based on subregion averages computed when necessary and reasonable.

Percent GNP in Education (+)

This estimate takes into account public and private expenditures at all levels of education—primary, secondary and post-secondary, including vocational education.

Source: UNESCO 1973, Table 5–1, 504–30; UNESCO 1980, Table 4–1, 659–83. Supplemented by United Nations 1975a. Estimates for missing data computed on the basis of subregion averages.

2.   HEALTH STATUS SUBINDEX

Rate of Infant Mortality Per 1000 Live Born (−)

The number of infants who die before reaching one year of age, per thousand live births in a given year.

Source: United Nations 1973a, Table 21, 89–94; United Nations 1981a, Series A., 4–15; United Nations 1973a, 94–100. Estimates for missing data computed on the basis of subregion averages.

Population in Thousands Per Physician (−)

These estimates were derived from World Health Organization (WHO) surveys that take into account the number of trained medical personnel residing in a country relative to the population size of that country.

Source: United Nations 1973b, Table 202, 747–51; United Nations 1979a, Table 207, 893–97. Data supplemented by Bacheller 1980, 504–710.

Male Life Expectation At One Year (+)

Indicates the number of years newborn male children would live if subject to the mortality risks prevailing for the cross section of population at the time of their birth.

Source: United Nations 1973a, Table 27, 600–619; United Nations 1980a, Table 4, 109–13.

3.   WOMEN STATUS SUBINDEX

Percent Age-Eligible Girls Attending First Level Schools (+)

Indicates the percentage of girls aged 6–11 years that are enrolled in primary schools.

Source: UNESCO 1981, Table 3–2.

Percent Children in Primary Schools—Girls (+)

Indicates the percentage of children enrolled in primary school that are girls.

Source: UNESCO 1980, Table 3.4, 231–51.

Percent Adult Female Illiteracy (−)

The percentage of women aged 15 years and older who cannot read and write.

Source: United Nations 1980b, Table 14, 12–13.

Years Since Women Suffrage (+)

Measures the number of years since women were granted the right to vote in the election of officials to various governmental and other public offices.

Source: United Nations 1963, Report #2. Data supplemented by a 1982 survey undertaken by this author of embassies for countries reporting no women suffrage in 1963.

Years Since Women Suffrage Equal to Men (+)

Indicates the number of years since men and women shared equally in the right to elect officials to office and, themselves, to stand for election to various governmental and other public offices.

Source: United Nations 1963, Report #2. Data supplemented by a 1982 survey undertaken by this author of embassies for countries reporting no women suffrage in 1963.

4. DEFENSE EFFORT SUBINDEX

Percentage GNP in Defense Spending (−)

Takes into account all expenditures made for military and defense purposes including the cost of new armaments, the cost to maintain soldiers in uniform, and so forth. These expenditures are reflected as a percentage of the total goods and services produced by a nation during a given year.

Source: Stockholm International Peace Research Institute 1978, Appendix 6A, 142–65; SIPRI 1981, Appendix 6A, 166–69.

5. ECONOMIC SUBINDEX

Per Capita Economic Growth Rate (+)

See definition of "Per Capita Estimated Income" below.

Source: United Nations 1971a, Table A–4, 186–88; World Bank 1980, Table 1, 110–11.

Per Capita Estimated Income ($) (+)

GNP estimates were calculated using the *World Bank Atlas* method: "GNP in national currency units was expressed first in weighted-average prices for the base period (1979–80), converted into dollars at the GNP-weighted average exchange rate for this period, and adjusted for U.S. inflation. The resulting estimate of GNP was then divided by the population in mid-1979. This method reduces the effect of temporary undervaluations or overvaluations of a particular currency and generally assures greater comparability of the estimates of GNP per capita among countries" (World Bank 1980, 158).

Source: United Nations 1973b, Table 187, 621–27; World Bank 1980, Table 1, 110–11. Data supplemented by subregional estimates when reasonable.

Average Annual Rate of Inflation (−)

"Calculated from the 'implicit gross domestic product (GDP) deflator,' which is calculated by dividing, for each year of the period, the value of GDP in current market prices by the value of GDP in constant market prices, both in national currency" (World Bank 1980, 158).

Source: World Bank 1978, Table 1, 110–11.

Per Capita Food Production Index (1970 = 100) (+)

"Shows the average annual quantity of food produced per capita in 1976–78 in relation to that in 1969–71. . . . These estimates were derived . . . by dividing indicies of the quantity of food production by indicies of the total population. . ." (World Bank 1980, 158).

Source: United Nations 1979b, Table 2, 3. Estimates for some countries made on basis of subregional average scores.

6.   DEMOGRAPHY SUBINDEX

Total Population (Thousands) (−)

Based on midyear estimates, sample surveys, and, in some cases, complete censuses undertaken by nations and reported to the United Nations and other international demographic data-collecting organizations.

Source: United Nations 1971b, Table 6, 166–399; United Nations 1980a, Table 3, 210–87.

Crude Birth Rate Per 1000 Population (−)

Indicates the number of live births per one thousand population in a year.

Source: United Nations 1971b, Table 3, 119–25; United Nations 1981a, Table 3, 210–87.

Crude Death Rate Per 1000 Population (−)

Indicates the number of deaths per one thousand population in a year.

Source: United Nations 1971c, Table 18, 80–92; United Nations 1979a, Table 18, 68–75.

Rate of Population Increase (−)

The number of persons added to a population per one thousand persons already in the population, ignoring immigration.

Source: United Nations 1970, Table 2, 116–22; United Nations 1979c, Table 3, 98–104.

Percent of Population Under 15 Years (−)

Computed by dividing total number of persons in a country 15 years of age and younger by total population of that country.

Source: United Nations 1971b, Table 6, 166–399; United Nations 1980a, Table 3, 210–87.

7. GEOGRAPHY SUBINDEX

Percent Arable Land Mass (+)

Includes arable land and land permanently planted in crops, plus permanent meadows and pastures, divided by total country area.

Source: United Nations 1971c, Table 26, 110–14.

Number Major Natural Disaster Impacts (−)

"A major disaster was defined as one which meets at least *one* of the following criteria: (1) a minimum of $1 million damage; (2) a minimum of 100 persons dead; (3) a minimum of 100 persons injured" (Regulska 1980, 1).

Note: Nation-specific raw score values for this indicator are reported in Appendix C.

Source: Regulska 1980. Missing data estimated for selected countries on the basis of subregional analysis (Reed 1981).

Lives Lost in Major Natural Disasters Per Million Population (−)

Reports loss of life from disaster impacts by country and by deaths divided by million persons in the population during year of event occurrence.

Note: Raw score values for this indicator are reported in Appendix C.

Source: Regulska 1980. Missing data estimated for selected countries computed on the basis of subregional analyses (Reed 1981).

8.   POLITICAL STABILITY SUBINDEX

Political stability data were gathered by Charles Taylor and David Jodice as part of their more comprehensive study of political events that took place in 155 nations between 1948 and 1977 (see Jodice and Taylor 1981). In the present study, only data for the years 1969 and 1977 were used. All Political Stability Subindex data reported in this analysis, then, reflect the actual frequency with which the selected indicators of political stability occurred within the 107 nations included in this study, but *only for the years 1969 and 1977*. Because of significant variations in the size of national populations, however, the "number of deaths from domestic violence" indicator was recomputed to reflect the "number of deaths from domestic violence *per one million population*" during each of the two study years.

Number of Political Protest Demonstrations (−)

". . . a non-violent gathering of people organized for the announced purpose of protesting against a regime, government, or one or more of its leaders; or against its ideology, policy, intended policy, or lack of policy; or against its previous action or intended action. . . . This category excludes election meetings, rallies, and boycotts" (Taylor and Hudson 1972, 66).

Number of Political Riots (−)

"A violent demonstration or disturbance involving a large number of people characterized by material damage or bloodshed" (Taylor and Hudson 1972, 67).

Number of Political Strikes (−)

". . . A work stoppage by a body of industrial or service workers or a stoppage of normal academic life by students to protest a regime or its leaders' policies or actions" (Jodice and Taylor 1981, 6). This variable excludes strikes directed primarily at economic goals (for example, higher wages, better working conditions, and so on).

Number of Armed Attacks (−)

"An act of violent political conflict carried out by (or on behalf of) an organized group with the object of weakening or destroying the power exercised by another armed group. It is characterized by bloodshed, physical struggle, or the destruction of property" (Taylor and Hudson 1972, 67).

Number of Deaths From Domestic Violence Per Million Population (−)

"Unlike the other indicators . . . [this indicator] is not an event variable but a body count. The deaths reported here occurred mainly in conjunction with armed attacks, but also in conjunction with riots and (to a much lesser extent) demonstrations" (Taylor and Hudson 1972, 68).

Note: Raw score values for this indicator are reported in Appendix C.

9. POLITICAL PARTICIPATION SUBINDEX

Years Since Independence (+)

Computed by subtracting year of official independence as an autonomous nation-state from the modal year of the study.

Source: Taylor and Hudson 1972, Table 2–1, 26–29.

Years Since Most Recent Constitution (+)

Computed by subtracting year of most *recent* constitution from modal year of the study.

Source: Paxton 1977.

Presence of Functioning Parliamentary System (+)

Reflects the extent to which nations have functioning and representative national political assemblies: $0 = $ no; $1 = $ questionable no; $2 = $ questionable yes; $3 = $ yes.

Note: This indicator reflects values only for the years 1972 and 1977; raw score values are reported in Appendix C.

Source: Blondel 1973, Appendix, 243–48; Gastil 1978, 223–325.

Presence of Functioning Political Party System (+)

Reflects the number of officially recognized *and* active political parties within a nation: 0 = no political party structure; 1 = single party system; 2 = multiple party system.

Note: This indicator reflects values only for the years 1972 and 1977; raw score values are reported in Appendix C.

Source: Blondel 1973, Appendix, 243–48; Gastil 1978, 223–325.

Degree of Influence of Military (−)

Reflects the decision-making influence of military authorities over civilian political affairs: 0 = none or limited influence; 1 = questionable influence; 2 = military in power, or exercises strong indirect influence.

Note: This indicator reflects values only for the years 1972 and 1977; raw score values are reported in Appendix C.

Source: Blondel 1973, Appendix, 243–48; Gastil 1978, 223–325.

Number of Popular Elections Held (+)

Measures the frequency with which regularly scheduled popular elections are held.

Source: Jodice and Taylor 1981, by special permission of the authors.

10.   CULTURAL DIVERSITY SUBINDEX

Largest Percentage Sharing Same Mother Tongue (+)

"Percentages calculated from absolute figures. . . . Where censuses . . . list bilinguals separately, these have been added to the speakers of the nonofficial languages . . ." (Rustow 1967, 284).

Source: Rustow 1967, 284–86.

Largest Percentage Sharing Same Basic Religious Beliefs (+)

These data are estimates only. Percentages are based on the number of persons in a country affiliated with a particular religious tradition, divided by the size of that country's population.

Source: Delury 1979, 513–98; Bacheller 1980.

Ethnic-Linguistic Fractionalization Index (−)

Measures the degree of ethnic and linguistic heterogeneity within a national population, two factors long associated with level of political stability within nations. For a discussion of this point, see Deutsch (1953) and Rice (1972). High fractionalization, that is, high ethnic-linguistic diversity, occurs as numbers approach 1.0; low fractionalization levels exist as the ratio moves closer to 0.0.

Source: Taylor and Hudson 1972, Table 4–15, 271–74.

11. WELFARE EFFORT SUBINDEX

"'First Law' is usually the first consolidated compulsory legislation extending protection against a specific risk to a substantial segment of the salaried labor force on an industry-wide or nation-wide basis, rather than to a particular occupational group such as seamen, miners, bank employees, etc." (USDHHS 1980, viii).

Years Since First Law—Old Age, Invalidity, Death (+)

Includes programs that provide pensions or lump-sum payments to help replace the income loss resulting from old age itself, from permanent retirement, . . . from a permanent or long-continuing and more or less total disablement, . . . or from the death of a working provider.

Source: USDHHS 1980.

Years Since First Law—Sickness & Maternity (+)

Includes: (1) cash benefits to replace wages lost as a result of relatively short-term sickness of non-occupational origin; (2) cash benefits to replace wages lost during maternity leave; and (3) medical benefits or services in the event of either of these contingencies.

Source: USDHHS 1980.

Years Since First Law—Work Injury (+)

Includes social security programs that provide cash payments and medical care during periods of temporary disability resulting from a work injury or occupational disease or illness.

Source: USDHHS 1980.

Years Since First Law—Unemployment (+)

Often structured independently of other social security measures, these programs provide cash benefits and reemployment services to claimants and beneficiaries. Such programs typically are linked with other employment services (career assessment, jobs location, training and retraining, and so on).

Source: USDHHS 1980.

Years Since First Law—Family Allowances (+)

". . . Family allowances are primarily regular cash payments to families with children. In some countries, these programs also include school grants, birth grants, maternal and child health services, and sometimes allowances for adult dependents" (USDHHS 1980, xxi). These programs are closely integrated with other social security measures in some countries; in others, they are entirely separate.

Source: USDHHS 1980.

Appendix B

Index and Subindex Computational Notes

INDEX COMPUTATIONAL NOTES

Index and subindex scores were computed in six steps.*

Step 1. Measures of Central Tendency and Dispersion

Raw score means, standard derivations, variance and other measures of central tendency and dispersion were computed for all 88 indicator observations (two observations for each of 44 indicators—1969–70 and 1979–80). The results of these computations are summarized in Table B–17.

Step 2. Raw Score Transformation into Standardized Units of Measurement

Indicator raw score values were transformed from *variable* units of measurement (rates per 1000, dollars, grams, percentages, ratios, and so on), into *standardized* units of measurement (Z-scores) using the following formula: ($(x_i\text{-}\overline{X})/SD$), where x_i is the original value of the ith case; $\overline{X}$ is the mean of the variable; and SD is the standard deviation. The Z-score generates a new variable with a group means of 0 and a group standard deviation of 1 (see Blalock 1979). Inasmuch as Z-scores are premised on the mathematical assumptions of the normal distribution, Z-scores for an individual nation reflect the relative position of that nation along the horizontal of the normal

---

*Statistical analyses were performed using the various analytical modules of the *Statistical Package for the Social Sciences* (Nie et al.).

curve, that is, in units of standard deviations from the group mean of 0 (-3, -2, -1, 0, $+1$, $+2$, $+3$, etc.).

The following table illustrates the Z-score data standardization procedure as applied to the Health Subindex for India (1969 only).

TABLE B–1   Illustration of Raw Score Transformation into Standardized Z-Scores (India, 1969–70)

Indicator	Raw Score (x_i)	Country - Group Mean Score $(x_i - \overline{X})$	Standard Deviation (SD)	Z-Score
ZV13. Rate Infant Mortality per 1000 Live Born ($-$)	139.0	(139.0–73.8)	55.3	$+1.1801$
ZV25. Population in Thousands per Physician ($-$)	4.8	(4.8–11.2)	17.7	-0.3620
ZV14. Life Expectation at 1 year, males ($+$)	48.4	(48.4–55.8)	11.8	-0.6266

Tables 4–4 and 4–5 report Z-scores for all ISP indicators. Both tables report Z-scores grouped by socioeconomic development level.

Step 3. Directionality of Indicators

The directional signs of many ISP variables had to be altered so that social progress "gains" and "losses" along these indicators of social development could be properly aggregated into overall ISP and subindex scores. In the above Z-score illustration for India, for example, both "rate of infant mortality ($-$)" and "population in thousands per physician ($-$)" are stated so that *decreases* in the numbers reported for these indicators actually reflect *increases* in overall level of national social provision, that is, lower rates of infant mortality and lower patient case loads for physicians are assessed more favorably than are higher rates of infant mortality or higher patient-physician caseloads. By design, 21 of the ISP's 44 indicators reflect *gains* in social progress by *decreasing* rather than increasing (see Chart 3–1 for the directional signs of all ISP and subindex indicators).

So as to accurately reflect gains and losses in social progress over time, the Z-scores for all inversely-stated indicators were multiplied by a constant value of −1. In effect, this procedure altered only the mathematical sign of these indicators and not their numerical value. In the data transformation illustration for India, for example, the signs of the first two indicators were reversed so that the Z-score values of these indicators could be properly subtracted (from +1.1801 to −1.1801) and added (from −0.3620 to +0.3620) to composite ISP scores. The Z-score for "Life expectation . . ." remained unchanged since increases in this indicator reflect positive increases in level of social progress. This procedure was repeated for all inversely stated ISP indicators as part of the statistical procedures required to compute subindex scores (see Step 4 for subindex formulae).

Step 4. Computation of Subindex Scores

Three arithmetic steps were required to compute subindex scores:

(a) The mathematical signs of negatively directional indicators were reversed for the reasons and in the manner described in Step 3 above;
(b) The unweighted Z-score values of all subindex indicators were totalled; and then
(c) The sum of the Z-scores was divided by the number of indicators contained in the subindex (three for the Health Subindex, six for the Political Participation Subindex, and so on.

The indicators and formulae used to compute each subindex are reprinted below. Essentially, these formulae produce subindex scores that are really statistical averages of the various indicators—ranging in number from one to six—that make up the subindex; for example, 1969 Health Subindex Score for India, $((−1.1801) + (0.3620) + (−0.6266)/3) = 0.4816$. In this way, each of the ISP's eleven subindexes contributes exactly 9.09 percent to composite ISP scores $(100\% ÷ 11$ subindexes $= 9.09\%)$.

1. EDUCATION SUBINDEX

COMPUTE ED69 = ((ZV45+(−1*ZV21)+(−1*ZV22)+ZV19)/4)†
COMPUTE ED79 = ((ZV945+(−1*ZV921)+(−1*ZV922)+ZV919)/4)

---

†Note: In the syntax of SPSS the asterisk (*) mark indicates multiplication, the slash (/) indicates division.

Where:

TABLE B–2   Education Subindex

Indicator	Modal Year	Var. No.
School enrollment ratio, First level (+)	1969–70	ZV45
	1980	ZV945
Pupil-teacher ratio, First level (−)	1969	ZV21
	1980	ZV921
Percent adult illiteracy (−)	1969	ZV22
	1980	ZV922
Percent GNP in education (+)	1969–70	ZV19
	1980	ZV919

2. HEALTH STATUS SUBINDEX

COMPUTE HL69 = (((−1*ZV13) + (−1*ZV25) + (ZV14))/3)
COMPUTE HL79 = (((−1*ZV913) + (−1*ZV825) + (ZV814))/3)

Where:

TABLE B–3   Health Status Subindex

Indicator	Modal Year	Var. No.
Rate infant mortality per 1000 live born (−)	1969	ZV13
	1980	ZV913
Population in thousands per physician (−)	1969	ZV25
	1978	ZV825
Life expectation at 1 year, males (+)	1969	ZV14
	1978	ZV814

3. WOMEN STATUS SUBINDEX

COMPUTE WOM69 =
((ZV6946 + ZV104 + (−1*ZV102) + ZCV10069 + ZCV10169)/5)

COMPUTE WOM79 =
$((ZV7946 + ZV105 + (-1*ZV103) + ZCV10079 + ZCV10179)/5)$

Where:

TABLE B–4   Women Status Subindex

Indicator	Modal Year	Var. No.
Percent age eligible girls attending First level schools (+)	1970 1979	ZV6946 ZV7946
Percent children in primary schools girls (+)	1970 1977	ZV104 ZV105
Percent adult female illiteracy (−)	1970 1980	ZV102 ZV103
Years since women suffrage (+)	1969 1979	ZCV10069 ZCV10079
Years since women suffrage equal to men (+)	1969 1979	ZCV10169 ZCV10179

4. DEFENSE EFFORT SUBINDEX

COMPUTE DE69 = $(-1*ZV80)$
COMPUTE DE79 = $(-1*ZV980)$

Where:

TABLE B–5   Defense Effort Subindex

Indicator	Modal Year	Var.No.
Percent GNP in defense spending (−)	1969 1979	ZV80 ZV980

5. ECONOMIC SUBINDEX

COMPUTE EC069 = $((ZV61 + ZV7 + (-1*ZV7017))/3)$
COMPUTE EC079 = $((ZV861 + ZV907 + (-1*ZV8017) + ZV992)/4)$

Where:

TABLE B–6   Economic Subindex

Indicator	Modal Year	Var. No.
Economic growth rate (+)	1967–68 1979	ZV61 ZV861
Per capita income (Est. U.S. Dollars) (+)	1969 1979	ZV7 ZV907
Average annual rate of inflation (−)	1960–70 1970–79	ZV7017 ZV8017
Per capita food production index (1970 = 100) (+)	1976–78	ZV992

6.   DEMOGRAPHY SUBINDEX

COMPUTE DEM69 = (((−1*ZV901)+(−1*ZV27)+(−1*ZV96)+
            (−1*ZV47)+(−1*ZAD70))/5)
COMPUTE DEM79 = (((−1*ZV902)+(−1*ZV927)+(−1*ZV896)+
            (−1*ZV847)+(−1*ZAD79))/5)

Where:

TABLE B–7   Demography Subindex

Indicator	Modal Year	Var. No.
Total annual population (Thousands) (−)	1970 1979	ZV901 ZV902
Crude birth rate per 1000 population (−)	1969 1980	ZV27 ZV927
Crude death rate per 1000 population (−)	1969 1974–78	ZV96 ZV896
Rate population increase (−)	1963–69 1978	ZV47 ZV847
Percent of population under 15 years (−)	1970 1979	ZAD70 ZAD79

7. GEOGRAPHY INDEX[a]

COMPUTE GE69 = ((ZV76 + (− 1*ZV891) + (− 1*ZV890))/3)
COMPUTE GE079 = GE69

Where:

TABLE B–8   Geography Subindex

Indicator	Modal Year	Var. No.
Percent arable land mass (+)	1971	ZV76
Number disaster impacts (−)	1947–79	ZV891
Lives lost in disaster per million population (−)	1947–79	ZV890

8. POLITICAL STABILITY SUBINDEX

COMPUTE STA69 = (((− 1*ZVT6900) + (− 1*ZVT6902) +
(− 1*ZVT6905) + (− 1*ZVT6903) +
(− 1*ZCV6916))/5)
COMPUTE STA79 = (((− 1*ZVT7700) + (− 1*ZVT7702) +
(− 1*ZVT7705) + (− 1*ZVT7703) +
(− 1*ZCV7716))/5)

Where:

TABLE B–9   Political Stability Subindex

Indicator	Modal Year	Var. No.
Political protest demonstrations (−)	1969	ZVT6900
	1977	ZVT7700
Political riots (−)	1969	ZVT6902
	1977	ZVT7702
Political strikes (−)	1969	ZVT6905
	1977	ZVT7705
Armed attacks (−)	1969	ZVT6903
	1977	ZVT7703
Deaths from domestic violence (−)	1969	ZCV6916
	1977	ZCV7716

9. POLITICAL PARTICIPATION SUBINDEX

COMPUTE PAR69 = ((ZCV73669 + ZCV3269 + ZV58 + ZV55 +
                               (− 1*ZV59) + ZVT6912)/6)
COMPUTE PAR79 = ((ZCV73679 + ZCV73279 + ZV758 + ZV755 +
                               (− 1*ZV759) + ZVT7712)/6)

Where:

TABLE B–10   Political Participation Subindex

Indicator	Modal Year	Var. No.
Years since independence (+)	1969	ZCV73669
	1979	ZCV73679
Years since most recent constitution (+)	1969	ZCV3269
	1979	ZCV73279
Functioning parliamentary system (+)	1972	ZV58
	1977	ZV758
Functioning political party system (+)	1972	ZV55
	1977	ZV755
Influence of military (−)	1972	ZV59
	1977	AV759
Number of popular elections held (+)	1969	ZVT6912
	1977	ZVT7712

10. CULTURAL DIVERSITY SUBINDEX[a]

COMPUTE CUL69 = ((ZV351 + ZV352 + (− 1*ZV35))/3)
COMPUTE CUL79 = CUL69

Where:

TABLE B–11   Cultural Diversity Subindex

Indicator	Modal Year	Var. No.
Largest percent sharing same mother tongue (+)	1952–66	ZV351
Largest percent sharing same basic religious beliefs (+)	1980	ZV352
Ethnic-linguistics fractionalization index (−)	1964	ZV35

11.   WELFARE EFFORT SUBINDEX[a]

COMPUTE WEL69 = ((ZX49 + ZX50 + ZX51 + ZX52 + ZX53)/5)
COMPUTE WEL79 = WEL69

Where:

TABLE B–12   Welfare Effort Subindex

Indicator	Modal Year	Var. No.
Years since first law—old age, invalidity, death (+)	1969	ZX49
Years since first law—sickness and maternity (+)	1969	ZX50
Years since first law—work injury (+)	1969	ZX51
Years since first law—unemployment (+)	1969	ZX52
Years since first law—family allowances (+)	1969	ZX53

Step 5.   Computation of Composite Index Scores (ISP, INSP)

Index of Social Progress (ISP) scores were computed through simple addition of the eleven unweighted, but averaged, subindex scores.

COMPUTE ISP69 = WOM69 + HL69 + LD69 + DE69 + DEM69
                 + GE69 + CUL69 + STA69 + PAR69 + WEL69
                 + ECO69
COMPUTE ISP79 = WOM79 + HL79 + ED79 + DE79 + DEM79 +
                 GEO79 + CUL79 + STA79 + PAR79 + WEL79
                 + EC79

Index of Net Social Progress (INSP) scores, however, exclude Geographic Subindex values from their calculations:

COMPUTE INSP69 = (ISP69-GE69)
COMPUTE INSP79 = (ISP79-GEO79)

---

[a]Data reported in these subindexes were treated as statistical constants for both modal time periods.

The result of these calculations is illustrated in the following table that reports 1969 subindex and composite index scores for India:

TABLE B–13   Averaged Index of Social Progress Scores, India (1969)

1. Education	$= (-0.6317)$	7. Geography	$= (-0.2970)$
2. Health Status	$= (-0.4816)$	8. Political Stability	$= (-0.7372)$
3. Women Status	$= (-0.2351)$	9. Political Participation	$= (+0.5281)$
4. Defense Effort	$= (+0.1521)$	10. Cultural Diversity	$= (-0.8849)$
5. Economic	$= (-0.5441)$	11. Welfare Effort	$= (-0.2823)$
6. Demography	$= (-2.0016)$		

Index of Social Progress (ISP = $(1 \rightarrow 11)$ = (-5.4153)
Index of Net Social Progress (INSP) = $(1 \rightarrow 6 + 8 \rightarrow 11)$ = (-5.1183)

Step 6.   Standardization of Index (ISP + INSP) And Subindex Scores

The size and awkwardness of the numbers resulting from the various Z-score transformations and summations of Steps 2 through 5 proved to be too small to handle conveniently, even within a computer. Also, addition of the subindex Z-score averages resulted in approximately one-half of the 107 nations having negative ISP and INSP scores [(ISP Range = (-9.657) to $(+9.843)$, Mean = 0.000]. In the preceding Z-score illustration for India (1969), for example, the initial Composite ISP score was -5.4153.

To solve the dual problems of number size and awkwardness, and to eliminate negative mathematical signs from ISP composite totals, three mathematical operations were performed on all Index and Subindex scores:

(a)   All subindex scores were multiplied by a constant value of $+10$. This procedure increased the size of the numbers to make them more visually manageable.

(b)   A constant value of 9.0909 was added to each subindex score after completion of Step 6a, that is, the proportionate share of each subindex in the composite ISP.

(c)   The product resulting from Step 6b was then rounded to the nearest whole number in order to eliminate decimals.

TABLE B–14   Formulae for Standardized Subindexes

COMPUTE	STNED69 = RND(9.0909 + (10*ED69))
COMPUTE	STNED79 = RND(9.0909 + (10*ED79))
COMPUTE	STNHL69 = RND(9.0909 + (10*HL69))
COMPUTE	STNHL79 = RND(9.0909 + (10*HL79))
COMPUTE	STNWOM69 = RND(9.0909 + (10*WOM69))
COMPUTE	STNWOM79 = RND(9.0909 + (10*WOM79))
COMPUTE	STNDE69 = RND(9.0909 + (10*DE69))
COMPUTE	STNDE79 = RND(9.0909 + (10*DE79))
COMPUTE	STNECO69 = RND(9.0909 + (10*EC069))
COMPUTE	STNEC79 = RND(9.0909 + (10*EC79))
COMPUTE	STNDEM69 = RND(9.0909 + (10*DEM69))
COMPUTE	STNDEM79 = RND(9.0909 + (10*DEM79))
COMPUTE	STNGE69 = RND(9.0909 + (10*GE69))
COMPUTE	STNGE079 = RND(9.0909 + (10*GE079))
COMPUTE	STNSTA69 = RND(9.0909 + (10*STA69))
COMPUTE	STNSTA79 = RND(9.0909 + (10*STA79))
COMPUTE	STNPAR69 = RND(9.0909 + (10*PAR69))
COMPUTE	STNPAR79 = RND(9.0909 + (10*PAR79))
COMPUTE	STNCUL69 = RND(9.0909 + (10*CUL69))
COMPUTE	STNCUL79 = RND(9.0909 + (10*CUL79))
COMPUTE	STNWEL69 = RND(9.0909 + (10*WEL69))
COMPUTE	STNWEL79 = RND(9.0909 + (10*WEL79))

The same set of procedures was followed in standardizing ISP and INSP scores except that a constant value of 100—the average for all 107 nations—was added to the original summated composite index scores. Standardized ISP and INSP scores for individual nations also were rounded to the nearest whole number.

TABLE B–15   Formulae for Standardized Composite Indexes (ISP, INSP)

COMPUTE	STNDEV69 = (100 + (10*SDEV69))
COMPUTE	STNDEV79 = (100 + (10*DEV79))
COMPUTE	RSTNDEV6 = RND(STNDEV69)
COMPUTE	RSTNDEV7 = RND(STNDEV79)
COMPUTE	STNNET69 = RND(100 + (10*NETDEV69))
COMPUTE	STNNET79 = RND(100 + (10*NETDEV79))

The standardized versions of Index and Subindex scores for India are as follows:

TABLE B–16   Standardized Index and Subindex Scores for India (1969)

Subindex	Initial Score	Standardized Score
1. Education	−0.6317	3.0
2. Health Status	−0.4816	4.0
3. Women Status	−0.2351	7.0
4. Defense Effort	+0.1521	11.0
5. Economic	−0.5441	4.0
6. Demography	−2.0016	−11.0
7. Geography	−0.2970	6.0
8. Political Stability	−0.7372	2.0
9. Political Participation	+0.5281	14.0
10. Cultural Diversity	−0.8849	0.0
11. Welfare Effort	−0.2823	6.0
Index of Social Progress (ISP)	−5.4153	46.0
Index of Net Social Progress (INSP)	−5.1183	49.0

Table B–17 reports measures of central tendency and dispersion for standardized versions of all index and subindex scores. Table B–18 contains interindex correlation coefficients for all subindexes with one another and with the ISP and INSP for 1969 observations. Interindex correlation coefficients for 1979–80 did not differ appreciably for those in 1969 and, therefore, are not reprinted here.

The reader should note that, unless otherwise indicated, only the standardized versions of the ISP and its component subindexes are reported in the narrative portion of this book.

TABLE B–17 Measures of Central Tendency and Dispersion on the Standardized Indexes of Social Progress (ISP, INSP) by Year and Subindex (N = 107)

		Measures of Central Tendency		Measures of Dispersion				
		Mean	Standard Deviation	Minimum	Maximum	Range	Skewness	Kurtosis
Index of Social Progress (ISP) (RSTNDEV)	1969	99.99	50.11	3.0	198.0	195.0	.22	−1.06
	1979	100.02	51.12	−12.0	201.0	213.0	.18	−0.98
Index of NET Social Progress (INSP) (STNNET)	1969	99.99	48.8	−1.0	201.0	202.0	.14	−1.01
	1979	99.99	50.3	−19.0	196.0	215.0	.08	−0.88
1. Education Subindex (STNED)	1969	9.12	7.51	−8.0	23.0	31.0	−.09	−.81
	1979	9.09	7.42	−11.0	23.0	34.0	−.29	−.53
2. Health Status Subindex (STNHL)	1969	9.09	8.75	−5.0	26.0	37.0	−0.89	−0.05
	1979	9.10	8.68	−18.0	19.0	33.0	−0.76	−0.38
3. Women Status Subindex (STNWOM)	1969	9.10	8.3	−7.0	27.0	34.0	.05	−1.05
	1979	9.11	8.0	−5.0	26.0	31.0	−.02	−1.00

TABLE B–17   Continued

		Measures of Central Tendency		Measures of Dispersion				
		Mean	Standard Deviation	Minimum	Maximum	Range	Skewness	Kurtosis
4. Defense Effort Subindex (STNDE)	1969	9.07	9.97	−50.0	17.0	67.0	−3.46	14.94
	1979	9.08	9.98	−32.0	19.0	51.0	−2.14	5.23
5. Economic Subindex (STNEC)	1969	9.08	6.16	−24.0	22.0	46.0	−1.83	9.12
	1979	9.15	5.70	−18.0	20.0	38.0	−1.04	3.70
6. Demography Subindex (STNDEM)	1969	9.07	6.97	−11.0	23.0	34.0	.38	−.69
	1979	9.10	6.77	−9.0	22.0	31.0	.28	−.91
7. Geography Subindex* (STNGEO)	1969	9.13	6.15	−21.0	18.0	39.0	−1.89	6.16
	1979							
8. Political Stability Subindex (STNSTA)	1969	9.16	6.25	−24.0	12.0	36.0	−3.53	13.56
	1979	9.04	6.95	−29.0	12.0	41.0	−3.70	15.67
9. Political Participation Subindex (STNPAR)	1969	9.10	6.50	−3.0	32.0	35.0	.00	.48
	1979	9.07	6.90	−2.0	32.0	34.0	.58	.11

10. Cultural Diversity Subindex* (STNCUL)	1969	9.08	8.72	-13.0	20.0	33.0	-.62	-.71
	1979							
11. Welfare Effort Subindex* (STNWEL)	1969	9.09	8.58	-4.0	29.0	33.0	.82	-.54
	1979							

*These subindexes were treated as statistical constants for 1969–70 and 1979–80.

TABLE B–18   Matrix of Standardized Index of Social Progress and Subindex Intercorrelation Coefficients, 1969 (N = 107)

Indexes	Index of Social Progress (ISP)	Education Subindex	Health Subindex	Women Subindex	Defense Subindex	Economic Subindex	Demographic Subindex	Geographic Subindex	Political Stability Subindex	Political Participation Subindex	Cultural Diversity Subindex	Welfare Effort Subindex	Index of Net Social Progress (INSP)
Education	.85	1.00											
Health	.81	.82	1.00										
Women	.85	.79	.77	1.00									
Defense	.18	-.17	-.16	.03	1.00								
Economic	.56	.49	.49	.41	-.11	1.00							
Demographic	.84	.75	.69	.71	-.03	.48	1.00						
Geographic	.24	.06	.01	.08	.03	.08	.28	1.00					
Political Stability	.04	-.10	-.20	-.19	.26	-.04	-.14	.15	1.00				
Political Participation	.66	.52	.53	.60	.13	.34	.47	-.03	-.12	1.00			
Cultural Diversity	.57	.52	.56	.44	-.15	.20	.44	-.09	-.03	-.12	1.00		
Welfare Effort	.84	.72	.62	.77	.04	.43	.26	.26	-.16	.52	.40	1.00	
Net Social Progress (INSP)	.99	.86	.82	.86	.18	.56	.82	.12	.02	.68	.60	.79	1.00

Note: Correlation coefficients greater than ± .19 are significant at the $p < .05$ level with 107 degrees of freedom (df).

Appendix C

Raw Score Values of Selected Indicators on the *Political Stability, Political Participation,* and *Geographic* Subindexes by Economic Development Grouping and Nation

Two data sources used to compile the statistics in this study are not yet widely available in the print medium (Regulska 1980; Jodice and Taylor 1981). For this reason, the author has included in this appendix raw score values for 11 of the 14 indicators used to create the subindexes of *Political Stability, Political Participation,* and *Geography.* Both the sources of these data and their coding as used in the present study are reported at the end of Table C–1. For supplementary information concerning the methodological treatment of these variables in constructing both the Index of Social Progress (ISP) and the Index of Net Social Progress (INSP), the reader is referred to the relevant sections in Appendix A and Appendix B.

TABLE C–1   Raw Score Values of Selected Indicators Contained on the Political Stability, Political Participation, and Geographic Subindexes for Modal Years 1970–80 by Economic Development Grouping and Nation (N = 107)

	Political Stability Subindex					Political Participation Subindex				Geographic Subindex		
Index of Social Progress (Vulnerability Zones)	Political Protest Demonstrations	Politically Motivated Riots	Politically Motivated Strikes	Politically Motivated Armed Attacks	Deaths From Domestic Violence Per Million Population	Functioning Parliamentary System	Functioning Political Party System	Role of Military	Number Popular Elections Held	Number Major Natural Disasters	Lives Lost/Mil in Natural Disasters	Index of Net Social Progress (Vulnerability Zones)
Developed Market Economies (N = 24)												
160.4[a]	10.8[c]	3.8[c]	1.9[c]	8.0[c]	0.05[e]	2.9[g]	1.8[i]	0.1[k]	1.3[m]	21.7[o]	70.3[p]	158.8
161.4[b]	10.3[d]	4.6[d]	1.4[d]	22.8[d]	0.32[f]	2.9[h]	2.0[j]	0.1[l]	1.1[n]			159.8
Austria												
186(1)	1	0	0	1	.27	3	2	0	0	8	43	184(1)
192(1)	2	0	0	0	.00	3	2	0	0			189(1)
Australia												
173(2)	7	0	0	3	.00	3	2	0	1	14	22	168(2)
184(1)	3	0	0	2	.00	3	2	0	2			179(1)
Belgium												
175(1)	1	0	0	0	.00	3	2	0	0	9	2	171(2)
178(1)	0	0	0	0	.00	3	2	0	1			174(2)
Canada												
157(2)	5	0	2	12	.00	3	2	0	0	12	19	161(2)
170(2)	1	0	0	0	.00	3	2	0	6			174(2)
Denmark												
198(1)	1	0	0	0	.00	3	2	0	0	1	5	191(1)
201(1)	0	0	0	1	.00	3	2	0	1			194(1)
Finland												
169(2)	0	0	0	0	.00	3	2	0	0	(3.5)[q]	171	173(2)
174(2)	0	0	0	0	.00	3	2	0	0			178(1)

France	172(2)	7	4	4	2	.00	3	2	0	4	11	19	168(2)
	165(2)	14	1	6	19	.09	3	2	0	0			161(2)
FDR Germany	179(1)	13	11	0	20	.05	3	2	0	2	13	10	175(1)
	174(2)	12	0	0	6	.20	3	2	0	0			170(2)
Greece	136(3)	3	0	0	36	.00	0	0	0	0	11	529	133(3)
	146(3)	4	2	1	13	.11	3	2	0	1			144(3)
Ireland	185(1)	3	0	0	2	.10	3	2	0	1	1	65	178(1)
	183(1)	3	0	0	5	.63	3	2	0	1			176(1)
Israel	87(5)	2	0	1	1	.00	3	2	0	1	2	3	81(5)
	92(5)	9	2	4	1	.86	3	2	0	1			86(5)
Italy	160(2)	9	15	14	11	.38	3	2	0	0	7	93	155(2)
	158(2)	32	21	0	91	.27	1	2	0	0			152(2)
Japan	149(3)	14	6	5	4	.00	3	2	0	1	55	278	157(2)
	157(2)	1	1	0	3	.01	3	2	0	0			165(2)
Netherlands	187(1)	0	0	0	0	.00	3	2	0	0	5	133	182(1)
	190(1)	3	3	0	6	.65	3	2	0	1			186(1)
New Zealand	178(1)	0	0	0	0	.00	3	2	0	1	(4)	3	174(2)
	186(1)	0	0	0	0	.00	3	2	0	0			183(1)
Norway	186(1)	0	0	0	0	.00	3	2	0	1	(3)	7	189(1)
	193(1)	1	0	0	0	.00	3	2	0	1			196(1)
Portugal	131(3)	8	1	4	2	.00	3	1	0	1	4	64	127(3)
	146(3)	5	4	0	10	.00	3	2	1	0			142(3)
South Africa	121(4)	8	0	0	0	1.00	3	2	0	1	1	1	112(4)
	98(5)	20	16	3	28	2.49	3	2	0	1			89(5)
Spain	156(2)	13	0	1	1	.00	3	1	0	0	5	24	150(2)
	129(3)	48	44	10	54	.00	3	2	0	1			122(4)
Sweden	198(1)	0	0	0	0	.00	3	2	0	0	(4)	0.4	201(1)
	189(1)	1	1	0	0	.00	3	2	0	0			192(1)

TABLE C–1   Continued

| | Index of Social Progress (Vulnerability Zones) | Political Stability Subindex | | | | | Political Participation Subindex | | | | Geographic Subindex | | Index of Net Social Progress (Vulnerability Zones) |
		Political Protest Demonstrations	Politically Motivated Riots	Politically Motivated Strikes	Politically Motivated Armed Attacks	Deaths From Domestic Violence Per Million Population	Functioning Parliamentary System	Functioning Political Party System	Role of Military	Number Popular Elections Held	Number Major Natural Disasters	Lives Lost/Mil in Natural Disasters	
Switzerland	164(2)	1	0	0	0	.00	3	2	2	2	2	9	159(2)
	170(2)	0	0	0	1	.00	3	2	0	2			165(2)
United Kingdom	171(2)	28	31	2	69	.29	3	2	0	13	21	89	165(2)
	145(3)	36	9	10	296	.16	3	2	0	7			139(3)
United States	91(5)	133	24	13	28	.15	3	2	0	0	326	46	121(4)
	116(4)	51	7	0	12	.01	3	2	0	0			146(3)
Yugoslavia	140(3)	2	0	0	0	.05	3	1	0	1	4	51	136(3)
	137(3)	1	0	0	0	.19	3	1	1	0			133(3)
Eastern Trading Area (N = 7)	155.9	19.1	0.7	0.0	0.1	0.14	3.0	1.0	0.1	0.6	2.4	12.4	151.9
	148.4	5.9	0.1	0.1	0.3	0.00	2.3	1.0	1.0	0.3			144.3
Albania	137(3)	0	0	0	0	.00	3	1	0	0	2	18	134(3)
	108(4)	0	0	0	0	.00	2	1	1	0			106(4)
Bulgaria	167(2)	0	0	0	0	.00	3	1	0	0	1	2	163(2)
	155(2)	0	0	0	0	.00	3	1	1	0			151(2)
Czechoslovakia	151(2)	112	4	0	1	.90	3	1	1	0	3	0.6	147(3)
	163(2)	4	1	0	0	.00	2	1	1	0			158(2)

Hungary	173(2)	1	0	0	0	.10	3	1	0	0	2	1	166(2)
	169(2)	0	0	0	0	.00	2	1	1	0			161(2)
Poland	168(2)	1	0	0	0	.00	3	1	0	1	5	1	163(2)
	168(2)	7	0	0	0	.00	2	1	1	0			163(2)
Rumania	163(2)	0	0	0	0	.00	3	1	0	1	2	64	158(2)
	163(2)	3	0	1	0	.00	2	1	1	0			158(2)
USSR	132(3)	20	1	0	0	.01	3	1	0	1	(1.8)	0.4	132(3)
	113(4)	27	0	0	2	.02	3	1	1	2			113(4)
Developing Countries (N = 58)	85.3	2.3	1.8	1.0	28.6	496.94	2.3	1.2	0.7	0.5	6.4	369.6	86.9
	89.0	1.7	1.1	0.5	5.3	10.25	1.9	1.0	1.0	0.4			88.6
Algeria	87(5)	0	0	0	0	.00	3	1	2	0	3	102	89(5)
	96(5)	0	0	0	0	.00	0	1	2	1			97(5)
Argentina	116(4)	15	20	19	41	1.33	0	0	2	0	9	26	110(4)
	124(4)	4	0	0	20	107.00	0	0	2	0			119(4)
Bolivia	84(5)	1	0	0	1	.21	0	0	2	0	1	1	85(5)
	92(5)	0	0	0	1	.00	0	0	2	0			93(5)
Brazil	123(4)	2	0	1	7	.07	3	2	2	0	20	66	127(3)
	137(3)	5	2	2	0	.00	3	2	1	0			141(3)
Burma	80(5)	1	0	0	7	6.59	0	0	2	0	9	136	81(5)
	70(6)	0	0	0	14	7.48	2	1	2	0			71(6)
Cameroon	62(6)	0	0	0	0	.00	3	2	0	0	(1.4)	100	62(6)
	65(6)	0	0	0	0	.00	3	1	1	0			66(6)
Chile	135(3)	2	2	2	0	.00	3	2	0	1	9	578	140(3)
	90(5)	1	0	0	0	.00	2	0	2	0			95(5)
Colombia	117(4)	1	2	0	1	.34	3	2	0	0	12	62	120(4)
	130(3)	0	7	1	7	.82	3	2	0	0			133(3)

TABLE C-1 Continued

| | Political Stability Subindex | | | | | | Political Participation Subindex | | | | Geographic Subindex | | |
	Index of Social Progress (Vulnerability Zones)	Political Protest Demonstrations	Politically Motivated Riots	Politically Motivated Strikes	Politically Motivated Armed Attacks	Deaths From Domestic Violence Per Million Population	Functioning Parliamentary System	Functioning Political Party System	Role of Military	Number Popular Elections Held	Number Major Natural Disasters	Lives Lost/Mil in Natural Disasters	Index of Net Social Progress (Vulnerability Zones)
Costa Rica	138(3)	0	1	0	0	.00	3	2	0	0	4	15	138(3)
	152(2)	0	0	0	0	.00	3	2	0	0			152(2)
Cuba	140(3)	1	0	0	2	2.17	0	2	0	0	9	138	138(3)
	141(3)	0	0	0	0	.00	3	1	1	0			139(3)
Dom. Republic	113(4)	2	1	0	1	.95	3	2	0	0	1	185	112(4)
	118(4)	1	0	0	0	.00	3	2	0	0			117(4)
Ecuador	108(4)	1	1	0	4	1.86	3	2	1	0	4	1045	116(4)
	105(4)	1	2	2	0	3.84	0	0	2	0			113(4)
Egypt	72(6)	0	0	0	0	.00	3	1	0	1	(3)	1	75(5)
	81(5)	4	1	0	9	1.18	3	1	0	1			84(5)
El Salvador	115(4)	1	0	0	0	.00	3	2	0	0	3	90	110(4)
	109(4)	6	0	0	3	4.63	0	0	2	1			104(4)
Ghana	58(6)	1	1	1	0	3.02	0	0	2	1	(1.5)	57	54(6)
	39(7)	0	1	3	0	.00	0	0	2				36(7)
Guatemala	66(6)	0	0	0	7	2.00	3	2	0	0	5	3317	88(5)
	72(6)	1	0	0	0	.00	3	2	0	0			94(5)
Honduras	86(5)	2	2	0	0	.40	3	1	0	0	4	2047	100(4)
	80(5)	0	0	0	0	.00	0	0	2	0			92(5)

India	46(7)	13	17	2	40	1.72	3	2	0	4	65	162	49(7)	
	53(6)	17	8	1	2	.03	3	2	0	3			56(6)	
Indonesia	28(7)	0	1	0	3	.00	2	2	2	2	11	39	32(7)	
	71(6)	0	0	0	0	.00	2	1	2	1			75(5)	
Iran	66(6)	2	1	0	0	.25	3	0	0	0	32	1482	81(5)	
	69(6)	0	1	0	1	.00	2	1	1	0			83(5)	
Iraq	64(6)	1	0	0	7	20.00	0	1	2	0	1	17	63(6)	
	66(6)	1	2	0	4	.17	0	1	2	0			65(6)	
Ivory Coast	68(6)	1	0	1	0	.00	3	1	0	0	(1.1)	90	64(6)	
	73(6)	0	0	0	0	.00	3	1	1	0			69(6)	
Jamaica	130(3)	0	0	0	1	.00	3	2	0	0	4	141	128(3)	
	132(3)	0	1	0	0	7.14	3	2	0	0			130(3)	
Jordan	42(7)	1	0	0	3	.00	3	0	1	0	1	69	44(7)	
	54(6)	0	0	0	0	.00	2	0	1	0			56(6)	
Kampuchea	49(7)	0	0	0	4	14.48	3	0	2	0	(1)	894	56(6)	
	49(7)	0	0	0	0	.00	2	1	1	0			55(6)	
Kenya	68(6)	5	5	0	8	1.71	3	1	0	1	1	10	70(6)	
	56(6)	0	0	0	0	.00	0	1	1	0			58(6)	
Korea, South	102(4)	8	0	0	2	.00	3	2	0	3	16	1040	110(4)	
	107(4)	8	1	0	1	.00	3	2	0	0			115(4)	
Lebanon	112(4)	5	11	3	26	60.38	3	2	0	0	4	153	112(4)	
	93(5)	1	2	6	126	166.33	3	2	0	0			93(5)	
Liberia	69(6)	0	0	0	0	.00	3	1	0	0	(1.4)	302	69(6)	
	65(6)	1	0	0	0	.00	3	1	0	0			65(6)	
Libya	49(7)	0	0	0	0	.00	0	0	2	0	1	87	52(6)	
	86(5)	0	1	0	1	.00	2	1	2	0			90(5)	
Madagascar	83(5)	0	0	0	0	.00	3	1	0	0	2	86	78(5)	
	79(5)	0	0	0	0	.00	3	1	1	0			74(6)	

TABLE C–1 Continued

	Index of Social Progress (Vulnerability Zones)	Political Stability Subindex					Political Participation Subindex				Geographic Subindex		Index of Net Social Progress (Vulnerability Zones)
		Political Protest Demonstrations	Politically Motivated Riots	Politically Motivated Strikes	Politically Motivated Armed Attacks	Deaths From Domestic Violence Per Million Population	Functioning Parliamentary System	Functioning Political Party System	Role of Military	Number Popular Elections Held	Number Major Natural Disasters	Lives Lost/Mil in Natural Disasters	
Malaysia	81(5)	1	0	0	6	63.13	3	2	0	1	2	4	32(5)
	92(5)	0	0	0	0	.00	3	2	0	0			95(5)
Mauritania	63(6)	0	0	0	0	.00	3	1	0	0	2.3	1379	70(6)
	27(7)	0	0	0	2	.00	1	1	1	0			34(7)
Mexico	120(4)	2	1	0	5	.41	3	1	0	0	23	66	118(4)
	121(4)	6	2	3	15	.55	2	1	0	0			120(4)
Morocco	72(6)	1	0	2	0	.00	0	0	0	1	2	576	74(6)
	73(6)	0	0	0	0	.00	2	2	0	1			76(5)
Nicaragua	83(5)	1	0	0	0	.00	3	1	0	0	3	2490	101(4)
	87(5)	0	0	0	6	13.64	2	1	1	0			105(4)
Nigeria	3(8)	2	1	0	106	14,890.28	0	0	2	0	2	3	–1(8)
	33(7)	0	1	0	1		0	0	2	0			28(7)
Pakistan	40(7)	20	23	8	13	2.52	2	1	2	0	1	433	41(7)
	31(7)	29	14	5	1	2.11	1	0	2	1			32(7)
Panama	128(3)	0	0	0	0	.00	3	2	0	0	(3)	300	131(3)
	122(4)	3	1	0	0	.00	2	0	2	1			125(3)
Paraguay	115(4)	0	0	0	0	.00	3	1	1	0	(3)	10	115(4)
	125(3)	0	0	0	0	.00	3	1	1	1			125(3)

Peru	82(5)	2	0	0	4	.00	0	0	2	0	12	1251	91(5)
	76(5)	1	5	7	1	2.24	2	0	2	0			85(5)
Philippines	98(5)	11	3	0	7	.75	3	2	0	1	14	280	100(4)
	91(5)	3	0	0	12	13.81	1	0	1	2			93(5)
Senegal	75(5)	2	2	2	0	.26	3	1	0	0	(3)	1	70(6)
	68(6)	0	0	0	0	.00	1	1	0	1			63(6)
Sierra Leone	80(5)	0	0	0	0	.00	3	2	0	10	1	191	72(6)
	62(6)	1	1	0	1	2.26	3	1	1	1			54(6)
Singapore	106(4)	0	0	0	1	.00	3	1	0	0	(3)	0.5	106(4)
	107(4)	0	0	0	0	.00	3	1	0	1			107(4)
Sri Lanka	119(4)	0	0	1	0	.00	3	2	0	0	4	15	118(4)
	118(4)	0	6	1	0	10.14	3	2	0	2			117(4)
Syria	71(6)	0	0	0	0	.00	0	1	2	0	(5)	3	66(6)
	115(4)	0	0	0	7	1.58	2	1	2	1			110(4)
Thailand	104(4)	1	0	0	11	.29	3	0	2	2	4	33	105(4)
	99(5)	2	1	0	10	1.88	1	0	2	0			100(4)
Togo	41(7)	0	0	0	0	.00	0	0	2	0	(1.5)	430	41(7)
	46(7)	0	0	0	0	.00	0	1	2	0			46(7)
Trinidad/ Tobago	123(4)	0	0	0	0	.00	3	2	0	0	(1)	17	123(4)
	126(3)	0	0	0	0	.00	3	2	0	0			125(3)
Tunisia	109(4)	0	0	0	0	.00	3	1	0	1	2	95	106(4)
	119(4)	1	0	0	0	.00	2	1	1	0			116(4)
Turkey	99(5)	10	6	1	5	.23	3	2	1	1	17	508	98(5)
	112(4)	2	4	0	15	1.57	3	2	1	1			110(4)
Uruguay	137(3)	5	3	13	7	1.72	3	2	0	0	1	14	128(3)
	140(3)	0	0	0	0	.00	0	0	2	0			131(3)
Venezuela	128(3)	2	0	0	10	1.80	3	2	0	0	4	32	129(3)
	137(3)	0	0	0	1	.48	3	2	0	0			138(3)

TABLE C–1   Continued

	Index of Social Progress (Vulnerability Zones)	Political Stability Subindex					Political Participation Subindex				Geographic Subindex		Index of Net Social Progress (Vulnerability Zones)
		Political Protest Demonstrations	Politically Motivated Riots	Politically Motivated Strikes	Politically Motivated Armed Attacks	Deaths From Domestic Violence Per Million Population	Functioning Parliamentary System	Functioning Political Party System	Role of Military	Number Popular Elections Held	Number Major Natural Disasters	Lives Lost/Mil in Natural Disasters	
R. Vietnam	8(8)	4	1	0	1318	13,743.02	3	0	2	0	11	304	10(8)
	53(6)	0	0	0	0	.00	2	1	1	0			54(6)
Zaïre	43(7)	1	0	0	0	.70	2	1	2	0	(1.5)	37	42(7)
	52(6)	0	0	0	8	3.91	2	1	1	0			51(6)
Zambia	73(6)	0	2	0	0	.00	3	2	0	0	(2.3)	263	71(6)
	37(7)	1	0	0	2	.00	1	1	1	0			35(7)
Zimbabwe	80(5)	2	0	0	0	.00	3	2	0	1	(2)	163.5	82(5)
	33(7)	0	0	0	35	241.85	3	2	0	1			35(7)
Least Developing Countries (N = 18)	44.4	0.2	0.1	0.0	1.0	28.29	1.5	0.6	1.0	1.7	1.7	191.4	43.4
	40.8	0.6	0.1	0.2	3.7	37.92	1.1	0.7	1.6	0.3			39.7
Benin	44(7)	0	0	0	0	.00	0	0	2	0	(1.5)	286	47(7)
	42(7)	0	0	0	0	.00	0	1	2	0			45(7)
Burundi	36(7)	0	0	0	0	.00	0	1	2	0	(1.5)	143	32(7)
	24(8)	0	0	0	0	.00	0	1	2	0			20(8)

Cen. Afr. Rep.	35(7)	0	0	0	0	.00	0	0	2	0	(1.3)	373	40(7)
	45(7)	0	0	0	0	.00	0	1	2	0			50(6)
Chad	25(7)	0	0	0	4	484.86	3	1	0	2	1	3	23(8)
	14(8)	0	0	0	1	1.95	0	0	2	0			11(8)
Ethiopia	36(7)	1	0	0	2	.12	3	0	0	0	1	0	30(7)
	−12(8)	8	1	0	62	452.72	0	0	2	0			−19(8)
Guinea	43(7)	0	0	0	0	.26	3	1	2	0	(1.7)	195	43(7)
	57(6)	0	0	0	0	.00	3	1	1	2			56(6)
Haiti	75(5)	0	0	0	3	11.04	3	1	0	0	7	1184	82(5)
	77(5)	0	0	0	0	.00	3	1	1	0			84(5)
Malawi	44(7)	0	0	0	0	.00	3	1	0	0	(2.5)	286	45(7)
	37(7)	0	0	0	0	.00	3	1	1	0			38(7)
Mali	46(7)	0	0	0	0	.00	0	0	2	0	(2)	96	45(7)
	35(7)	0	2	0	0	.00	2	1	2	0			34(7)
Nepal	49(7)	2	0	2	0	1.57	3	0	0	0	2	144	49(7)
	57(6)	2	0	0	1	.31	3	0	0	1			57(6)
Niger	34(7)	0	0	0	0	.00	3	1	0	0	(1.6)	229	38(7)
	34(7)	0	0	0	0	.00	0	0	2	0			37(7)
PDR Yemen	39(7)	0	0	0	6	4.92	0	1	0	0	(1)	30	37(7)
	71(6)	0	0	0	0	.00	2	1	1	0			69(6)
Rwanda	61(6)	0	0	0	0	.00	3	2	0	0	(1.5)	143	55(6)
	59(6)	0	0	0	0	.00	0	1	2	1			53(6)
Somalia	58(6)	0	0	0	0	.11	0	0	2	1	1	55	57(6)
	50(6)	0	0	0	0	.00	1	1	2	0			49(7)
Sudan	49(7)	0	0	0	1	.20	0	0	2	0	2	109	52(6)
	60(6)	0	0	0	1	.62	2	1	2	1			63(6)
Tanzania	43(7)	0	0	0	2	.16	3	1	0	0	(2)	34	37(7)
	29(7)	1	0	1	0	.00	1	1	1	0			23(8)

TABLE C–1   Continued

| | Political Stability Subindex | | | | | Political Participation Subindex | | | | Geographic Subindex | | |
Index of Social Progress (Vulnerability Zones)	Political Protest Demonstrations	Politically Motivated Riots	Politically Motivated Strikes	Politically Motivated Armed Attacks	Deaths From Domestic Violence Per Million Population	Functioning Parliamentary System	Functioning Political Party System	Role of Military	Number Popular Elections Held	Number Major Natural Disasters	Lives Lost/Mil in Natural Disasters	Index of Net Social Progress (Vulnerability Zones)
Uganda												
45(7)	1	0	0	0	.00	0	0	2	0	(1)	12	42(7)
21(8)	0	1	0	1	226.97	0	0	2	0			19(8)
Upper Volta												
37(7)	0	0	0	0	.00	0	0	2	0	(1.3)	124	28(7)
34(7)	0	0	0	0	.00	0	0	2	1			25(7)

[a]Values reported are for modal years 1968–70.

[b]Values reported are for modal years 1978–80.

[c]Values reported are for 1969 only (Jodice and Taylor 1981).

[d]Values reported are for 1977 only (Jodice and Taylor 1981).

[e]Values reflect number of deaths from domestic violence for the year 1969 only per million persons in the national population in 1969 (Base values from Jodice and Taylor 1981).

[f]Values reflect number of deaths from domestic violence for the year 1977 only per million persons in the national population in 1977 (Base values from Jodice and Taylor 1981).

[g]Values reported are for 1972 only (Blondel 1973). The variable is coded as follows: (0) = no functioning parliamentary system; (1) = ? no; (2) = ? yes; (3) = yes, that is, a parliamentary system of government in place and functioning.

[h]Values reported are for 1977 only (Gastil 1978). Coding is same as in note "g" above.

[i]Values reported are for 1972 only (Blondel 1973). The variable is coded as follows: (0) = no political party system in place or functioning; (1) = single party, or forced coalition, in place and functioning; (2) = two or more political parties in place and functioning.

[j]Values reported are for 1977 only (Gastil 1978). Coding is the same as in note "i" above.

[k]Values reported are for 1972 only (Blondel 1973). The variable is coded as follows: (0) = no or little influence of military in civilian affairs; (1) = ? no; (2) = military in power or exercises strong influence over civilian affairs.

[l]Values reported are for 1977 only (Gastil 1978). Coding is the same as in note "k" above.

[m]Values reported are for *1969 only* (Jodice and Taylor 1981).

[n]Values reported are for *1977 only* (Jodice and Taylor 1981).

[o]Values reported are for the 32-year period 1947–79 (Regulska 1980). Numbers in parentheses are estimates based on sub-regional averages, that is, the incidence of natural disasters that took place over the period within at least two nations in close geographic proximity to a nation with data missing on this variable were averaged to provide a reasonable estimate of the number of natural disasters that took place, but were not reported, for these nations.

[p]Values reflect the total number of deaths from all natural disasters for the entire 32-year period of the study, divided by a nation's population size in 1969 (Base values from Regulska 1980).

[q]Parentheses ( ) indicate data estimated using geographic subregional averages.

Bibliography

Adelman, I., and C. T. Morris. 1971. *Society, Politics and Economic Development.* Baltimore: Johns Hopkins University Press.

Alter, Jonathan et al. 1984. Homelessness in America. *Newsweek* (January 2):20–29.

Andrews, Frank, and Ronald Inglehart. 1979. The Structure of Subjective Well-Being in Nine Western Societies. *Social Indicators Research* 6(1):73–90.

Anner, Sylvia. 1982. *The Consequences of the Economic Crisis for the Present and Future Development of Social Welfare.* Regional Expert Meeting, Baden/Wien, Austria, September 6–11, 1981. Vienna: European Centre for Social Welfare Training and Research.

Arenson, Karen W. 1982. Epidemic of Recession Poses Hard Choices for All Nations. *New York Times* (November 25):1, 32.

Bacheller, Martin A., ed. 1980. *The Hammond Almanac, 1981.* Maplewood, NJ: Hammond Almanac, Inc.

Badgley, John. 1971. *Asian Development: Problems and Programs.* New York: The Free Press.

Banks, Arthur, and Robert B. Textor, eds. 1963. *A Cross-Polity Survey.* Cambridge, MA: MIT Press.

Baster, Nancy. 1969. *Level of Living and Economic Growth: A Comparative Study of Six Countries.* Geneva: UNRISD.

Baster, Nancy, and Wolf Scott. 1967. *Social and Economic Growth, Growth Patterns and Productivity Effect.* Geneva: UNRISD, Research Report #8.

———. 1969. *Level of Living and Economic Growth: A Comparative Study of Six Countries.* Geneva: UNRISD.

Bauer, Raymond, ed. 1966. *Social Indicators.* Cambridge, MA: MIT Press.

Beck, Melinda et al. 1983. Who Has the Bomb? *Newsweek* (December 5):56, 58.

Beckerman, Wilfred. 1978. *Measures of Leisure, Equality and Welfare.* Paris: OECD.

Bennett, M. K. 1951. International Disparities in Income Levels. *American Economic Review* 41 (September):632–49.

Berkol, Faruk N. 1976. Natural Disasters: A Neglected Variable in National Development Strategies. *International Social Science Journal* 28(4):730–35.

Berry, R. Albert, and Ronald Soligo. 1979. Some Welfare Aspects of International Migration. *Journal of Political Economy* 77:778–94.

Blalock, Hubert M. 1979. *Social Statistics.* Rev. 2nd ed. New York: McGraw-Hill.

Blondel, Jean. 1972. *Comparing Political Systems.* New York: Praeger Publishers.

Boudreau, Tom. 1980. *A New International Diplomatic Order.* Muscatine, Iowa: The Stanley Foundation, Occasional Paper No. 24.

Brandt, Willy et al. 1980. *North-South: A Program for Survival.* Cambridge, MA: MIT Press.

Brissimi, Hari. 1980. An Overview of the Refugee Situation in South East Asia. In *Social Development in Times of Economic Uncertainty*, ed. International Council on Social Welfare. New York: Columbia University Press.

Bubeck, Eric A., ed. 1972. *International Perspectives on Social Welfare Research: Report of an International Symposium.* Washington, DC: Brookings Institution.

Burton, Ian. 1978. *The Environment Hazard.* New York: Oxford University Press.

Center for Defense Information (CDI). 1983. *The World at War.* Washington, DC: CDI.

Christian, David. 1974. International Social Indicators: The OECD Experience. *Social Indicators Research* 1(2):169–88.

Commission on International Development. 1969. *Partners in Development.* New York: Praeger.

Connor, Walter. 1972. *Deviance in Soviet Society.* New York: Columbia University Press.

Cox, Idris. 1970. *The Hungry Half: A Study in the Exploitation of the Third World.* London: Laurence and Wishart.

Coyle, David Cushman. 1960. *The United Nations and How It Works.* New York: Mentor Books.

Cummings, Robert E. 1983. Social Development: The Economic, the Political and the Normative Emphases. *International Social Work* 26(1):13–25.

Dahl, Robert A. 1971. *Polyarchy: Participation and Opposition.* New Haven: Yale University Press.

Davis, Joseph S. 1945. Standards and Content of Living. *American Economic Review* 35(March):1–15.

Delury, George E., ed. 1979. *The World Almanac and Book of Facts, 1980*. New York: Newspaper Enterprise Association.

Deutsch, Karl. 1953. *Nationalism and Social Communication*. New York: Wiley.

Djukanovic, V., and E. P. Mach, eds. 1975. *Alternative Approaches to Meeting Basic Health Needs in Developing Countries*. Geneva: World Health Organization.

Dolmatch, Theodore B. 1981. *Information Please Almanac, 1982*. New York: Simon and Schuster.

Drenowski, Jan. 1970. *Studies in the Measurements of Levels of Living and Welfare*. Report No. 70.3. Geneva: United Nations Research Institute for Social Development.

———. 1972. Social Indicators and Welfare Measurement. *Journal of Development Studies* 8(3):77–89.

———. 1974. *On Measuring and Planning the Quality of Life*. The Hague: Mouton.

Editorial. 1982. The Withering of Europe's Welfare States. *The Economist* (October 16):67–68.

———. 1983. A Social Price. *Scientific American* 248(4):69A.

———. 1983. Pope's Address to Science Academy: "Work For the Building up of Peace." *Chronicle of Higher Education* 27(13):9–12.

———. 1983. The Debt-Bomb Threat. *Time* (January 10):42.

———. 1984a. Scientists Move Up Doomsday. *Time* (January 2):59.

———. 1984b. On the Record. *Time* (January 9):57.

———. 1980a. The Dispossessed. *World Press Review* 27(12):4.

———. 1980b. The Nuclear Club. *World Press Review* 27(12):6.

———. 1981. Nigeria Thinks Nuclear. *World Press Review* 28(1):22.

Ehrlich, Paul R., and Anne H. Ehrlich. 1972. *Population, Resources, Environment*. 2nd ed. San Francisco: W.H. Freeman and Co.

Estes, Richard J. 1983. Education for Comparative Welfare Research. In *Education for International Social Welfare*, ed. Daniel S. Sanders. Honolulu: University of Hawaii Press.

———. 1984. World Social Progress, 1969–1979. *Social Development Issues* 8(1).

Estes, Richard J., and John S. Morgan. 1976. World Social Welfare Analysis: A Theoretical Model. *International Social Work* 19(2):29–41.

Falk, Richard. 1971. *This Endangered Planet: Prospects for Human Survival*. New York: Random House.

Falk, Richard et al. 1982. *Toward a Just World Order*. Vol. 1. Boulder, CO: Westview Press.

Fidel, Kenneth, ed. 1975. *Militarism in Developing Nations*. New Brunswick, NJ: Transaction Books.

Friedman, Milton. 1983. "No" to More Money for the IMF. *Newsweek* (November 14):96.

Gastil, Raymond. 1978. *Freedom Around the World*. New York: Freedom House.

George, V., and P. Wilding. 1976. *Ideology and Social Welfare*. London: Routledge and Kegan Paul.

Gostkowski, Zygmunt, ed. c.1973. *Toward a System of Human Resource Indicators for Less Developed Countries*. OSSOLINEUM: The Polish Academy of Sciences, Institute of Philosophy and Sociology.

Gottlieb, Henry. 1982. Welfare Reductions in Europe. *Honolulu Star-Bulletin* (February 7):A–12.

Goulet, Dennis. 1971. *The Cruel Choice*. New York: Atheneum.

Grant, James P. 1983. *The State of the World's Children, 1982–1983*. New York: Oxford University Press.

Graycar, Adam. 1979. Political Issues in Research and Evaluation. *Evaluation Quarterly* 3:460–71.

Gutierrez, Gustav. 1973. *A Theology of Liberation*. New York: Orbis Books.

Hansen, Roger D. 1971. *The Politics of Mexican Development*. Baltimore: Johns Hopkins Press.

Harbison, Frederick H. 1970. *Quantitative Analyses of Modernization and Development*. Princeton: Princeton University, Industrial Relations Section, Department of Economics.

Hardiman, Margaret, and James Midgley. 1982. *The Social Dimensions of Development: Social Policy and Planning in the Third World*. Chichester: John Wiley.

Henriot, Peter J. 1972. *Political Aspects of Social Indicators: Implications for Research*. New York: Russell Sage Foundation.

Hewitt, Kenneth, and Ian Burton. 1971. *The Hazardness of a Place: A Regional Ecology of Damaging Events*. Toronto: University of Toronto Press.

Hogendorn, Jan S., and Wilson B. Brown. 1979. *The New International Economics*. Reading, MA: Addison-Wesley.

Horowitz, Irving L. 1966. *Three Worlds of Development: The Theory and Practice of International Stratification*. New York: Oxford University Press.

Hoselitz, Bert. 1960. *Sociological Aspects of Economic Growth*. Glencoe, IL: Free Press–Macmillan.

Howard, Donald S. 1969. *Social Welfare: Values, Means, and Ends*. New York: Random House.

Hunt, Chester. 1966. *Social Aspects of Economic Development*. New York: McGraw–Hill.

International Council on Social Welfare (ICSW). 1978. *Human Well-Being: The Challenge of Continuity and Change*. New York: ICSW.

International Labor Organization (ILO). 1977. *Meeting Basic Needs: Strategies for Eradicating Mass Poverty and Unemployment*. Geneva: ILO.

————. 1981. *The Cost of Social Security*. Geneva: ILO.

Jalee, Pieree. 1968. *The Pillage of the Third World*. New York: Monthly Review Press.

Jenkins, Shirley, ed. 1969. *Social Security in International Perspective*. New York: Columbia University Press.

Jodice, David A., and Charles L. Taylor. 1981. *Political Protest and Government Change, 1948–1977*. Berlin: International Institute for Comparative Social Research. (Raw data used with permission of investigators.)

Juster, F. Thomas. 1977. Alternatives to GNP as a Measure of Economic Progress. In *U.S. Economic Growth from 1976 to 1986: Prospects, Problems and Patterns*. Vol. 10. Prepared for U.S. Congress, Joint Economic Committee, May 20, 12–24.

Kahn, Alfred J., and Sheila B. Kamerman. 1976. *Social Services in International Perspective*. Washington, DC: USDHEW, Social and Rehabilitation Service.

Kennedy, Leslie et al. 1978. Subjective evaluation of Well-Being: Problems and Prospects. *Social Indicators Research* 5(4):457–74.

Knight, Robin. 1983. The Desperate Straits of Black Africa. *U.S. News & World Report* (February 14):28.

Kruzas, Anthony T. 1982. *Social Service Organizations and Agencies*. Detroit: Gale.

Lally, Dorothy. 1970. *National Social Service Systems*. Washington, DC: USDHEW, Social and Rehabilitation Service.

Lane, Hanne et al. 1983. *The World Almanac and Book of Facts 1984*. New York: Newspaper Enterprise Association.

Laslo, Ervin, coordinator. 1977. *Goals for Mankind: A Report to the Club of Rome on the New Horizons of Global Community*. New York: E.P. Dutton.

LeMoyne, James et al. 1983. Nigeria's Outcasts: The Cruel Exodus. *Newsweek* (February 14):32–34.

Leontieff, Wassily et al. 1977. *The Future of the World Economy: A United Nations Study*. New York: Oxford University Press.

Makler, Harry et al. 1982. *The New International Economy*. Beverly Hills, CA: Sage.

Maloney, John C. 1973. *Social Vulnerability in Indianapolis*. Indianapolis, IN: Community Service Council of Metropolitan Indianapolis.

Maslow, Abraham. 1968. *Toward a Psychology of Being*. 2nd ed. Princeton: Van Nostrand.

McGranahan, Donald et al. 1972. *Contents and Measurement of Socioeconomic Development*. New York: Praeger.

Meadows, Dennis. 1972. *The Limits to Growth*. New York: Universe Books.

Mendelsohn, Stefan. 1983. External Public Debt in the LDCs: No Reason to Panic. *Report of the World Bank* (June–July).

Merritt, Giles. 1982. The Job Gap: The West's Prospects for 1985. *World Press Review* (December):37–38.

Merritt, R.L., and Stein Rokkan eds. 1966. *Comparing Nations: The Use of Quantitative Data in Cross-National Research*. New Haven: Yale University Press.

Mische, Gerald, and Patricia Mische. 1977. *Toward a Human World Order*. New York: Paulist Press.

Morgan, John S. ed. 1966. *Welfare and Wisdom*. Toronto: University of Toronto Press.

Morris, Morris David. 1979. *Measuring the Conditions of the World's Poor*. New York: Pergamon.

Myrdal, Gunnar. 1968. *Asian Drama: An Inquiry into the Poverty of Nations*. New York: Random House.

————. 1970. *The Challenge of World Poverty*. New York: Pantheon.

Naipaul, V.S. 1977. *India: A Wounded Civilization*. New York: Knopf.

Nash, June. 1977. Women in Development: Dependency and Exploitation. *Development and Change* 8.

National Urban League. 1977. *The State of Black America, 1977*. New York: National Urban League.

Nie, Norman et al. 1975. *Statistical Package for Social Sciences (SPSS)*. 2nd ed. New York: McGraw–Hill.

Niewiarkoski, D. H. 1965. The Level of Living of Nations: Meaning and Measurement. *Estadistica: Journal of The InterAmerican Statistical Institute* 23(86): March.

Nordheimer, Jon. 1983. Belt-Tightening in Europe Squeezes Welfare State. *New York Times* (December 8):A–2.

Ominde, Simeon H. 1975. The Integration of Environmental and Developmental Planning for Ecological Crisis Areas in Africa. *International Social Science Journal* 27(3):499–516.

Organization for Economic Cooperation and Development (OECD). 1973. *List of Social Concerns Common to Most OECD Countries*. Paris: OECD.

————. 1976b. *The Use of Socio-Economic Indicators on Developing Planning*. Paris: OECD.

————. 1977a. *Measuring Social Well-Being: A Progress Report on the Development of Social Indicators*. Paris: OECD.

————. 1977b. *Basic Disaggregation of Main Social Indicators*. Special Studies, No. 4. Paris: OECD.

————. 1977c. *1976 Progress Report on Phase II: Plan for Future Activities*. Paris: OECD.

————. 1981. *The Welfare State in Crisis: An Account of the Conference on Social Policies in the 1980s*. Paris: OECD.

————. 1982. *The OECD List of Social Indicators*. Paris: OECD.

Organski, A. F. K. 1967. *The Stages of Political Development*. New York: Knopf.

Paiva, F. X. 1977. A Conception of Social Development. *Social Service Review* 51(3):327–36.

Paxton, John, ed. 1977. *Statesman Yearbook, 1977–1978*. London: Macmillan.

Pentland, Charles. 1981. Building Global Institutions. In *Issues in Global Politics*, ed. Gavin Boyd and Charles Pentland. New York: Free Press.

Pestel, Edward, and Mihaljo Mesarovic. 1974. *Mankind at the Turning Point*. New York: E.P. Dutton.

Piettre, Andre. 1968. Human Rights as the Basis of Social Welfare. *International Social Work* 11(3):2–9.

Przeworski, Adam, and Henry Teune. 1970. *The Logic of Comparative Social Inquiry*. New York: John Wiley.

Pryor, Frederick. 1968. *Public Expenditures in Communist and Capitalist Nations*. Homewood, IL: Richard D. Irwin.

Pusic, Eugene. 1972. *Social Welfare and Social Development*. Paris: Mouton.

Radask, Ronald. 1976. *The New Cuba: Paradoxes and Potentials*. New York: William Morrow.

Reed, Edward, ed. 1968. *Beyond Co-existence: The Requirements of Peace*. New York: Grossman.

Reed, John L. 1981. *A Comparative Analysis of Natural Disasters Upon Nations*. Unpublished MSW thesis, University of Pennsylvania, School of Social Work.

Regulska, Joanna. 1980. *Global Trends in Natural Disasters*. Denver: Natural Hazard Research Institute, University of Colorado (mimeo).

Reubens, Beatrice. 1970. *The Hard to Employ: European Programs*. New York: Columbia University Press.

Rice, Frank A. 1962. *Study of the Role of Languages in Asia, Africa and Latin America*. Washington, DC: Center for Applied Linguistics of the Modern Language Association of America.

Rimlinger, Gaston. 1971. *Welfare Policy and Industrialization in Europe, America, and Russia*. New York: John Wiley.

Rodgers, Barbara et al. 1968. *Comparative Social Adminstration*. London: George Allen and Unwin.

———. 1979. *The Study of Social Policy: A Comparative Approach*. London: George Allen and Unwin.

Rudov, Melvin H., and Nancy Santangelo. 1979. *Health Status of Minorities and Low-Income Groups*. Washington, DC: U.S. Department of Health, Education, and Welfare, Publication No. (HRA) 79–627.

Rustow, Dankwart A. 1967. *A World of Nations: Problems of Political Modernization*. Washington, DC: Brookings Institution.

Sancton, Thomas A. et al. 1981. Rendezvous in Cancun. *Time* (October 26):50.

Sanders, Daniel. 1982. *The Developmental Perspective in Social Welfare.* Honolulu: University of Hawaii.

Sauvant, Karl P., and Hajo Hasenpflug, eds. 1977. *The New International Economic Order: Confrontation or Cooperation Between North and South?* Boulder, CO: Westview Press.

Schlegel, John, ed. 1977. *Toward a Redefinition of Development.* London: Pergamon.

Schumacher, E. F. 1973. *Small is Beautiful: Economics As If People Mattered.* New York: Harper and Row.

Scrimshaw, Nevin, and John E. Gordon. 1968. *Malnutrition, Learning and Behavior: Proceedings of an International Conference.* Cambridge, MA: MIT Press.

Seers, Dudley. 1972. What are we Trying to Measure? *Journal of Development Studies* 8(3):21–36.

Sewell, John W. et al. 1977. *The United States and World Development: Agenda 1977.* New York: Praeger.

Shanas, Ethel. 1968. *Old People in Three Industrial Societies.* London: Routledge and Kegan Paul.

Sheldon, Eleanor, and Wilbert Moore, eds. 1968. *Indicators of Social Change.* New York: Russell Sage Foundation.

Singh, Jyoti S. 1977. *A New International Economic Order: Toward a Fair Distribution of the World's Resources.* New York: Praeger.

Smith, M. 1973. *The Geography of Social Well-Being in the United States.* New York: McGraw–Hill.

Squire, Lyn. 1979. *Labor Force, Employment and Labor Markets in the Course of Economic Development.* Washington, DC: The World Bank.

Sivard, Ruth L. 1983. *World Military and Social Expenditures, 1983.* Washington, DC: World Priorities.

Stockholm International Peace Research Institute (SIPRI). 1978. *World Armaments and Disarmaments, 1978.* London: Taylor and Francis.

———. 1981. *World Armaments and Disarmaments, 1981.* London: Taylor and Francis.

———. 1983. *World Armaments and Dissarmaments, 1983.* London: Taylor and Francis.

Taylor, Charles L., and Michael C. Hudson. 1972. *World Handbook of Political and Social Indicators.* 2nd ed. New Haven: Yale University Press.

Tennison, Debbie C. 1983. Homeless People Grow Numerous in Europe, Despite Welfare States. *Wall Street Journal* (April 25).

Tinbergen, Jan. 1976. *RIO: Reshaping the International Order.* New York: American Elsevier.

Treen, Joseph et al. 1983. Doctors Who Make Pain. *Newsweek* 102(5):27–8.

United Nations. 1954. *International Definition and Measurement of Standards and Levels of Living.* Sales No. 1954.IV.5. New York: UN.

———. 1961. *An Interim Report on the International Definition and Measurement of Levels of Living.* Doc. No. E/Cn.3/270/REV.1-E.CN.5/353. New York: UN.

———. 1963. *Political Rights of Women in Member Nations of the United Nations.* International Report #2: Women in the World Today. #A/5456. New York: UN.

———. 1964. *Handbook of Household Surveys: A Practical Guide for Inquires on Level of Living.* New York: UN.

———. *Demographic Yearbook, 1969.* 1970. Sales No. E/F.70.XIII.1. New York: UN.

———. 1971a. *World Economic Survey, 1969–70.* New York: UN.

———. 1971b. *Demographic Yearbook, 1970.* Sales No. E/F.71.XIII.1. New York: UN.

———. 1971c. *Statistical Yearbook, 1970.* Sales No. E/F.71.XVII.1. New York: UN.

———. 1973a. *Demographic Yearbook, 1972.* Sales No. E/F.73.XIII.1. New York: UN.

———. 1973b. *Statistical Yearbook, 1972.* Sales No. E/F.73.XVII.1. New York: UN.

———. 1975a. *Statistical Yearbook, 1974.* Sales No. E/F.75.XVII.1. New York: UN.

———. 1975b. *World Housing Survey, 1974.* Sales No. E.75.IV.8. New York: UN.

———. 1976. *Disaster Prevention and Mitigation: A Compendium of Current Knowledge.* Vols. 1–10. New York: UN Office of Disaster Relief Coordinator.

———. 1977a. *World Economic Survey, 1976.* Sales No. E.77.II.C.1. New York: UN.

———. 1977b. *Yearbook of the United Nations, 1975.* Sales No. E.77.I.1. New York: UN.

———. 1977c. *The Feasibility of Welfare-Oriented Measures to Supplement the National Accounts and Balances: A Technical Report.* Sales No. E.77.XVII.12. New York: UN.

———. 1978a. *Economic and Social Consequences of the Arms Race and of Military Expenditures: Updated Report of the Secretary-General.* Sales No. E.78.IX.1. New York: UN.

———. 1978b. *Human Rights: A Compilation of International Instruments.* Sales No. E.78.XIV.2. New York: UN.

———. 1979a. *Statistical Yearbook, 1978.* Sales No. E/F.79.XVII.1. New York: UN.

————. 1979b. *The State of Food and Agriculture, 1978*. Rome: UN Food and Agriculture Organization.

————. 1979c. *Demographic Yearbook, 1979*. Sales No. E/F.79.XIII.1. New York: UN.

————. 1979d. *1978 Report on the World Social Situation*. Sales No. E.79.IV.1 and E.79.IV.3. New York: UN.

————. 1979e. *World Population Trends and Prospects, 1977*. New York: UN.

————. 1979f. *Report of World Conference to Combat Racism and Racial Discrimination, Geneva 14–15 August, 1978*. Sales No. E.79.XIV.2. New York: UN.

————. 1980a. *Demographic Yearbook, 1979*. New York: UN.

————. 1980b. *World Conference of the U.N. Decade for Women: Equality, Development and Peace*. A/Conf.95/25. Copenhagen: 14–30 July.

————. 1981a. *Population and Vital Statistics Report Data Available as of April 1981*. Statistical Papers, Series A, Vol. XXXIII, No. 2. New York: UN.

————. 1981b. *Study on All the Aspects of Regional Disarmament*. Sales No. E.81.IX.2. New York: UN.

————. 1982. *Yearbook of Human Rights, 1977–78*. Sales No. E.81.XIV.1. New York: UN.

UNESCO. 1972. *Statistical Yearbook, 1971*. Paris: UNESCO.

————. 1973. *Statistical Yearbook, 1972*. Paris: UNESCO.

————. 1976. *The Use of Socio-Economic Indicators in Development Planning*. Paris: UNESCO.

————. 1977. *Statistical Yearbook, 1977*. Paris: UNESCO.

————. 1978. *Statistical Yearbook, 1978*. Paris: UNESCO.

————. 1980. *Statistical Yearbook, 1980*. Paris: UNESCO.

————. 1981. *Statistical Yearbook, 1981*. Paris: UNESCO.

United Nations European Social Development Programs. 1972. *Expert Group on Methods of Determining Norms and Standards for Planning and Policymaking in the Social Sectors*. (Sardinia, Italy) #GE.72-8594.

————. 1974. *Expert Group on Standard Setting in Social Welfare*. (Izmir, Turkey) #GE.74-10705.

————. 1976. *Minimum Levels of Living*. (Marianske Lazne, Czech.) #GE.78-6650.

United Nations High Commissioner for Refugees. 1973. *A Story of Anguish and Action*. Sales No. E.73.IV.2. New York: UN.

United States Department of Health and Human Services (USDHHS). 1980. *Social Security Programs Throughout the World, 1979*. Report #54, (SSA) 13-11805. Washington, DC: Social Security Administration.

United States Commissioner for Civil Rights. 1978. *Social Indicators of Equality for Minorities and Women*. Washington, DC: Government Printing Office.

Usher, John. 1983. Deaths of 15 Million Children Reported. *Honolulu Star-Bulletin and Advertiser* (December 11):I–6.

Veenhoven, Ruut et al. 1977. *Correlates of Happiness: An Inventory of the Results of Empirical Investigations on Happiness up to 1975*. Rotterdam: Erasmus University, Department of Sociology.

Vogel, Lynn H., and Michael S. Lund, eds. 1972. *Cross National Research in Social Policy*. Chicago: University of Chicago: School of Social Service Administration.

Ward, Barbara. 1971. *The Widening Gap: Development in the 70's*. New York: Columbia University Press.

Warwich, D. P., and S. Osherson, eds. 1973. *Comparative Research Methods*. Englewood Cliffs, NJ: Prentice–Hall.

Wendt, Paul. 1963. *Housing Policy—The Search for Solutions*. Berkeley: University of California Press.

Wilensky, Harold L. 1975. *The Welfare State and Equality*. Berkeley: University of California Press.

World Bank. 1978. *World Development Report, 1978*. New York: Oxford University Press.

———. 1979. *World Development Report, 1979*. New York: Oxford University Press.

———. 1980. *World Development Report, 1980*. New York: Oxford University Press.

———. 1983. *World Development Report, 1983*. New York: Oxford University Press.

Zapf, Wolfgang. 1975. Systems of Social Indicators: Current Approaches and Problems. *International Social Science Journal* 27(3):479–98.

Zanker, Alfred. 1983. Behind Mass Unemployment in Europe. *U.S. News & World Report* (January 31):82.

About the Author

Richard J. Estes is Associate Professor of Social Work at the University of Pennsylvania. He holds graduate degrees from the University of Pennsylvania and the University of California at Berkeley. Dr. Estes' research interests include international and comparative social welfare, employment and unemployment, mental health epidemiology, and small group dynamics. He has traveled extensively. During 1978–79, he was a Senior Fulbright lecturer to both the Institute for Advanced Social Work Education in Trondheim, Norway, and the Teheran School of Social Work, Teheran, Iran; during 1982–83 he was visiting Professor of Research and Social Policy at the University of Hawaii at Manoa, Honolulu, Hawaii.

Dr. Estes lectures and consults widely and is the author of numerous papers and research monographs on a variety of social work/social welfare topics. In addition to the present volume, Dr. Estes has written the *Directory of Social Welfare Research Capabilities* (Dorrance 1981), *Social Work Practice: A Pictorial Essay* (National Association of Social Workers 1981), and edited *Health Care and the Social Services* (Warren H. Green 1984).